Contents

Preface

This is the third book in a series of Surrey Seminars in Applied Economics and takes as its theme international aspects of economic development. As with the other books in the series, the volume comprises chapters written by acknowledged experts. The chapters focus on topical issues but endeavour to put them in a broader context. The intention is to produce, with a minimal publication lag, a major reference text which will be valuable to both students and teachers. Reviews of the earlier books in the series suggest that some success has been achieved in realizing this goal. This book is based on an international seminar held at the University of Surrey in September 1991.

Development economists often appear to be filled with self-doubt as to the legitimacy of their subdiscipline as an area of study, and possibly during the 1970s there was some evidence of a waning interest in development issues. However, this trend, if it existed, now appears to have been reversed. If one looks at the number of specialist journals and research centres, as well as the levels of recruitment on development courses, there is strong justification for feeling that development economics is alive and well.

Within the subject area there has always been a tendency to draw a distinction between domestic and international aspects: many well-known development economists argue that domestic issues are fundamentally more important and intellectually more interesting. A theme of this book is to take issue with this extreme view. Development is a process influenced by a complex combination of domestic and international factors. While it is certainly important not to ignore the domestic side of things, concentration on this dimension is bound to lead to only partial vision. Besides, it is increasingly difficult to sustain a distinction between the domestic and international aspects of economic development given the extent of interaction between them. This book examines areas of interaction as well as the strategic international factors which impinge on development in terms of both finance and trade. It should therefore be of interest to students of both development and international economics.

Thanks go to all the authors for keeping to a tight schedule and to Liz Blakeway who acted as Conference Administrator and helped to push the whole project through to fruition. Although she always remains happy and smiling I imagine that after each book in this series is produced her feelings must be rather like those of the mother of ten who after each birth says 'never again'! Future volumes in the Surrey Seminars in Applied Economics are envisaged!

Contributors

Graham Bird *Department of Economics, University of Surrey, Guildford, Surrey GU2 5XH, UK.*

Ricardo Gottschalk *Institute of Development Studies, University of Sussex, Falmer, Brighton, East Sussex, BN1 9RE, UK.*

Stephany Griffith-Jones *Institute of Development Studies, University of Sussex, Falmer, Brighton, East Sussex, BN1 9RE, UK.*

Sara Horrell *Department of Economics, University of Cambridge, Cambridge, CB3 9DE, UK.*

John Hudson *Department of Social Sciences, University of Bath, Bath, BA2 7AY, UK.*

Homi Katrak *Department of Economics, University of Surrey, Guildford, Surrey, GU2 5XH, UK.*

Matthew McQueen *Department of Economics, University of Reading, Reading, Berkshire, RG6 2AA, UK.*

Chris Milner *Department of Economics, Loughborough University of Technology, Loughborough, Leicestershire, UK.*

Paul Mosley *Institute for Development Policy and Management, Precinct Centre, Oxford Road, Manchester, M13 9QS, UK.*

S. Mansoob Murshed *Department of Economics, University of Surrey, Guildford, Surrey GU2 5XH, UK.*

Peter J. G. Pearson *Department of Economics, University of Surrey, Guildford, Surrey GU2 5XH, UK.*

P. N. Snowden *Department of Economics, The Management School, Lancaster University, Lancaster LA1 4YX, UK.*

Paul Stevens *Department of Economics, University of Surrey, Guildford, Surrey GU2 5XH, UK.*

International Aspects of Economic Development: A Contextual Introduction

GRAHAM BIRD

What causes some countries to develop more rapidly than others? Why do some developing countries earn a reputation for being the examples to emulate, while others become regarded as 'basket cases'? At a general level the answers to these questions are quite straightforward. Courses in economics usually begin by introducing the concept of the production possibility frontier and by identifying the factors that cause it to shift outwards. Crucial to demarcating the location of the frontier are resource endowments and the efficiency with which these are used. It is relatively easy to represent and extend these ideas in terms of aggregate supply. However, the full and efficient use of resources within an economy also depends on aggregate demand. Failure to balance aggregate demand and aggregate supply creates macroeconomic disequilibria. Economies will develop most satisfactorily where productive capacity expands and where aggregate demand is maintained at a level which fully utilizes but does not exceed productive potential.

However, generalizations such as this are operationally meaningless unless the processes by which aggregate supply is increased are well understood and unless aggregate demand may be effectively managed. Although most people would hold opinions as to what determines aggregate supply, there is no universally accepted paradigm. Moreover, it is increasingly recognized as being insufficient merely to identify relevant economic variables such as domestic saving, the marginal efficiency of capital, and industrial organization: political, social, cultural and institutional factors also need to be taken into account. This comment is, of course, relatively easy to make but in practice, it means that the development process is likely to be almost infinitely complex. Where a particular blend of economic, political, social, cultural and institutional factors is unique to an individual country it will become extremely difficult to generalize about the development process. What we end up with is a series of specific case studies.

However, while the development process is not fully understood, the challenge to secure sustained economic advancement in poor countries remains pressing. The data in Table I.1 show that for every regional and income subgroup the growth of GDP in developing countries in 1990 was

Table I.1 Growth of GDP in low- and middle-income economies, 1981–90.

Region or income group	Annual change in GDP (%)					1989 GDP (US$ billions)
	1981–6	1987	1988	1989	1990[a]	
Low- and middle-income economies	3.9	3.6	4.2	3.2	2.3	3560.3
By regional group						
Sub-Saharan Africa[b]	1.8	0.3	2.6	3.0	1.1	164.6
East Asia[c]	8.0	8.9	9.3	5.6	6.2	821.0
South Asia[d]	5.2	4.3	8.1	4.9	4.4	353.3
Europe, Middle East and North Africa[e]	3.7	0.6	2.1	2.0	0.4	1201.2
Latin America and the Caribbean[f]	1.5	3.1	0.6	1.4	−0.7	943.6
By income group						
Low-income economies[g]	6.4	6.1	7.8	4.5	4.3	930.8
Middle-income economies[h]	3.0	2.5	2.6	2.5	1.3	2652.1
Severely indebted, middle-income economies[i]	1.9	2.9	1.3	1.3	−1.6	1071.1

Source: World Bank Annual Report (1991).
[a] Preliminary.
[b] Excludes South Africa.
[c] China, Fiji, Indonesia, Democratic Kampuchea, Kiribati, Republic of Korea, Lao People's Democratic Republic, Macao, Malaysia, Mongolia, Papua New Guinea, the Philippines, Solomon Islands, Thailand, Tonga, Vanuatu, Viet Nam and Western Samoa.
[d] Bangladesh, Bhutan, India, Maldives, Myanmar, Nepal, Pakistan and Sri Lanka.
[e] Afghanistan, Algeria, Bulgaria, Czechoslovakia, Egypt, Greece, Hungary, Islamic Republic of Iran, Iraq, Jordan, Lebanon, Libya, Malta, Morocco, Oman, Poland, Portugal, Romania, Syrian Arab Republic, Tunisia, Turkey, Republic of Yemen and Yugoslavia.
[f] All American and Caribbean economies south of the United States, except Cuba.
[g] Economies with a GNP *per capita* of $580 or less in 1989.
[h] Economies with a GNP *per capita* of more than $580 but less than $6000 in 1989.
[i] Argentina, Bolivia, Brazil, Chile, the Congo, Costa Rica, Côte d'Ivoire, Ecuador, Egypt, Honduras, Hungary, Mexico, Morocco, Nicaragua, Peru, the Philippines, Poland, Senegal, Uruguay and Venezuela.

less than it had been during 1981–6. A similarly depressing picture emerges in relation to the data on GDP *per capita* (Table I.2). Only in the East Asia and South Asia regional groupings was there a positive growth in GDP *per capita* in 1990, and even here the growth was less marked than it had been in the 1980s. For developing countries in Sub-Saharan Africa and in Latin America and the Caribbean, living standards appear to have fallen almost unremittingly during the 1980s.

Table I.2 Growth of GDP *per capita* in low- and middle-income economies, 1981–90.

Region or income group	1989 population (millions)	Annual change in GDP *per capita* (%)				
		1981–6	1987	1988	1989	1990[a]
Low- and middle-income economies	4053.2	1.8	1.4	2.0	1.0	0.2
By regional group						
Sub-Saharan Africa[b]	480.4	−1.3	−2.8	−0.6	−0.2	−2.1
East Asia[c]	1552.4	6.4	7.1	7.4	3.8	4.3
South Asia[d]	1130.8	2.8	2.0	5.7	2.6	2.1
Europe, Middle East and North Africa[e]	433.2	1.6	−1.4	0.1	0.1	−1.3
Latin America and the Caribbean[f]	421.4	−0.6	1.0	−1.4	−0.6	−2.6
By income group						
Low-income economies[g]	2948.4	4.3	3.9	5.5	2.3	2.1
Middle-income economies[h]	1104.9	0.8	0.4	0.6	0.5	−0.6
Severely indebted, middle-income economies[i]	554.3	−0.3	0.8	−0.7	−0.6	−3.4

Source: World Bank Annual Report (1991).
For notes, refer to Table I.1.

In the absence of a perfectly articulated model it is still worthwhile to see how certain elements may make a contribution to development. Theoretically it is possible to perceive economic development as an exclusively domestic phenomenon. Appropriately chosen assumptions can remove all external constraints. Foreign exchange gaps can soon evaporate if one assumes a perfectly elastic supply of international capital, or perfect substitutability between capital and labour, or between domestic and foreign inputs. Furthermore, 'gaps' are, by definition, *ex ante* concepts. *Ex post* development will comply with effective constraints. Even *ex ante*, gaps may be removed simply by reducing targeted growth rates.

However, the relevant question is not whether it is possible to perceive a set of circumstances in which economic development would be a purely domestic phenomenon, but whether this set of circumstances is realistic. Taking the experience of the 1980s it is surely difficult to argue that the economic fortunes of developing countries were insulated from external and international influences. Economic development takes place within an international setting which may be either encouraging or discouraging.

While the spillover effects which macroeconomic policies in industrial countries have on each other are becoming more fully recognized and analysed within the context of the international coordination of macroeconomic policy, sight should not be lost of the implications that such policies have for the developing world. A simple but realistic example may be used to illustrate the point. The unbroken lines in Figure I.1(a) illustrate an original situation of macroeconomic equilibrium in the OECD (Organisation for Economic Cooperation and Development). A leftward shift in LM to LM* reflects the pursuit of contractionary monetary policy in the OECD. Depending on the slope of IS, this policy pushes up the rate of interest and pushes down income. These changes will have important implications for developing countries if they hold a large amount of floating interest rate debt and rely heavily on OECD countries as a market for their exports. Indeed, this is very much the course of events that the world witnessed at the beginning of the 1980s as rising interest rates and falling export receipts contributed to the Third World debt crisis.

Of course, while contractionary monetary policies in industrial countries create severe balance of payments and debt problems in developing countries, expansionary policies can accommodate adjustment with growth.

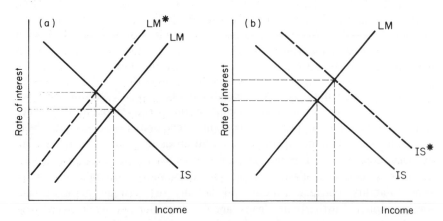

Figure I.1 A simple illustration of the effects of OECD policies on less developed countries. (a) Contractionary OECD monetary policy. (b) Expansionary OECD fiscal policy.

Yet even our very simple model illustrates certain complexities. Expansionary fiscal policy in the OECD will, according to Figure I.1(b), be a mixed blessing for developing countries. While they will benefit from any related increase in the demand for their exports, they will lose from the increase in world interest rates. To map out the detail of the relationship between economic performance in less developed countries and that in industrial countries requires much more sophisticated analysis, but the basic point that economic welfare in less developed countries is affected by international influences is surely made. The international aspects of economic development relate to both adjustment and financing and can impinge on both the demand and supply side of the domestic economy.

Faced with a desire to strengthen the balance of payments as might exist in a highly indebted developing country, economic adjustment may focus either on export expansion or import compression. The extent to which the first of these options is available will, in practice, depend not only on domestic policy but also on policies abroad. What access do developing countries have to markets in industrial economies; what levels of protection do they encounter and in what form? What happens if developing countries in general are successful in penetrating industrial country markets; is there a danger that this 'success' will induce an adverse movement in their terms of trade? Is it, in any case, legitimate to use the phrase 'in general' where developing countries are concerned or are there simply too many differences between them to warrant generalization?

It is clearly possible to paint both pessimistic and optimistic pictures. The pessimistic one might look as follows. At an early stage in its development the 'typical' developing country relies mainly on exporting primary products. While it encounters relatively few protectionist measures on these it also faces low price and income elasticities of demand. Success in increasing the volume of exports will, in these circumstances, be associated with reduced export earnings. The incentive will therefore exist to diversify away from primary products into processing or manufactured goods, where the relevant elasticities are higher. However, the country may now find that it encounters levels of protection which prevent it from exploiting the more conducive demand conditions. If this pessimistic picture is accurate, how does one account for the apparent trading success of the Newly Industrializing Countries? Discussion of these questions poses at least two others. First, what is the most desirable international trading system from the point of view of developing countries? Second, assuming that they do not at present face such a system, what is the developing countries' best strategy given the system that actually exists and bearing in mind the dynamics which suggest that their success within any particular system will result in that system being modified?

Many of these trading issues are discussed in the chapters in this book by Matthew McQueen (Chapter 1) and Chris Milner (Chapter 2). McQueen, for example, shows the sheer complexity of the European Community's trade preferences as they relate to various categories of developing countries. He draws attention to the declining relative importance of the EC in the exports of non-oil developing countries. However, he rejects the argument that trade preferences have little trade-stimulating effect on the exports of less developed countries. Instead, he suggests that, particularly for small developing countries and where trade preferences provide exemption from non-tariff barriers (NTBs) as well as from tariffs, trade preferences can provide an important complementary role, in conjunction with outward oriented (or neutral) trade strategies. He proposes that the newly industrializing countries should be graduated out of EC trade preferences, requiring them to conform to GATT rules in return for 'rolling back' NTBs, and that the EC's most generous scheme of preferences should be made available to all remaining less developed countries. His concern is that without such changes, and especially with the completion of the internal market and preoccupation with Eastern Europe, developing countries will become increasingly peripheral to EC trade and economic relations, to the detriment of both parties.

Milner examines the relevance of the 'new' international trade theories and of strategic trade policy for developing countries in terms of the design of their own commercial policy. He concludes that they would be mistaken to interpret these 'advances' as providing justification for greater selective intervention, and argues that international specialization is not arbitrary and that the existence of scale economies does not erode the importance of other sources of cost differential.

An impact on such cost disadvantages as developing countries encounter may, in principle, be achieved through importing technology from abroad. Imperfect substitutability between domestic labour and foreign machines has for a long time led developing countries to recognize that imports of capital goods will be an important component in strengthening the supply side of their economies and in promoting economic growth. However, it has also been recognized that machines designed for use in industrial countries may not be ideal for use in developing ones. Homi Katrak (Chapter 3) investigates various areas of concern and examines not only the problems of limited choice and inappropriateness in design, but also the question of how competition amongst machinery suppliers may affect the prices of both used and new machines. Finally, Katrak considers how the private and social benefits of imported machines may be affected by the structure of developing countries' markets.

It has commonly been argued that without diversification into more technologically advanced sectors, many developing countries will be exposed to adverse trend movements in their terms of trade and instability about this trend. Paul Stevens (Chapter 4) takes this analysis one stage further by examining the links (and incompatibilities) between the world energy market and economic development. What makes energy deserving of such attention? Stevens argues that it is the rapidity with which swings in price occur combined with the pervasive nature of energy in most economies. In the light of his claim that incompatibilities between energy markets and economic development will become more significant in the future, Stevens examines a range of policy options, some familiar and some less so. In particular he focuses on cooperation, and argues that, for the importers, this offers potential scope for minimizing the problems that arise from energy market characteristics.

Oil, and primary products in general, form one bridge between developing and developed countries. This linkage is a part of the model of North–South interaction constructed by Mansoob Murshed (Chapter 5). The model is essentially structuralist in lineage but incorporates asymmetries in as much as the North exhibits fix-price and the South flex-price characteristics. Murshed illustrates how the basic model may be extended to cover issues such as protectionism, developing country debt and the global environment, as well as the long-term North–South terms of trade.

Concern over global warming amongst developed countries is something that developing countries might seek to exploit. Peter Pearson (Chapter 6) undertakes a detailed examination of how the Third World fits into the global environmental picture. He points out that the transnational nature of a number of energy–environment problems implies that international cooperation will be needed and that, in the case of greenhouse gases, and given the rapidly increasing projected share of the Third World in global emissions, abatement by industrial countries on their own will be ineffectual. Yet it may be difficult to persuade developing countries to participate without some positive incentive to do so. This clearly leads to the question of foreign aid which, more generally, offers one way of attempting to close the financing gap that developing countries encounter.

Table I.3 provides a summary of financial flows to developing countries during the 1980s. A notable feature of the table is the increasing share of aid in resource transfers, although this is accounted for largely by the diminishing flows from other sources rather than by increasing aid flows. Many of the issues associated with aid have been well rehearsed recently in the literature. Given its increasing relative importance, however, a central issue is aid effectiveness. Paul Mosley, John Hudson and Sara Horrell (Chapter 7) examine this question and draw on econometric evidence concerning the connection between aid and the growth of GNP. The

Table I.3 Total net resource flows to developing countries, 1981–9 (current $ billion).[a]

Source	1981	1982	1983	1984	1985	1986	1987	1988	1989
Official Development Finance (ODF)	45.5	44.2	42.4	47.7	48.9	56.3	61.6	66.0	69.0
Official Development Assistance (ODA)	36.8	33.9	33.9	35.0	37.3	44.5	48.3	51.6	53.1
Of which: Bilateral disbursements	28.9	26.3	26.3	27.2	28.8	34.9	38.2	40.3	40.5
Multilateral disbursements	7.9	7.6	7.6	7.8	8.5	9.6	10.1	11.3	12.6
Other ODF	8.7	10.3	8.5	12.7	11.6	11.8	13.3	14.4	15.9
Of which: Bilateral disbursements	3.0	3.7	1.3	4.5	3.7	4.0	6.6	7.9	9.0
Multilateral disbursements	5.7	6.6	7.2	8.2	7.9	7.8	6.7	6.5	6.9
Total export credits	17.6	13.7	4.6	6.2	4.0	-0.7	-2.6	-0.5	1.2
DAC countries	16.2	12.7	3.9	5.2	3.4	-0.9	-2.9	-0.9	1.0
Of which: Short-term	2.9	3.0	-3.5	0.3	3.2	3.0	4.1	2.0	1.0
Other countries	1.4	1.0	0.7	1.0	0.6	0.2	0.3	0.4	0.2
Private flows	74.3	58.2	47.9	31.7	31.4	28.2	34.5	40.4	40.2
Direct investment	17.2	12.8	9.3	11.3	6.6	11.3	21.0	25.1	22.0
Of which: Offshore centres	4.1	4.1	3.7	3.8	3.7	6.8	13.5	9.9	–
International bank lending	52.3	37.9	35.0	17.2	15.2	7.0	7.0	5.8	8.0
Of which: Short-term	22.0	15.0	-25.0	-0.6	12.0	-0.4	5.0	2.0	4.0
Total bond lending	1.3	4.8	1.0	0.3	5.4	2.7	0.5	0.4	1.0
Other private	1.5	0.4	0.3	0.3	1.3	3.9	2.5	4.9	5.0
Grants by nongovernmental organizations	2.0	2.3	2.3	2.6	2.9	3.3	3.5	4.2	4.2
Total net resource flows	137.4	116.1	94.9	85.6	84.3	83.8	93.5	105.9	110.4

Source: Development Cooperation Report (OECD, Paris, 1990).
[a] Includes flows from all sources, i.e. DAC, Eastern European countries, Arab and other less developed country donors. Figures exclude Taiwan.

analysis of aid's contribution to economic development illustrates the synergistic relationship that exists between domestic and international factors. It also illustrates the difficulties in reaching general conclusions in circumstances where many of the factors that influence the effectiveness of aid are country-specific. Yet if aid is to represent the principal route through which resource transfers are to occur, it is vital that the key determinants of its effectiveness become better understood. As Mosley *et al.* point out, many of the old, but ill-substantiated, nostrums that used to pass for knowledge have been swept away without having been replaced by anything else.

During the 1970s, of course, many developing countries relied on private international capital markets as a source of finance. A legacy of this reliance was the developing country debt crisis of the 1980s; a problem which served to underline dramatically the interrelationship between developing and industrial economies. Stephany Griffith-Jones and Ricardo Gottschalk (Chapter 8) examine whether developing country debt remains a problem in the 1990s. They argue that, while difficulties still remain, substantial progress has been made. An important component of recent policy has been the so-called Brady Plan for debt reduction. Nicholas Snowden (Chapter 9) focuses on the specific but central question of how debt reduction will affect future capital inflows. Snowden argues that the answer depends on the implicit seniority structure of external claims, and suggests that the claims represented by exit bonds need to be separated more satisfactorily from those of future bond issues.

Continuing with this line of argument, if private lending cannot be resuscitated and if additional foreign aid is not forthcoming, is there not a role for the international financial institutions (IFIs) to play in helping to foster economic development? Graham Bird (Chapter 10) examines how the division of labour between the International Monetary Fund and the World Bank has become increasingly blurred during the 1980s and 1990s. Drawing on evidence to suggest that existing institutional arrangements are not working well, Bird identifies and assesses various alternative arrangements, favouring one that envisages an enhanced role for the World Bank.

A common theme that runs through all the chapters in this book may be identified. Developing countries can and do influence their own destiny: indeed, sustained economic development is most unlikely to be achieved if domestic policies are unwise and inappropriate. However, having said this, the international aspects of economic development are also important. International aspects will constrain the choice of domestic policies, will constrain the impact of domestic policies, and may even have a direct effect on the design of domestic policies through the conditionality attached to foreign loans. During the 1980s many developing countries found themselves in an unfriendly international economic environment, with the result that in many parts of the developing world economic (and social) development was arrested. Recession in industrial economies combined with increasing protectionism did not assist export expansion, while diminishing access to international finance limited the range of other policy options available. If, for whatever motives, the richer countries of the world are genuine in their commitment to assist the poorer ones, the chapters in this book suggest various avenues through which such a commitment may be translated into reality.

1 | European Community Trade Policies Towards the Developing Countries

MATTHEW McQUEEN*

I INTRODUCTION

The European Community affects the developing countries both directly through its trade and aid policies and indirectly through its internal policies, most notably through the Common Agricultural Policy (CAP). Both these policies and the complex linkages between them produce wide-ranging effects and the discussion must therefore be selective. This paper concentrates on an analysis of the empirical evidence on EC trade policies, because trade forms the fundamental linkage between the EC and the developing countries. This is not to deny the importance of aid to the developing countries, nor to regard trade and aid as substitutes, since clearly the latter involves a direct transfer of resources while trade simply offers the opportunity of transforming domestic resources into foreign resources. Trade, however, is quantitatively much more significant, particularly at the Community level. This may be illustrated by the fact that total aid disbursements by individual EC countries (excluding Greece, Luxembourg, Portugal and Spain) are equivalent to around 15% of EC imports from the non-oil developing countries, while Community aid (as opposed to the national aid programmes of the member states) is equivalent to around 2% of these imports. Trade policy, which is determined in principle at Community level, is therefore the 'key area in which the Community as such can bring its influence to bear on the immense task of

* I am grateful to Chris Milner, University of Loughborough, for comments on a draft of this paper.

INTERNATIONAL ASPECTS OF
ECONOMIC DEVELOPMENT
ISBN 0–12–099742–8

generating a sustained improvement in the economic condition of the Third World' (Hine, 1985, p. 156).

Developing countries are increasingly exhorted and persuaded—through making aid flows conditional on the implementation of World Bank structural adjustment programmes—to adopt outwardly oriented industrialization strategies. There are, however, two opposing views regarding the prospects for developing country exports to the industrialized countries. Optimists emphasize the static and dynamic gains from trade and envisage an increasing interdependence not only in traditional exports of raw materials, energy and foodstuffs, but also increasingly in manufactured goods, especially in the context of a rapid growth in intra-industry trade. Pessimists are sceptical of the possibilities of increasing the international division of labour and emphasize that increased competition from imports of manufactured goods and processed raw materials (e.g. petroleum products) from the developing countries can be expected to meet increased protectionism. In addition, electronics-based technological change can be expected to reverse the international division of labour of the 1970s and return production closer to the markets in the industrialized countries (Kaplinsky, 1984).

This debate involves complex and unresolved issues but, since the EC accounts for one-third of the non-oil exports of the developing countries to the industrialized countries, this paper seeks to shed some light on the issues by analysing trends in the imports of the EC and in its import-stimulating and import protection measures.

II TRENDS IN EC IMPORTS FROM THE NON-OIL-EXPORTING DEVELOPING COUNTRIES

Imports by the EC from the non-oil-exporting developing countries (NODCs) increased four-fold in real terms[1] over the period 1963–88 and doubled during 1980–8. World trade also grew rapidly over much of this period and so, as Figure 1.1 shows, the 1989 share of NODCs in EC imports from third countries (extra-EC imports) was still only marginally above its 1965 level. It should be noted, however, that this import share has recovered substantially since declining over the period 1960–77, despite the fact that EC import growth rates were significantly lower in 1980–8 compared to 1960–70. This suggests that developing countries have become more competitive in the EC market in the last decade and that they have been able to benefit from an increasing international division of labour.

Figure 1.2 decomposes the share of NODCs in extra-EC imports into various groupings by countries. The five newly industrializing countries (Brazil, Hong Kong, Singapore, South Korea and Taiwan) doubled their

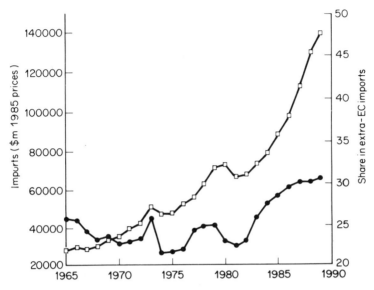

Figure 1.1 EC imports from non-oil developing countries. —□—, Real EC imports from NODC ($m); —●—, NODC share in extra-EC imports (%).

share of extra-EC imports over the period 1975–89 and clearly underpin the rapid growth of NODC exports. Other NODCs, however, also increased their share of extra-EC imports from under 18% to over 22%, implying that increased competitiveness was not confined simply to the five NICs. The Latin American countries, excluding Venezuela, showed a parallel increased share, reflecting to a significant extent the exports of Brazil (accounting for approximately 40% of exports), while the shares of the ASEAN countries and the non-oil Mediterranean countries[2] slowly increased from low levels. EC imports from the ACP countries recorded declining shares from low levels and this is analysed separately in the discussion of the impact of the Lomé Convention.

Figure 1.3 analyses the evolution of the separate shares of the five NICs in EC imports from the NODCs, and indicates that this increased from 20% in 1975 to 27% in 1989. Within this group there were significant changes in relative shares: although Brazil has the largest share (6.9%), its importance has declined since the mid-1980s with the rapid growth in imports from Taiwan and South Korea.

These generally favourable trends in EC imports from the NODCs need to be interpreted in the context of trends in the world exports of these countries, as indicated in Table 1.1. First, intra-NODC trade increased from 17.5% of total exports in 1970 to 21.2% in 1988, and the share of the industrialized countries decreased from just under 70% to 64.4%. Second,

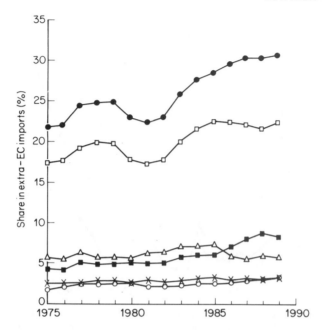

Figure 1.2 Shares in extra-EC imports, 1975–89. —●—, Total share of non-oil
developing countries in extra-EC imports (%); —×—, share of non-
oil developing Mediterranean countries in extra-EC imports (%);
—△—, share of Latin American countries (less Venezuela) in extra-EC
imports (%); —○—, share of ASEAN countries in extra-EC imports
(%); —■—, share of 5 NICs in extra-EC imports (%); —□—, share of
non-oil developing countries less 5 NICs in extra-EC imports (%).

the EC has been a substantially more important market for food beverages
and tobacco, agricultural raw materials, ores and metals, while the US has
been a more important market for fuels and manufactured goods. The latter
group of products has grown at more than twice the rate of the former, and
the share of manufactured goods in total NODC exports has increased from
26% to 65%. As a result, whereas US imports from the NODCs in 1970
were approximately three-quarters those of the EC, relative import levels
had reversed by 1988. The decrease in the relative importance of the EC
compared to the US was true for all the main geographical regions but was
particularly marked in the case of Asia, where the share of exports to the
EC declined from 26% to 17%, while the share of the US increased from
14% to 23%.

In the case of manufactured goods, whereas both countries each
imported just over $2 billion in 1970, by 1988 the US imported more than
twice the level ($39.6 billion) of the EC ($18.2 billion). Also, while the EC

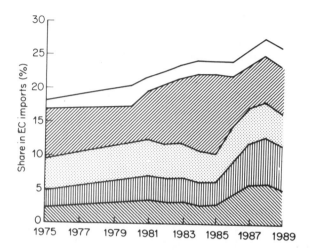

Figure 1.3 Shares of NICs in EC imports from non-oil developing countries. □, Singapore; ▨, Brazil; ▩, Hong Kong; ▥, Taiwan; ▧, South Korea.

share in NODC exports of manufactures stayed constant at 19%, that of the US increased to just under one-third. The substantial decrease in the relative importance of the EC compared to the US in the export of manufactured goods by the developing countries cannot be explained by differential rates of growth of imports. On the contrary, EC imports of manufactured goods grew at an annual rate of 13.4%, while US imports of manufactured goods increased at 11.8%. Possible explanations may be found in terms of differences in the comparative advantages of the EC and the US in manufactured goods, stronger US trade links with the NICs and the more industrialized countries in South East Asia and Latin America, and differences in trade policies towards imports of manufactures from the developing countries.

III REGIONAL TRADE AGREEMENTS

One of the hallmarks of EC trade policy has been its willingness to differentiate between different groups of non-member countries in its trade relations. This is not only contrary to the basic GATT principle of non-discrimination (as indeed was the formation of the EC itself) but also reflects a strong mercantalist influence on the formulation of EC trade policy (it may be noticed, in passing, that the EC *Statistical Yearbook on*

Table 1.1 Export structure by destination for non-oil developing countries, 1970–88.

Commodity groups	Share in exports 1970–88	Industrialized countries	EC	USA	Japan	Non-oil developing countries
All products						
1970		69.9	29.9	22.0	9.4	17.5
1988		64.4	21.0	26.8	10.6	21.2
Average growth	(14.7)	(14.2)	(12.5)	(16.0)	(15.5)	(16.0)
Food items						
1970	35.6	73.5	35.6	23.8	5.4	13.4
1988	15.8	62.6	30.1	15.6	12.0	17.0
Average growth	(9.7)	(8.7)	(8.7)	(7.1)	(14.6)	(11.2)
Agriculture and raw materials						
1970	13.0	62.9	29.9	7.4	17.7	20.3
1988	4.4	52.6	24.1	7.2	18.2	30.1
Average growth	(8.1)	(7.0)	(6.8)	(7.9)	(8.3)	(10.5)
Ores and metals						
1970	17.3	86.4	43.1	16.6	19.7	5.1
1988	5.4	68.0	31.9	11.8	20.3	20.1
Average growth	(7.5)	(6.1)	(5.8)	(5.5)	(7.7)	(16.1)
Fuels						
1970	7.4	63.1	11.8	30.8	7.8	28.0
1988	8.4	60.5	12.9	25.2	19.0	29.5
Average growth	(15.6)	(15.3)	(16.2)	(14.3)	(21.5)	(15.9)
Manufactured goods						
1970	26.2	59.8	18.7	27.7	4.4	26.8
1988	64.6	65.9	18.8	32.3	7.9	20.5
Average growth	(20.6)	(21.3)	(20.6)	(21.7)	(24.6)	(18.8)

Source: UNCTAD Handbook of International Trade and Development Statistics 1990 (UN, New York, 1991).

External Trade includes tables on EC trade balances with every country in the world). The 'hierarchy of trade preferences' (Weston *et al.*, 1980) for the developing countries may be summarized as follows:

(1) The Lomé Convention—ACP Group
Africa (46 countries)
Caribbean (15 countries)
Pacific (8 countries)
(2) Association Agreements—providing 'eventual' full EC membership
Cyprus, Turkey, Malta

(3)   Preferential Trade and Co-operation Agreements
         Maghreb (Algeria, Morocco and Tunisia)
         Mashraq (Egypt, Jordan, Lebanon, Syria)
         Israel
         Yugoslavia
(4)   Generalized System of Preferences
         42 developing countries (not covered by above)
         9 least developed countries (not covered by above)
         Hong Kong, Macao
         Bulgaria, Hungary, Mongolia, Poland

These trade agreements only give a margin of preference over non-EC and, for most manufactured goods, non-EFTA sources of supply.

Economists tend to concentrate on the margin of *tariff* preference offered by these schemes and conclude that since successive rounds of tariff reductions have resulted in a low average EC tariff, preferential trade arrangements can have little or no trade-stimulating effect. This argument is, however, misleading. First, the average tariff on manufactured goods exported by the developing countries is higher than that for the developed countries (e.g. EC tariffs on clothing vary from 8% to 14%), while tariffs on agricultural and fisheries products regarded as sensitive by the EC are almost invariably within the range 13–24%. Second, given the general escalation of nominal tariffs with the degree of processing and manufacturing, effective tariff rates (measuring the effective degree of protection of domestic producers) are a multiple of nominal rates. Third, as the general level of tariff has decreased, so the developed countries have sought to protect certain sensitive sectors of their economies from particularly competitive countries, some of which are developed countries (e.g. Japan), but a substantial proportion of these instruments of 'new protectionism' are directed at the developing countries. It is difficult to determine which developing countries are affected by these measures and by how much, but it is important to appreciate that the *possibility* of such action being taken, as a result of a rapid growth of imports of a particular product from a developing country, increases the already high risks associated with investment for exports. The potential value of a trade preference agreement to beneficiaries must therefore be assessed in terms of the total or partial guarantee of exemption which it offers against *all* trade restrictions. This is best illustrated by contrasting the terms of the Lomé Convention with those of the Generalized System of Preferences.

III.1   Lomé Convention

The Lomé Convention originated from the preferential schemes of Britain, France and Belgium for their ex-colonies (although, in the case of Britain, its ex-colonies in Asia were excluded from the Convention). It is regarded by the EC as the most important of its preferential trade agreements, both in terms of its comprehensive coverage of trade and aid and because it is a negotiated contractual agreement between the ACP countries and the EC. Indeed, it is described in the Convention as a 'model for relations' between developed and developing states (*Article 1*). The Fourth Lomé Convention was signed in December 1989 for a 10-year period and the main provisions were as follows:

(1) Products originating in the ACP are imported into the EC free of customs duties and quotas.

(2) (a) For 40 CAP products, there is either total exemption from customs duties or partial exemption, sometimes within a marketing timetable and within a reference quantity, and total or partial reduction of third country levies;

  (b) for beef and veal, there is access free of customs duties and 90% of levies, subject to quotas, for Botswana, Kenya, Madagascar, Swaziland and Zimbabwe;

  (c) for sugar, guaranteed quantities are imported from 13 ACP countries at a price negotiated annually within the price range obtaining in the EC.

(3) A Protocol on rum and bananas seeks to protect traditional ACP suppliers from competition from third countries.

(4) Rules of origin avoid third countries benefiting from Lomé preferences by requiring all ACP exports to the EC to qualify as 'originating' products. These rules are more or less identical across all EC preferential trade agreements in terms of process and value added criteria but, in addition, the ACP are the only group allowed to count imports of intermediate products both from the EC and from each other as 'originating' and, in addition, can obtain temporary exemption (derogation) from the rules for a 5-year period, either automatically if value added reaches 45% or through submitting a case for exemption if value added is below this level.

(5) Aid commitments for 1990–5 of Ecu 12 000 m were allocated as follows:

	(Ecu millions)	
European Investment Bank	1200	
European Development Fund	10 800	
Of which: STABEX[3]	1500	
SYSMIN[4]	480	
Risk capital	825	
Grants	7995	
Of which:Emergency		350

Interest subsidies	280	
Structural adjustment	1150	
Other grants	6215	
Of which: Regional cooperation		1250
Projects		4965

III.2   Generalized System of Preferences

Dissatisfaction with the operations of the GATT (referred to as the 'rich nations' club') led to the establishment of the first United Nations Conference on Trade and Development (UNCTAD) in 1964. Central to the debate at the conference was the Prebisch Report (after the author Raul Prebisch, who became the first Secretary-General of UNCTAD) in which two major problems were addressed: first, the slow and unstable growth of export earnings from primary products; and second, the need for developing countries to diversify their exports into manufactured goods. To achieve the latter in the face of what were perceived to be high discriminatory tariffs against imports from developing countries, a system of preferential tariffs was demanded which would serve the twin objectives of eliminating tariffs and obtaining a competitive advantage over suppliers in developed countries (Langhammer and Sapir, 1987). The need for more favourable treatment for the developing countries was particularly emphasized by Prebisch on the grounds of infant industry and economies of scale arguments (the theoretically superior alternative of subsidies to those industries financed by the developed countries was regarded as politically infeasible). The initial concept was for a uniform scheme implemented by all developed countries but, in practice, each donor country introduced its own scheme, the EC in 1971 and the US (the last industrialized country to do so) in 1976.

From the outset, donor countries have been concerned to protect domestic producers from the most competitive developing countries and this concern has grown with the rapid industrialization of the NICs. Protection has been achieved both by limiting the range of products available for preferences and by placing restrictions on the extent to which particular developing countries may benefit from preferences. These restrictions take the form of either a 'competitive need' criterion as operated by the US, or a system of predetermined tariff quotas as operated by the EC and other donor countries. Under the US system, Generalized System of Preferences (GSP) eligibility on a product is removed from a beneficiary if its exports to the US in the previous year accounted for either 50% or more of the value of US imports of that product, or exceeded a certain dollar value. Product/country combinations are reconsidered for eligibility if US imports of the product from the affected country fall below the competitive need limitation in a subsequent year. This system provides a guarantee of preferential treatment in any one year but creates uncertainty for competitive exports beyond this period. The EC scheme seeks to create a greater degree of certainty of treatment for beneficiaries by operating a system of tariff quotas. This increasingly complex system is now set at Community level, and establishes value or volume limits for preferential treatment for individual beneficiaries (to ensure that the most competitive countries do not 'crowd out' the less competitive). In practice, however, it has been very difficult for individual importers and exporters to obtain sufficiently accurate and up-to-date information on the level of exhaustion of these quota limits, particularly in the case of sensitive goods, and as a result of this uncertainty the exemption from duties for the most competitive countries has become more in the nature of a 'windfall gain' than a quantifiable competitive advantage.

During the 1980s, the EC and the US introduced 'graduation' measures to remove those countries which they consider competitive from the list of GSP beneficiaries on a product-by-product basis. Indeed, the enabling clause, which was added to the GATT in 1979 to authorize an exception to the MFN clause in favour of 'special and differential' treatment for the developing countries, envisaged that as countries became more developed, so they would 'return to GATT norms'. The Group of 77, representing the developing country interests in UNCTAD, have strongly resisted such graduation from eligibility for preferences and question the absence of open and agreed objective criteria for graduation. The developed countries defend graduation not simply on grounds of equity (for example, Hong Kong and Singapore have a *per capita* GNP more than double that of Greece and Portugal and substantially greater than Ireland), but also because the more industrialized developing countries have more to gain, both in terms of exports and internal resource allocation, from mutual reductions in barriers to trade than from special but limited preferences.

A further pressure for improvements to the GSP has been the progression of development strategy away from the ideas of the 1960s, which concentrated on industrialization as the sole means for accelerating economic development, towards recognizing the important and often complementary role of the agricultural sector, particularly in the earlier stages of development. As a result, the EC has gradually extended its GSP offer on dutiable primary products. An important constraint on this, however, has been the desire not only to protect EC producers but also to maintain more favourable treatment for the Mediterranean and particularly the ACP group of developing countries. This has limited not only the range of products listed but also the value of the offer. For example, the GSP offer on cocoa paste and cocoa butter allows only a 4% reduction on tariffs of 15% and 12% respectively, while the reduced tariff on tinned pineapples is subject to a strict volume limit. The whole offer on GSP products states that 'the temporary and non-binding nature of the system means that the offer may be withdrawn wholly or in part at a later stage, thus maintaining the possibility of remedying any unfavourable situations which may arise, including the ACP States, following the implementation of the system' (*Official Journal*, 1990, L.370).

The main features of the 1991 GSP scheme can be summarized as follows:

(1) Industrial products, with the exception of textiles and steel which are subject to separate regulations, enter tariff-free within certain limits and for a period of one year and this offer is available to all members of the Group of 77 and certain other countries in Eastern Europe.

(2) In practice, the offer has been renewed each year since its inception, but the autonomous and annual nature of the scheme allows the EC to make frequent changes to the scheme.

(3) The limits also apply, in practice, to some 145 sensitive products (i.e. those that compete strongly with EC manufacturers), with the remaining non-sensitive products (about 95% of the total number of products) subject only to statistical surveillance and with free access without limit for the least developed countries.

(4) GSP imports of sensitive products are controlled in a number of ways:

(a) a ceiling (mostly stipulated in Ecu) is calculated for each product and customs duties *may* be reimposed on a beneficiary once this ceiling is exhausted and at the request of a member state;

(b) in the case of certain NICs, 'fixed duty-free amounts' are calculated which, in a number of cases, are smaller than the ceiling and where the full customs duty is automatically reintroduced once the quota is exhausted;

(c) since 1986, the differentiation of the scheme has increased still further by designating certain product/countries where the GSP limit referred to in (b) is reduced by 50%, while in other cases (where the 50% reduction has applied in the past) product/country combinations have been removed (graduated out) from the GSP offer. Since 1987, South Korea has been suspended from the EC scheme over a dispute concerning intellectual property rights.

(5) The more limited offer on textiles is open only to the 33 signatories (1990) of the Multi-Fibre Arrangement (MFA) or similar bilateral export restraint agreements and is subject to a complex system of 6-monthly tariff quotas (for the most competitive countries) or annual ceilings apportioned among the 12 member states.

(6) A list of 350 agricultural products are given partial or in some cases total suspension of duties, with the additional provision of duty-free entry for the least developed countries.
(7) Exports must quality under the rules of origin.
(8) A safeguard clause is present.

IV   TRADE EFFECTS OF THE SCHEMES

IV.1   Lomé Convention

Despite being at the apex of the EC hierarchy of trade preferences, the share of the ACP countries[5] in EC imports from the non-oil developing countries has declined since the first Lomé Convention was signed in 1975 from a level of 21% to 10% in 1989. A recent study (Moss and Ravenhill, 1987) also found that, although the ACP countries have been relatively successful in maintaining or increasing their share of EC imports of their most important exports, this has often taken place in a declining overall market and in some cases there have been major decreases in the value of exported commodities. The only grain of comfort was that the non-oil Commonwealth countries did manage to increase their shares in the imports of the six founder members of the Community (where prior to 1975, they did not have preferential access except through the GSP in the period 1971–4). This evidence led a recent survey of preferential schemes offered by the OECD countries to conclude that 'on balance the Lomé Convention appears to have done little to stimulate industrialisation of the beneficiaries through export incentives' (Brown, 1988, p. 345).

The key question, however, is what would have been the experience of the ACP countries without Lomé, but with the prevailing internal policies of the ACP countries and external trading conditions. In view of the difficulties which Sub-Saharan Africa has faced over the period since 1975, it seems likely that their performance would have been even less satisfactory. First, most of these economies have maintained high tariff and non-tariff barriers on imports and this, combined with fiscal, social security and pricing policies, has generated a strong bias against exporting. Trade preferences, at best, can reinforce trade-oriented policies but it is unreasonable to expect preferences to more than offset the tax on the export sector produced from protectionist policies. Second, during the 1970s, Africa's export volume fell by almost 1% annually, while that of other developing countries increased, and this trend accelerated in the first half of the 1980s, with a wide difference in the growth of export volume that persisted into the second half of the 1980s. Some of the factors causing these adverse trends were probably the consequence of the domestic policies pursued by these countries. At least as important, however, were the effects of the two increases in the price of oil, which produced world recession and a sharp fall in demand for primary products. Lomé preferences were clearly powerless to reverse the effects of these forces. Third, valid generalizations regarding the effects of Lomé on the exports to the EC of such a heterogeneous group of (now 69) developing countries are difficult to sustain. In addition, exports to the EC are concentrated among a relatively few countries and products. Within the non-oil products there are divergent trends: copper, iron ore, vegetable oils, non-ferrous metals, iron and steel, fertilizers, animal feedstuffs, oil seeds and wood show stagnant or declining growth rates, while agricultural products (coffee, tea, cocoa, bananas, beef, fruit and vegetables) and fishery products have shown positive growth rates. Exports of manufactured products, particularly clothing, textile fabrics and wood veneers, have also shown rapid growth rates.

Rather than analysing broad aggregates, it therefore seems more useful to concentrate on those sectors in which the preferences under Lomé for manufactured goods (tariff and quota-free access) and agricultural products (duty-free plus concessions for CAP products) could potentially enable the ACP countries to diversify into non-traditional exports to the EC. This research was first carried out by Stevens and Weston (1984) and subsequently extended using published trade data (McQueen and Stevens, 1989) and case studies of Jamaica, Kenya and Ethiopia (Stevens, 1990), Mauritius (McQueen, 1990) and Zimbabwe (Riddell, 1990).

The analysis of trade data identified 70 products (6-digit level of classification) in eight broad groups: fisheries (canned tuna), leather goods, fresh flowers, vegetables, processed tropical agricultural products, wood products, yarns and fabrics, clothing and linen, which were either new exports or had developed rapidly from a small base in 1975. These exports had a total value of Ecu 826 million (1987), equivalent to 7% of total ACP non-fuel exports to the EC. Altogether, 28 ACP countries were identified and, although many exported only a small number of products, one-third of the countries exported six or more products and five exported more than 15 products. It was also of interest that these countries included not only relatively more developed countries such as Kenya, Mauritius and Zimbabwe, but also poorer countries such as Ethiopia, Sudan and Ghana.

It was not possible from the trade statistics alone to link export success in non-traditional products with Lomé preferences but the field studies provided reasons to suppose that its provisions had, at the very least, been helpful. Government policies towards the export sector, particularly changes in policies towards greater liberalization (or at least some compensation for protectionist policies), were crucial, while the recovery of growth in the international economy in the 1980s was also important.

These factors may be illustrated by the case of Mauritius (which has shown the most rapid degree of export diversification), where substantial changes in government policy after 1982, combined with a well-educated labour force and traditional links with the EC (France and UK), enabled Lomé to act as a key instrumental factor in the development of non-traditional exports. The benefits of Lomé to Mauritius may be summarized as follows (McQueen, 1990):

'(1) Exports of sugar have been the mainstay of the economy. The EC has consistently produced a surplus of beet sugar over its domestic consumption and, if the UK had not insisted on a guaranteed quota for Mauritius (and other Commonwealth sugar cane exports) at the time of entry into the EC, this market would, almost certainly, have been eventually closed to Mauritius. The world market for sugar has been generally depressed and the EC price has been, on average, three times the world price. These revenues provided the basis for local investment in the EPZ (export processing zone).

(2) Tariff and (MFA) quota-free entry into the EC stimulated 'infant' industries in a number of ways. First, exemption from duties of 8% to 14% gave a substantial effective subsidy to production over non-preferred countries, where value added levels are around one-third of the value of the exported product. Second, exemption from MFA quotas and guaranteed market access have been fundamental in attracting investment from the NICs (particularly Hong Kong), whose exports have been limited by quotas. The significance of exemption from quotas is particularly illustrated by the case of pullovers, where the import share of Mauritius in the EC market has been allowed greatly to exceed that of any other developing country (the fact that this still only accounts for a very small share of intra-EC trade indicates the extent of protection of the EC market). Third, quotas have also raised EC prices and thus enhanced the export earnings of Mauritius.

(3) Financial assistance under the Conventions, however, has only been of some indirect benefit to the EPZ, while technical cooperation can best be described as symbolic.'

Mauritius also illustrates the point that trade preferences should not be interpreted simply as tariff preferences: at least as important was the *guarantee of market access* which the Convention has provided.[6] The safeguard clause which could limit access has never been used, while the imposition of 'voluntary' export restraints by the UK and France in the late 1970s was regarded as so politically inept (at a time when the Lomé

Convention was being held up as a 'model for the new international economic order') by the other member states of the EC that the voluntary restraints were quietly forgotten in the 1980s.

It seems clear, therefore, that an export processing zone based on exports of clothing would not have grown to anything like its present level without preferences. This does not, of course, mean that Mauritius would not have been able to develop non-traditional exports of other products in the absence of preferences, as well as a lower volume of exports of clothing subject to MFA quotas. Indeed, the structure of preferences may have been such as to generate a misallocation of resources compared to an optimal situation of free trade prices (i.e. a welfare loss consequent on overproduction in line with 'false' comparative advantage). It might also be argued that preferences have induced a potentially unstable degree of concentration on a narrow range of clothing exports parallel to the country's dependence on sugar. Without preferences, the industrial structure may have been more diversified and less liable to instability. These points, however, simply underline the fact that preferences are second-best policies to free trade and, unless the view is taken that without preferences the developed countries would by now have removed barriers to imports from the developing countries, it seems reasonable to assume that most developing countries are probably better off with preferences than without, given protectionism in developed countries. It should also be noted that all export processing zones seem to develop first as 'industrial monocultures' (ILO/UNCTC, 1988) but that the share of the dominant industry declines over time, as shown for example by the older zones in South Korea and Mexico. Also, without preferences the export processing zones would certainly have grown at a much lower rate and, given the rapid growth of population in the 1960s and early 1970s, this would have created high levels of unemployment, with all the social costs and potential unrest that this entails. In the case of Zimbabwe, the closure of the South African market provided the pressure for the development of new products and markets, and Lomé provided the necessary degree of preferences to establish a foot-hold in such competitive areas as clothing and high-quality vegetables and flowers.

Jamaica illustrates some of the important weaknesses in Lomé, particularly regarding the restrictive effects of rules of origin. The US has positively encouraged at least a partial shift in the international division of labour and, as a result of this and preferences under the Caribbean Basin Initiative, Jamaica has been able to expand greatly exports of clothing to the US and Canada. Exports to the EC, however, have hardly grown at all because most do not qualify for preferences under the process criteria of the rules of origin.

No small group of studies can be taken as representative of a group as diverse as the ACP countries and this was not the intention of the study. Equally, in none of the cases can an unambiguous causal link be drawn between the Lomé Convention and the development of non-traditional exports. A host of factors is at work to explain both the success in exporting these new products and the failure to export others for which Lomé preferences are also substantial. Government policy in the exporting state is clearly a critical factor. In the cases of both Jamaica and Kenya, the lateness of the move into non-traditional exports can be explained in part by the unsupportive nature of government policies in the early period. Equally significant was the sharp change of direction of policies in Mauritius in the early and mid-1980s.

Nonetheless, there is some circumstantial evidence to suggest that a link exists. The degree of preference that the ACP countries enjoy over third-party exporters to the EC market is linked directly to the level of protection. The higher the level of protection for a particular commodity, the greater the scope for the EC to provide preferences to the ACP group, and indeed the studies found that the export diversification of all five countries has been precisely into those commodities on which EC protectionism is particularly strong and, hence, the Lomé preference is most marked. The result of EC protection is to limit supply onto the European market and, therefore, to raise prices. The ACP countries, as privileged exporters, gain part of the economic rent in these high prices. Because the markets are competitive, the ACP countries have to be efficient if they are to sell at all, but if they do reach this threshold efficiency level, their revenues are greater than they would be under free-market conditions. In a sense, therefore, the combination of EC protection plus Lomé preferences provides something akin to 'infant industry' protection for the domestic market, but with the added element that competition is not suppressed completely, thus reducing the possibility that the economic rent will be absorbed in production inefficiency.

If there is some evidence that the Lomé preferences have been helpful, there is also evidence that imperfections in the Convention have been a constraint on more rapid diversification. The rules of origin have been a clear impediment to some export diversification in Jamaica and Mauritius. The rules of origin have been amended in the Fourth Lomé Convention and if the EC is willing to abide by the spirit of the new provisions, it is possible that this barrier could be reduced. In addition to the rules of origin, the quotas that apply to many of the CAP concessions may become a constraint in the future. In the past, the quotas appear to have been sufficiently large to accommodate most non-traditional ACP exports of CAP products (i.e. excluding beef, rice, sugar and tobacco). However, if, as seems possible, the small group of existing exporters is joined by other ACP states as significant exporters to the EC, the group quotas could well become binding.

IV.2 Generalized System of Preferences

The extent to which developing countries can obtain preferences depends upon the tariff structure of the donor country, the structure of the preferential scheme (country coverage, product coverage, quota limitations, administration rules), the range and value of products exported to the donor country, and the degree of knowledge of exporters of the scheme. All of these factors will vary both between donor and recipient countries and over time (for example, measured in Ecu, the proportion of zero-duty EC imports from GSP countries fell from 74% in 1981 to 41% in 1989 *not* because duties had been extended to a wider range of imports but because of the fall in oil prices and the depreciation of the US$ against the Ecu). Statistics on preferential imports must therefore be interpreted with considerable caution.

Table 1.2 provides details of GSP imports in 1988 from the three donors responsible for 90% of GSP-receiving imports of $56b: the EC (33%), Japan (25%) and the USA (32%). A first approximation of the extent to which exports from developing countries may benefit from preferential treatment is to consider the proportion of dutiable imports included in the scheme. This is relatively high (81%) for the EC compared to the other main donors and OECD countries in general. As mentioned above, this ratio will vary from year to year, partly as a result of factors outside the structure of the GSP scheme itself; however, this 'coverage' ratio only once dropped below 70% in the period 1978–88. In contrast, the coverage ratio is much lower for the US, and has been consistently below 40%. In the case of Japan, the coverage ratio varied between 60% and 66% over the period 1978–87, almost certainly due to the changes in the commodity composition of imports, measured in US$. The utilization ratio (the proportion of

Table 1.2 Imports of preference-giving countries from beneficiaries of their schemes, 1988.

Country	Total imports ($b)	Dutiable ($b)	Proportion of dutiable imports covered (%)	Utilization ratio (%)	Ratio of preferential to dutiable imports (%)
EC	101.1	62.4	81.1	36.8	29.8
Japan	90.3	62.3	42.6	53.4	22.7
USA	153.0	140.3	35.6	36.7	13.1
OECD	370.9	281.9	49.8	41.0	20.0

Source: UNCTAD.

products covered by the GSP which actually received preferential treatment) in all cases is substantially less than 100% (although it may be noted that the cost in terms of the reduction in customs duties in the EC scheme was of the order of Ecu 1 000 million). The low utilization ratios reflect restrictions on access to GSP benefits for sensitive products, country/product-specific exclusions, inability to fulfil rules of origin, lack of familiarity with the schemes, and costs of information gathering and compliance with the regulations governing the schemes being greater than the margin of tariff preference. For all three donor countries, these low utilization ratios tended to decrease in the 1980s, reflecting increasingly stringent limitations on the most competitive suppliers of sensitive products (variations between Japan and the other two schemes can be explained largely by the exclusion of certain sensitive items—subject to quota limits and competitive need exclusion in the EC and US sectors—from their offer). The even lower ratio of preferential imports to dutiable imports suggests that there is considerable scope for improvements in all the preferential schemes, in terms both of product coverage and of access to the schemes.

Since the introduction of the GSP, all preference-giving countries have provided special measures for the least developed countries and, in the case of the EC, this applies to all of the 41 countries designated by the UN (Japan covers 38 of these countries, and the US 32). Table 1.3, however, reveals a marked difference between the EC and the US, where the broader product coverage of the EC scheme results in a relatively much higher level of dutiable imports from the least developed countries receiving preferences ($325 m) than in the US ($42 m), despite the US having a level of dutiable imports from these countries one-third greater than the EC.

Table 1.3 Imports of preference-giving countries from the least-developed countries, 1988.

Country	Total imports ($m)	Dutiable ($m)	Proportion of dutiable imports covered (%)	Utilization ratio (%)	Ratio of preferential to dutiable imports (%)
EEC	1043	571	94.2	60.4	56.9
Japan	715	450	52.0	99.1	51.6
USA[a]	1184	756	26.8	20.7	5.6
OECD	3472	1976	55.6	58.9	32.8

Source: UNCTAD.
[a] 1987.

The effects on the least developed countries reflect the fundamentally different approach of the EC, which has been to widen the product coverage of the scheme and protect EC producers by targeting restrictions on the most competitive countries. This also has the effect of ensuring (at least in the post-1981 schemes) that the less industrialized beneficiaries are not 'crowded out' by the NICs. The US, in contrast, protects vulnerable domestic industries largely by the exclusion of sensitive product lines in areas such as textiles and clothing (subject to MFA restrictions), footwear, electronic goods and steel goods, but has no *a priori* limits on imports, making the scheme more transparent and easier to administer (and therefore easier for exporters to understand).

The lack of transparency of the EC scheme is not only an obstacle to potential exporters but may also lead to an exaggeration of the restrictions of the scheme and consequently discourage exporters from applying for duty-free treatment. Considering aggregate trade flows, 52% of dutiable imports in 1989 were classified by the EC as 'sensitive' (broadly defined to include products subject not only to quotas and ceilings but also to statistical surveillance at the request of a member state), and of these only 41% received tariff-free entry into the EC market. Even in the case of non-sensitive goods, only 51% received duty-free treatment. The low proportions receiving preference were not, however, due to the widespread use of tariff quotas and ceilings on industrial goods. Inevitably a large proportion of the GSP benefits are concentrated in a relatively few developing countries (although the list of countries has changed as the decreased price of oil has removed most oil exports from the 'top ten', while countries such as China have significantly expanded their exports) with a substantial industrial base and with industries competitive in world markets. Table 1.4 lists the top ten beneficiaries from the EC scheme in 1989, accounting for 72% of GSP-receiving imports, and it should be noted that only in the case of Hong Kong and Singapore (and South Korea, prior to exclusion in 1987) is their ranking on GSP benefits significantly less than their ranking in covered trade, implying that these countries have been less successful in obtaining preferences due to quotas and ceilings.

More light is shed on the impact of GSP limitations on preferential treatment in Table 1.5, where it can be seen that in the two years 1989 and 1990, between 46 and 47 industrial products (defined at the 6-digit level of classification), excluding MFA products, were subject to duties being reimposed as a result of the exhaustion of quotas and ceilings and, of these, one-quarter were accounted for by China. Table 1.6 provides details of graduation (i.e. out of the GSP) and differentiation (stricter quotas on the most competitive beneficiaries) in the EC scheme of 1991 and, according to the EC Commission, these restrictions were applied mostly on the basis of a

Table 1.4 Main GSP beneficiaries from the EC scheme, 1989.

Country	Share in covered trade (%)	Share in GSP benefits (%)
China	15.5	15.3
Brazil	10.6	12.9
India	6.5	9.4
Thailand	5.6	6.4
Indonesia	4.1	4.9
Hong Kong	6.9	4.8
Singapore	8.5	4.6
Kuwait	2.2	4.6
Romania	3.3	4.5
Malaysia	4.9	4.3
Total	68.1	71.7

Source: Commission of the European Communities (1990).

Table 1.5 Re-establishment of duties on GSP imports (6-digit classification) in the EC scheme for industrial products, 1989/90.

Country	1989 Sensitive products	1989 Non-sensitive products	1990 Sensitive products	1990 Non-sensitive products
Argentina	—	—	1	—
Brazil	5	2	6	—
China	10	2	9	2
Colombia	1	—	—	—
Hungary	—	—	3	—
India	3	1	3	—
Indonesia	2	1	2	—
Malaysia	4	—	3	1
Mexico	4	—	6	—
Pakistan	2	—	2	—
Philippines	2	—	2	—
Poland	—	1	2	—
Romania	—	1	—	—
Singapore	1	1	—	—
Thailand	3	1	2	1
Venezuela	—	1	—	—
Total	37	10	42	4

Source: EC Commission.

Table 1.6 Graduation and differentiation in the EC scheme, 1991.[a]

Country	Number of products with 50% reduction in preferential amounts	Number of products excluded from the scheme
Saudia Arabia	1	7
Libya	1	1
Brazil	2	—
Hong Kong	5	9
Singapore	3	—

Source: EC Commission.
[a] South Korea suspended from scheme over 'discriminatory measures in respect of the Community in the sphere of protection of intellectual property'.

share of at least 20% in extra-EC imports. Again, it can be seen that only a small number of products are involved, and that most of these restrictions concern Saudi Arabia (petroleum products) and Hong Kong.

Thus, although limits are set for all beneficiaries and for all sensitive products and are, in addition, available on request by an EC member state for non-sensitive products, for the vast majority of products and beneficiaries the GSP offers unlimited duty-free entry for industrial goods. In the case of agricultural goods, although only 57% of dutiable imports are covered by the scheme, over 60% of these covered products receive preferential treatment (though often only to a limited extent).

The major sector reducing the overall proportion of GSP-covered imports that receive preference is textiles and clothing: although 84% of these products are covered by the scheme (one-quarter of total GSP-covered imports), less than one-third received preferential treatment in 1989. These quantitative restrictions, however, are derived directly from the MFA quotas, and liberalization therefore depends entirely upon changes (or progressive elimination) in the MFA and not in the GSP scheme as such. Also, it should be noted that the inclusion of textiles and clothing in the EC's GSP, although reducing the average share of GSP-receiving imports in dutiable and GSP-covered imports, is an important reason why the EC performs most favourably with respect to the least developed countries.

The substantial gap between the appearance of restrictions and the reality of openness of the EC's GSP for most products and countries is puzzling, as it would appear to defeat the objective of the scheme—to encourage exporters in the developing countries. It may be a product of the mercantilist philosophy which appears to underly much of EC trade policy and its consequent desire to 'manage' trade. An alternative explanation may be expressed in terms of an objective function for the Commission which seeks to maximize the export opportunities of the developing countries, subject to the constraints of (a) protecting domestic producers against the perceived 'threat' from particularly competitive exporters in particular developing countries, (b) overcoming general hostility to preferences from influential industrial and political lobbies in the Community (by creating a 'smokescreen' of restrictions on preferential imports), and (c) preserving the differential levels of preferential treatment in the hierarchy of preferences because the latter is the main instrument of Community (as opposed to member states') foreign policy. The cost of this approach, however, has been to create a substantial lack of clarity and stability which creates uncertainty both for exporters and for importers in the EC. The unpredictability of the scheme is most marked in the case of textiles and clothing, where there are two quotas each year allocated among each of the 12 member states. It is also, however, present in the case of non-sensitive products under surveillance where duties can (but not necessarily will) be reimposed once a 'reference threshold' is reached, while in the case of ceilings, duties are reimposed only if a member state puts up a sufficiently strong case on commercial or political grounds. Such uncertainty, combined with the annual nature of the scheme, must make long-term planning difficult and greatly reduce the capacity of the scheme to encourage investment in developing countries in export-oriented industries.

Empirical studies of the trade effects of the GSP fall broadly into three categories. First, *ex ante* partial equilibrium models estimate trade creation effects from the price elasticity of demand for imports, the initial value of imports from beneficiaries before the introduction of preferences, and the proportional decrease in the price of imports as a result of the decrease in tariffs. Trade diversion effects are estimated from cross-price elasticities of demand between beneficiary and non-beneficiary sources of supply, initial market share and estimated trade creation effects. Second, *ex post* models use data for trade flows both before and after preferences are introduced. These models use two methods. The first method is a constant market shares approach, which compares the exports of beneficiaries to a donor country with a "control" of non-preference-receiving exports, either of the beneficiaries to other markets or of comparable non-beneficiaries to the same market. The second method uses cross-sectional gravity models which show whether the margin of tariff preference has increased exports to a statistically significant degree. Third are general equilibrium models which incorporate terms of trade and exchange rate movements and general macroeconomic effects consequential on changes in trade flows.

These estimates of GSP trade expansion produce large variations in results due not only to differences in methodologies, specification of models and time periods, but also to small differences in the estimates of key parameters (for a survey, see Borrmann *et al.*, 1981 and Brown, 1988). Some of these studies also operate at a high level of aggregation in their analysis. Two recent studies, however, overcome some of these deficiencies and cast doubts on the more pessimistic estimates of the effects of the Community's GSP. The first is the *ex ante* study by Karsenty and Laird (1987) which reduced aggregation bias by carrying out all computations at the level of the tariff line, while also allowing for annual changes in product coverage, limitations and beneficiaries. Net trade gains were found to be as follows: EC, 19.1% of covered imports (excluding trade gains in clothing, on the basis that MFA quotas make tariffs redundant); US, 21%4; and Japan, 13.9%. Simulations of the elimination of restrictions on all goods by all donors yielded an additional direct trade gain of $20.6b, three times the benefits that are currently enjoyed. This illustrates both the possibilities for further benefits and the fact that preferences are always second-best policies to complete trade liberalization. The second study, by MacPhee and Rosenbaum (1989), was *ex post* and, unlike previous studies, tested for the effects of denial and restoration of preferential treatment on exports to the EC. The results suggested that beneficiaries respond positively to preferential tariff reductions and that equally, denial of preferences holds market shares of affected countries below what they would otherwise have been. Furthermore, this was as true for the competitive countries (Brazil, Hong Kong, South Korea, Yugoslavia) as for the less industrialized countries.

None of these studies, however, addressed the fundamental rationale for preferences in a world of trade barriers and in terms of general economic development. One example of this concerns the direct and indirect effects of preferences in stimulating output and employment in the export sector and in sectors closely linked to exports. Another example is the partial protection which preferences give to infant industries in developing countries whilst still stimulating gains in 'x efficiency' through the requirement to compete in the markets of the developed countries that offer the preferences. These studies also do not identify these dynamic gains in terms of differences in the size of the country and its resource endowments. For example, the growth-stimulating effects of preferences would be expected to be very small in the case of a large economy such as Brazil (though possibly significant in particular sectors of the economy), simply because exports are a small proportion (7%) of GDP. Conversely, in the majority of developing countries, where a small population[7] is combined with relatively low levels of *per capita* income and hence a small size of domestic market, exports are a much larger proportion of GDP and hence preferences have a potentially much greater capacity to have a growth-stimulating effect. The key word is 'potentially' because preferences, as seen in the case of Mauritius, can be only one factor in stimulating export expansion, and the resource endowments, trade regime and general economic environment of the country will be crucial determinants of export capacity.

IV.3   Rules of origin

Since the partners to the preferential trade agreement preserve their tariff autonomy, the origin of traded goods has to be determined to prevent third countries deflecting exports to the EC via ACP countries with a lower tariff on these goods than the Community. Such trade deflection would undermine the Community Common External Tariff and therefore the margin of tariff preference received by the developing countries. In this respect the EC and the developing countries have a mutual interest in preserving the integrity of the rules of origin. There may, however, be a conflict of objectives between the partners to the agreement. It is to be expected that developing countries will wish to increase their exports of labour-intensive manufactured goods and attract foreign investment into export-oriented manufacturing sectors. The EC, however, may be expected to limit such an increase in imports, not only through tariff quotas but also through its definition of an 'originating product'. For example, a study (McQueen, 1982) of the rules of origin showed that over 90% of the products defined under the GSP as 'sensitive' and 30% of the semi-sensitive products were subject to the most restrictive elements of the rules of origin.

In the case of goods produced wholly from local resources, no problem of definition arises. Such a situation is, however, unusual, particularly for a small developing country, and once goods are processed or manufactured, it is likely that at least some intermediate products have to be imported. All countries granting preferences approach this problem by stating first that 'substantial transformation' of the non-originating input must have taken place and define this as a change of 4-digit tariff heading. However, since the tariff schedules have not been drawn up specifically to provide a definition of substantial transformation, the EC has supplemented the 'tariff jump' criterion to cover cases where there is a change of tariff heading but where it considers that there has been insufficient transformation.

In the context of this study, there are four particularly contentious additional criteria. The first is the exclusion of 'simple assembly of parts and articles to constitute a complete article'. The second is to define minimum process criteria for textiles and clothing specifying that the starting material must be yarn. The third is to define maximum percentage criteria for non-originating materials of 40% or 50% of the ex-works price of the finished product. Fourth, for fishery products to qualify, they must be 'taken from the sea' by ships registered in the EC or in the developing country, at least 50% owned by nationals of the EC or ACP states, and further restrictions apply to the nationality of the captain and crew. A potentially useful concession, available only to the ACP states, is that they are able to include imports from the EC or other ACP states as 'originating' products. The only concession available to non-ACP countries is that if they are members of a regional grouping of developing countries they may include imports from each other as originating products.

With regard to the first criterion, a possible first step for countries with a small domestic market, limited natural resources and a low level of industrialization, such as many developing countries, is to encourage the establishment of assembly industries, with the long-term objective of moving into higher value added production once the industrial base has developed. Such exports to the EC would be denied preferences under the 'simple assembly' rule. The EC defends this position by claiming that it acts for the benefit of the developing countries by excluding 'footloose' industries but, since in the case of the ACP countries the cumulation rules permit EC companies to establish simple assembly industries, it is clear that this rule is meant to exclude only third countries, and is therefore tantamount to a form of 'reverse preference' for the EC. It also acts to the particular disadvantage of the Caribbean and Pacific ACP countries where assembly is most likely to involve US, Japanese and Australian companies.

The second criterion involves very substantial transformation of the non-originating material (yarn) and goes beyond what could reasonably be regarded as necessary to avoid trade deflection. As noted earlier, a number of the more developed ACP countries and those with the necessary manu-facturing base have rapidly increased their exports of textiles and clothing under the Convention. More realistic process criteria would offer a wider range of developing countries the chance to participate in this typical first stage of industrialization.

The severity of the third (value added) criterion, particularly for low-income developing countries, has been indicated in the context of the ACP countries (McQueen, 1982) by calculating the proportion of domestic value added in gross output for those 3-digit sectors in which the ACP countries might be able to export to the EC. Of the 265 observations, only 61 (23%) had a share of value added in gross output of 50% or more, while even relatively industrialized ACP states such as Kenya and the Côte d'Ivoire recorded only one sector exceeding the 50% threshold. The only exception to this pattern was Zimbabwe.

The fourth criterion (ownership of vessels) may also be considered restrictive because the developing countries generally do not operate their own deep-sea fishing fleets. They have no option, therefore, but to use alternative arrangements such as leasing or chartering vessels or providing fishing rights for foreign vessels, all of which fall foul of the rules of origin.

An important concession applying only to the ACP countries is that they can apply for derogations (exemptions) from the rules of origin. In the EC view, this procedure makes it unnecessary to change the rules of origin for the ACP group, as any significant economic problems can be dealt with in this pragmatic way. Furthermore, since only five derogations have been sought and all were granted, the EC concludes that the rules of origin are operating satisfactorily. Until 1990, however, derogations were granted only after an exhaustive examination of the evidence taking several months and then only for 3 years (renewable for a further 2 years for the least developed countries). Not surprisingly, where potential investors have found that they did not conform to the rules of origin, they have not asked for derogations because the high cost of submitting a case, together with uncertainty regarding the outcome, was not worth the short-term benefit of remission from the rules (McQueen, 1990; Stevens, 1990). The Fourth Lomé Convention has sought to improve on procedures by granting automatic derogations for 45% value added, speeding up the processing of applications, doubling the margin of tolerance for non-originating products to 10%, abolishing the double threshold rule for some products and reducing the percentage value added in some others.

Such modifications to the EC's rules of origin could be of considerable benefit if they were available to all other developing countries eligible for preferences (including the ability to 'cumulate' origin through trade from other developing countries), but they are no substitute for a thorough revision of the rules which takes account of the large changes in the structure of international production and of production conditions in developing countries.

V   NON-TARIFF BARRIERS ON IMPORTS FROM DEVELOPING COUNTRIES

Successive rounds of multilateral trade negotiations have reduced tariffs from an average of 40% in the late 1940s to a post-Tokyo Round (1979) figure of 6.5%; a successful completion of the Uruguay Round will lead to further tariff reductions. The average tariff facing developing countries is somewhat higher than this figure, whilst there are still high residual tariffs on agricultural goods exported by developing countries. In addition, tariffs generally escalate with the degree of processing and so developing countries can still face substantial effective tariff rates on processed and manufactured goods.

As tariffs have been reduced, however, non-tariff barriers (NTBs) have increased, particularly in the 1970s and 1980s, as increased competition from imports from the NICs was added to the recessionary effects of the rise in oil prices. The rapid increase in non-tariff barriers is important not only because they give rise to considerable economic inefficiency compared to tariffs, but also because they are concentrated on particular products and have been implemented in a discriminatory manner against particular countries or groups of countries and as such threaten the fundamental GATT principle of non-discrimination.

Quantifying the range and effects of NTBs is, however, beset with conceptual and practical difficulties, not least because there is no agreed definition of an NTB. A useful classification is provided by Laird and Yeats (1990). The authors divide measures into those which operate quantitatively and those which operate on prices or costs (either as a tax on importers, for example variable levies, or a subsidy to import competitors, for example tax incentives). These are then identified under three headings: Type I measures, so-called 'hard-core measures', whose intention is to reduce imports; Type II measures, which have 'secondary trade restrictive intent' (e.g. health and safety regulations); and Type III measures, which have 'spillover effects on trade' (e.g. public sector purchasing policies, regional policies). Anti-dumping measures and countervailing duties are governed by GATT rules and may therefore be regarded as falling outside the other measures, which are of dubious legality under international trade law. In practice, however, the threat of this legal action (or even an investigation) is sufficient to damage the competitive position of exporters who may therefore respond to the threat by concluding a 'voluntary' export restraint or price undertaking.

Laird and Yeats estimate that a total of $169.1 billion of EC imports in 1986 were affected by Type I and II NTBs and that the share of imports so affected increased from 21% in 1966 to 54% in 1986 (Table 1.7). This clearly illustrates the sharp increase in the use of NTBs (similar calculations using the number of transactions rather than the value of imports affected, produce broadly similar results), with particularly sharp increases in textiles and clothing, ferrous metals and electrical machinery. Furthermore, the increase in the share of trade affected by NTBs was highest in the EC due, in part, to the extension of the CAP to the UK.

Not all of these measures have been directed at the developing countries, while the inclusion of Type II measures in 'affected trade' may be regarded as controversial. A recent study (UNCTAD, 1990) using the UNCTAD Database on Non-Tariff Measures (described by Laird and Yeats, 1990)

Table 1.7 Non-tariff barriers on EC imports, 1966–86.

Product	Percentage of trade affected[a]	
	1966	1986
All products	21	54
Food	61	100
Agriculture and raw materials	4	28
Fuels	11	37
Ores and metals	0	40
Manufactures		
Textiles and clothing	20	100
Ferrous metals	8	96
Chemicals	13	55
Non-electrical machinery	1	29
Electrical machinery	0	67
Transport equipment	39	31

Source: Laird and Yeats (1990, pp. 312 and 314).
[a] Value of imports by 4-digit SITC group subject to Type I or II non-tariff barriers. It should be noted that this measure does not indicate the intensity of application of the non-tariff barriers.

concentrated on the 'hard-core measures' applied to imports from developing countries. This study concluded that, excluding MFA-covered goods, about $12.5 billion of imports (calculated using 6-digit HTS product categories) from developing countries into the EC were affected by 'hard' non-tariff measures in 1986. Further details of these products (covering 80% of non-MFA-affected imports) are given in Table 1.8.

In terms of the value of imports affected by non-tariff measures, footwear is the largest sector at $2100m, followed by manioc, bovine meat (canned, frozen and fresh) and sugar. Such indicators may, however, underestimate the effect of NTBs on exports by the developing countries because NTBs, if effective, will lower the value of imports of the affected products into the protected market. The UNCTAD study therefore attempted to indicate the 'true' restrictive effect of NTBs by comparing actual exports to the protected market with hypothetical exports (computed from import shares in an unprotected developed country market). The results are summarized in Table 1.9.

Clearly, because of the methodology used, these estimates can be regarded only as broadly indicative of the potential gains from import liberalization. They do suggest, however, that in the products analysed, export earnings could double, while in cases such as steel products, where the estimated trade losses are significantly greater than the present trade flows, liberalization could be particularly beneficial for the developing

Table 1.8 EC imports from developing countries of non-MFA products subject to non-tariff barriers.

Product	Imports ($m)	Percentage affected
Manioc	1157	9.2
Sugar	855	7.1
Footwear, leather uppers	799	6.4
Footwear, textile uppers	595	4.7
TV receivers	522	4.2
Bovine, fresh meat	383	3.1
Bovine, preserved meat	323	2.6
Oranges, fresh	300	2.4
Footwear, uppers and parts	237	1.9
Footwear, rubber	236	1.9
Bovine, frozen meat	234	1.9
Footwear, textile uppers	229	1.8
Molasses	218	1.7
Magnetic tapes	212	1.7
Video recorders	189	1.5
Apples, fresh	169	1.3
Animal feed	161	1.3
Tuna, frozen	152	1.2
Rice, husked brown	149	1.2
Bovine, live	148	1.2
Grapes, dried	138	1.1
Squid	135	1.1
Steel, semi-finished	128	1.0
Grapes, fresh	113	0.9
Sweet potatoes	100	0.8
Steel bars and rods	95	0.7
Olive oil	95	0.7
Non-alloy pig iron	93	0.7
Ferro-alloys	89	0.7
Tomatoes, fresh	86	0.7
Pears and quinces, fresh	85	0.7

Source: UNCTAD (1990).

countries concerned. It is also important to note that this exercise could not be carried out for such important exports to the EC as footwear, beef and sugar, because these are generally subject to restrictions and no 'control' developed country could therefore be identified for comparison.

A number of attempts, however, have been made to model the effects of liberalization of agricultural trade on developing countries. Zietz and Valdés (1988) considered the potential effects of full trade liberalization in beef and sugar by all industrialized countries and, depending on assumptions

Table 1.9 Estimated loss of non-MFA exports by developing countries as a result of the EC use of non-tariff measures.

Product[a]	Estimated loss[b] ($m)	Value of imports subject to non-tariff barriers ($m)
Animal feed (IL)	163.1	161.5
Steel pipes (AD)	162.1	60.7
Steel pipes (IS)	145.6	31.0
Steel, structural (VER)	130.5	41.1
Ball-bearings (AD)	116.6	25.1
Ferro-alloys (VER)	109.0	89.3
Grapes, dried (RP)	107.0	138.3
Steel bars and rods (VER)	105.3	94.5
Ferro-silicon (VER)	96.7	26.5
Magnetic tapes (ADD)	88.5	211.5
Fertilizer (ADD)	85.8	45.1
Video recorders (AD)	59.1	188.7
Steel, tin-coated (VER)	59.0	37.6
Magnetic tapes (AD)	57.2	45.6
Fibreboard (AD)	56.9	27.0
Steel, hot-rolled (VER)	51.2	21.4
Steel, stainless (VER)	51.0	18.4
Silicon (AD)	41.5	26.5
Steel, finished (VER)	41.0	127.9
Molasses	38.7	217.7
Total	$1765.8	$1635.4

Source: UNCTAD (1990).
[a] AD, anti-dumping action; ADD, anti-dumping duty; IL, import licence; IS, import surveillance; RP, reference price; VER, voluntary export restraint.
[b] See text for explanation of methodology.

regarding supply elasticities in developed and developing countries, concluded that (given the regime of protection in 1983), in the case of sugar, the export earnings of the developing countries could increase by between $3.4b (236%) and $7.4b (516%) and in the case of beef, by $4.4b to $5.1b, measured at 1980 prices. The significance of this can be judged from the fact that such gains would be equivalent to 30–49% of the foreign aid received by exporters of these products. Not all developing countries would gain from liberalization. Argentina, Brazil and India would be the main beneficiaries, while a number of other smaller developing countries would obtain substantial increases in their export earnings. Losses to Mauritius, Guyana, Fiji, Swaziland, Jamaica and Trinidad (who, under Lomé, obtain CAP prices for varying proportions of their exports) were estimated at

$380m (1980), while no estimates were given of the effects on important ACP exporters of beef covered by the protocol of the Convention (Botswana, Zimbabwe, Madagascar and Swaziland). The total gains may appear to be high, but the authors justified the upper level estimates by pointing out that long-term elasticities of supply in developing countries may be substantially higher than short-term elasticities, as producers can be expected to respond to permanently eliminated barriers to exports.

The possibilities for liberalization in world trade in agricultural products, of course, concern not simply beef and sugar (though these two products would have the greatest effect on the export earnings of developing countries) but also oilseeds and vegetable oils, coffee and associated products, cocoa and associated products, tea, tobacco and cotton. Simulations of various policy alternatives in the base period 1984-6 produced for the GATT negotiations on these products (covering the bulk of world agricultural trade) illustrate the difficulty of making valid generalizations about the effects of liberalization of trade in agricultural products.

Full liberalization of trade by the developed countries in temperate agricultural and tropical products would lead to increases in the world price of these products, particularly for the former (there would be a significant fall in supply coupled with increased demand). These price changes would produce positive or negative foreign exchange effects (depending on whether countries became net exporters or importers) and welfare effects (a rise in prices would increase producer surpluses and decrease consumer surpluses, and welfare changes for a country are the net effects of these two forces over affected products which are imported and exported). Table 1.10 attempts to summarize these effects over broad regions of the developing world (a positive net welfare effect indicates that there is a potential for gainers to compensate those who lose from the price changes and still be better off). Full trade liberalization produces substantial benefits for Latin America and the Caribbean (particularly Argentina, Brazil, Uruguay, Cuba, Columbia and Mexico), while Asia (particularly Thailand, India and Pakistan) benefits from liberalization in tropical products but not in temperate agricultural products. Africa has a net welfare loss in both temperate and tropical products (the zero change in foreign exchange earnings is due to the offseting effect of increased earnings from coffee and, to a lesser extent, tea and cocoa).

Fewer countries gain if export subsidies alone are abolished, while there is a significant loss of welfare to consumers in Africa and Asia. Even this effect is not unambiguous from the point of view of the economic development of the countries concerned. The availability of cheap agricultural imports (for example, in 1991, imported wheat was available in

Table 1.10 Indicators of effects of trade liberalization in agricultural products by the main developed countries. [a]

Region	Full liberalization				Abolition of export subsidies			
	Agriculture		Tropical products		Agriculture		Tropical products	
	Foreign exchange	Welfare	Foreign exchange	Welfare	Foreign exchange	Welfare	Foreign exchange	Welfare
Africa	–	–	0	–	–	–	–	–
Latin America and Caribbean	++	+	+	+	+	0	+	0
Asia and Pacific	–	–	+	+	–	–	0	–
Total	+	–	++	+	–	–	0	0

[a] –, negative effect; +, positive effect; 0, little or no effect.

the markets of Burkina-Faso at just over half the price of locally grown sorghum) from the surplus production of developed countries has undoubtedly enabled some governments to discriminate against the agricultural sector in their development strategies and in the allocation of resources, despite the fact that a thriving agricultural sector is, for most of these countries, an essential prerequisite for sustained development, particularly in Sub-Saharan Africa. Low internal prices have also, paradoxically, added to the problem of hunger in Africa by substantially reducing the incomes of the mass of poor farmers and therefore their capacity both to purchase food and to invest in order to increase its future supply. The liberalization of agricultural policies in the developed countries would therefore have complex direct and indirect effects that would require adjustment assistance to producers both in the developed countries and in certain developing countries. In the long term, however, the benefits would certainly be large.

Textiles and clothing have been the most protected manufacturing sectors of the developed countries in the post-war period, starting with the Long Term Arrangement on Cotton Textiles and subsequently in 1974 with the MFA under the GATT. The initial concept was for a controlled liberalization of world trade in textiles and clothing, but in practice an increasing number of developing countries have faced a more complex array of quotas across a wider range of closely defined product categories. Developing countries subject to binding quotas have reacted in various ways to these restrictions, for example by moving into other product categories not (at that moment) subject to restraints, by compensating for loss of volume by moving 'up-market' into higher-priced goods, or by shifting production to developing countries not subject (at that moment) to quotas (for example, Hong Kong's investment in the Mauritius clothing industry). Also, to varying degrees, the bilateral agreements which the EC has with 33 developing countries allow for the transfer of underutilized quotas on certain product lines to overutilized quotas on other products. In addition, the restrictions on imports raise prices in the country imposing quotas and thus create 'quota rents' which are available to be shared between importers and exporters. It is therefore very difficult to quantify the restrictive effects of the MFA (for a survey, see Cline, 1987). Table 1.11 compares the evolution over the 1980s of shares in apparent consumption (domestic production plus imports minus exports, i.e. a measure of the size in the market) for the EC and the US. The production of textile fibres is more capital-intensive than clothing and smaller market shares would therefore be expected for developing countries. In the case of clothing, market shares of developing countries are not only higher but have increased, especially in the US. Conversely, the market shares of imports from other developed

Table 1.11 Share of imports in apparent consumption of textiles and clothing by the EC and US.

Region	Textiles		Clothing	
	1981–2	1987–8	1981–2	1987–8
EC[a]				
Share of imports (%)	11.85	11.03	24.55	26.32
Developing countries (%)	4.49	4.88	15.26	19.14
NICs (%)	1.40	1.47	9.80	10.10
Other less developed countries (%)	2.68	2.94	5.29	8.69
Developed countries (%)	6.04	4.76	6.31	3.30
US/Canada[b]				
Share of imports (%)	5.30	7.83	20.74	36.81
Developing countries (%)	2.21	3.56	15.98	27.94
NICs (%)	1.10	2.08	13.02	20.84
Other less developed countries (%)	0.95	1.33	7.48	6.57
Developed countries (%)	2.52	3.38	7.66	5.33

Source: UNCTAD Handbook of International Trade and Development Statistics (1988, 1990).
[a] The value of EC imports of textiles from less developed countries in 1987–8 was $4.95b and for clothing was $17.38b.
[b] The value of US imports of textiles from less developed countries in 1987–8 was $3.27b and for clothing was $27.46b.

countries in the two markets are substantially smaller and have declined. There is a sharp contrast, however, between the experience of the NICs and other developing countries in the two markets for clothing. In order to protect the competitive position of clothing manufacturers, the US regulations permit 'outward processing' whereas the EC does not, in general, provide such concessions and implicitly discriminates in favour of smaller suppliers. This may explain why the NICs' share of the market in the US has almost doubled but has barely increased in the EC, while the share of other developing countries has declined in the US market and has increased by 64% in the EC. The overall effect is to suggest first, that despite an increasingly restrictive MFA regime, the developing countries have increased their market shares in clothing and second, that the EC is a more protected market for clothing than the US.

VI PROSPECTS FOR THE FUTURE

Any discussion of future trade relations between the EC and the rest of the world almost inevitably moves quickly to a discussion of the effects of 1992.

A recent survey (Winters, 1991) of the empirical evidence suggests the following. First, that the static trade creation and trade diversion effects will be low because existing barriers to intra-EC trade are small. More important effects from the complete integration of markets could arise from the consequent break-up of oligopolies, which would significantly drive down prices within the EC. Improved access to the whole EC market could also enable firms to achieve greater economies of scale. Second, both greater competition within the EC and lower long-term average costs of production can be expected to reduce imports of competing goods from the rest of the world. Third, against this may be set a once and for all increase in incomes arising from greater economic efficiency, which will increase the demand for all goods, including imports, depending on income elasticities of demand for these goods. There is no agreement, however, regarding these effects. Smith and Venables (1986) estimated that strong trade diversion effects will arise from increased EC competition. Neven (1990), on the other hand, estimated only small effects as regards goods produced by northern EC members (and hence against capital, skill and R & D intensive goods exported by developed countries) on the grounds that there is little currently unexploited comparative advantage between them, but considerable scope for increased labour-intensive exports from southern EC members. The latter view was also put forward by McQueen and Read (1987) and, if correct, would imply significant trade diversion against imports from developing countries.

In addition to the general economic effects of 1992, the single market will also have specific implications for different groups of developing countries. A number of trade-restricting measures used by the EC have been and, in certain cases, still are implemented at the level of the individual EC member states. These national quotas are directly contrary to the operation of a common market but they have, for political reasons, been surprisingly resilient. For example, tariff quotas for sensitive products under the GSP used to be allocated strictly between the member states and were removed only in 1987 after the European Court ruled them unlawful. *Article 115* of the *Treaty of Rome* also permits national restrictions and these, as has been seen, are operated for MFA products and sensitive products such as footwear, but these are also scheduled for removal by 1993. Hamilton (1991) investigated the effects of *Article 115* quotas by France against imports of clothing from Hong Kong over the period 1980–9 and concluded that *Article 115* played no *independent* role in producing price differences: the price differences observed could be explained solely by the maintenance of barriers against EC partner-country produced imports of perfect substitutes. As pointed out by McQueen and Read (1987), however, the increased competition in intra-community trade from southern EC countries, combined with the requirement for Spain and Portugal to adopt the full commercial policy of the EC by 1993 (and hence open up their previously highly protected markets to imports from the EC, other developed countries and developing countries—including imports under the preferential trade agreements of the EC) and the abolition of *Article 115* provisions, could, especially in times of a reduction or recession in the growth of world trade, lead to increased demands for the use of NTBs at Community level. Even limited concessions to such demands would more than offset the beneficial effects of the abolition of national restrictions. Particular problems also arise for the, mostly high-cost, ACP exporters of bananas who currently have privileged access to the French and UK markets over other developing country exporters and where 1992 will expose them to competition from much lower-cost exporters in South America.

The developing countries have therefore good cause to be apprehensive about whether the EC is 'de-linking' from them, not only in the technological sense of the export pessimism argument put forward by Kaplinsky (1984), but also because of uncertainties regarding the effects of 1992 and the future preoccupation of the EC with the economic and political development of Eastern Europe (which will not only absorb substantial resources from the EC countries, but also potentially increase competition in many of the goods currently exported to the EC by the developing countries). It is in this context that the future trade policy of the EC is a particularly important factor affecting growth and structural change in the developing countries.

The European Commission has put forward proposals (EC, 1990) for the GSP which seeks to simplify the scheme by abolishing quantitative restrictions and offering duty-free entry for most products, with reductions in duties for sensitive products and the exclusion of product/country pairs for the most competitive. The advantage of this proposal is that it would make the GSP more transparent and remove much of the uncertainty of treatment faced by exporters, as well as reducing the costs of administering the system. The disadvantage of the proposal is that it is doubtful whether a small reduction in tariffs would have any significant trade-stimulating effect. Also, as Table 1.5 indicates, if product/country pairs are removed for the most competitive, then there is no need to restrict duty-free entry, as quotas are not binding on the remaining developing countries.

An alternative and more radical proposal is to recognize that the EC is irrevocably committed to graduating the NICs out of special preferences and into accordance with full GATT norms. *Provided* that this commitment worked in both directions—i.e. that both the developed countries as well as the NICs reduced tariff and non-tariff barriers to trade—then all the evidence suggests that both should obtain substantial benefits. In addition, other developing countries would gain increased access to the rapidly expanding markets of the NICs.

The combination of such graduation with the exclusion of product/ country pairs for the most competitive would clear the way for abolishing the EC's hierarchy of preferences in favour of one scheme, modelled on that of the Lomé Convention. A good case can be made for special preferences for the less industrialized developing countries. Equally, as this chapter has sought to demonstrate, the benefits of preference have been substantially underestimated by the simplifications necessary to measure the global effects of preferences (especially where studies concentrate on the margin of *tariff* preferences). At present this hierarchy of privilege makes the schemes exceedingly complex to administer and, as has been seen, creates an aura of restrictiveness which is not true in reality but which greatly inhibits the utilization of the schemes by the developing countries in Asia and Latin America. In addition, the need to maintain differential treatment between the different levels of the hierarchy inhibits the EC in negotiations on trade liberalization. This was most clearly seen in the EC offer on tropical products in the Uruguay Round, where the proposal, particularly for coffee and cocoa, was simply to reduce MFN tariffs to the GSP rates but without any proposal to maintain correspondingly the margin of preference under the GSP. Since the GSP rates determine the effective margin of preference for the ACP countries, it is difficult to escape the conclusion that the offer was constrained by the need to preserve ACP preferences. The cost of this differential treatment for six tropical products (cocoa beans, coffee beans, tobacco, rice, tropical vegetable oils and cassava) in terms of the maintenance of tariffs, levies and quotas to GSP beneficiaries has been estimated at over Ecu 1 billion (Davenport and Stevens, 1990) against a cost of liberalization, in terms of net export loss to the ACP, of just under Ecu 16 million—a sum which could easily be provided as compensation by the EC.

It has always been difficult for the EC to justify the less favourable treatment of the lower-income countries of South and South East Asia and Latin America in favour of the ACP and Mediterranean countries. The extension of the trade provisions of the Lomé Convention either to all of these countries or with modifications in the case of the larger and more industrialized countries such as India and China, together with improvements to the rules of origin, would in a world of non-tariff barriers, provide the assurance of unrestricted access to the EC market for a period of time (10 years) sufficient to encourage investment in export industries. A single preferential scheme of this structure would undoubtedly be politically difficult to implement, but without such a trade policy instrument it is difficult to see how the Community can reconcile the pressure from the member states on developing countries to adopt structural adjustment programmes and export-oriented policies, with the increasing restrictions on non-tariff barriers on imports from the developing countries and the limitations of the GSP.

NOTES

1 Nominal values of EC imports deflated by the IMF index of non-oil developing country export unit values.
2 Defined as excluding EC imports from Algeria, Libya, Yugoslavia and Israel.
3 A system of compensation to ACP governments for shortfalls in earnings from exports to the EC of 49 agricultural-based products.
4 A special financing facility for mining sectors which face difficulties.
5 Sixty-six ACP countries, less oil-exporting countries (Nigeria, Gabon, Cameroon).
6 The importance of considering *trade* preferences and not simply *tariff* preferences in a world of selective and discriminatory non-tariff barriers implies that the trade diversion effects of preferences will tend to be greater than those traditionally estimated from *ex ante* import elasticity based models and that the incidence of such effects between different developing countries cannot be ignored.
7 Excluding China and India, only 17 developing countries have a population greater than 28 million (i.e. half the size of the UK) and most of the remaining 90 developing countries have a population less than 10 million.

REFERENCES

Borrmann, A., C. Borrmann and M. Steger (1981) *The EC's Generalised System of Preferences*, Institüt fur Wirtshaftsforschung, Hamburg.
Brown, D.K. (1988) 'Trade Preferences for Developing Countries: A Survey of Results', *Journal of Development Studies* **24**, 335–63.
Cline, W.R. (1987) *The Future of World Trade in Textiles and Apparel*, Institute for International Economics, Washington.
Davenport, M. and C. Stevens (1990) 'The Outlook for Tropical Products' in C. Stevens and D.C. Faber (eds), *The Uruguay Round and 1992*, European Centre for Development Policy Management, Maastricht.
EC (1990) 'Generalised System of References: Guidelines for the 1990s', *COM(90)329 Final*, Commission of the European Communities, Brussels.
Hamilton, C.B. (1991) 'European Community External Protection and 1992', *European Economic Review* **35**, 378–87.
Hine, R.C. (1985) *The Political Economy of European Trade*, Harvester Press, Brighton.
ILO/UNCTC (1988) *Economic and Social Effects of Multinational Enterprises in Export Processing Zones*, ILO, Geneva.
Kaplinsky, R. (1984) 'The International Context for Industrialisation in the Coming Decade', *Journal of Development Studies* **21**, 75–96.

Karsenty, G. and S. Laird (1987) 'The GSP, Policy Options and the New Round', *Weltwirtschaftliches Archiv* **123**, 262–95.

Laird, S. and A. Yeats (1990) 'Trends in Non-Tariff Barriers of Developed Countries', *Weltwirtschaftliches Archiv* **126**, 299–323.

Langhammer, R.J. and A. Sapir (1987) *The Economic Impact of Generalised Tariff Preferences*, (*Thames Essay No. 49*), Gower, London.

MacPhee, C.R. and D.I. Rosenbaum (1989) 'Has the European Community GSP Increased LDC Exports?', *Applied Economics* **21**, 823–41.

McQueen, M. (1982) 'Lomé and the Protective Effect of Rules of Origin', *Journal of World Trade Law* **16**, 119–32.

McQueen, M. (1990) *ACP Export Diversification: the Case of Mauritius*, Working Paper 41, Overseas Development Institute, London.

McQueen, M. and R. Read (1987) 'Prospects for ACP Exports to the Enlarged Community' in C. Stevens and J. Verloren van Themaat (eds), *EEC and the Third World, A Survey. 6. Europe and the International Division of Labour*, Hodder and Stoughton, London.

McQueen, M. and C. Stevens (1989) 'Trade Preferences and Lomé IV: Non-Traditional ACP Exports to the EC', *Development Policy Review* **7**, 239–60.

Moss, J. and J. Ravenhill (1987) 'The Evolution of Trade under the Lomé Conventions: The First Ten Years' in C. Stevens and J. Verloren van Themaat (eds), *EEC and the Third World, A Survey. 6. Europe and the International Division of Labour*, Hodder and Stoughton, London.

Neven, D.J. (1990) 'EC Integration Towards 1992: Some Distributional Aspects', *Economic Policy* **10**, 13–62.

Riddell, R. (1990) *ACP Export Diversification: Non-Traditional Exports from Zimbabwe*, Working Paper 88, Overseas Development Institute, London.

Smith, A. and A.J. Venables (1986) 'The Costs of Non-Europe: An Assessment Based on a Formal Model of Imperfect Competition and Economies of Scale' in *The Economics of 1992*, Commission of the European Communities, Brussels.

Stevens, C. (1990) *ACP Export Diversification: Jamaica, Kenya and Ethiopia*, Working Paper 40, Overseas Development Institute, London.

Stevens, C. and A. Weston (1984) 'Trade Diversification: Has Lomé Helped?' in C. Stevens (ed), *EEC and the Third World, A Survey. 4*, Hodder and Stoughton, London.

UNCTAD (1990) *Costs and Consequences of Non-Tariff Measures which Adversely Affect Exports of Developing Countries*, TD/B/1284, Geneva.

Weston, A., V. Cable and A. Hewitt (1980) *The EC's Generalised System of Preferences*, Overseas Development Institute, London.

Winters, A. (1991) 'International Trade and 1992', *European Economic Review* **35**, 367–87.

Zietz, J. and A. Valdés (1986) 'The Potential Benefits to LDCs of Trade Liberalisation in Beef and Sugar by Industrialised Countries', *Weltwirtschaftliches Archiv* **122**, 93–111.

2 | International Trade and Economic Development: The Implications of the 'New Trade Theory'

CHRIS MILNER*

I INTRODUCTION

Over a number of decades a debate has been conducted between the advocates of inward- and outward-oriented development strategies. The 1980s witnessed a growing ascendancy among the economics profession and policy-makers in developing economies of the latter, that is, export promotion strategy. Whether this ascendancy among policy-makers was the product of conviction or expediency is a matter of debate. There are a number of prominent, liberal economists, however, who claim that the debate ended in a clear and decisive victory for outward-oriented development strategies (Bhagwati, 1988; Riedel, 1991).

Much, though by no means all, of the debate was conducted by liberal economists within a neoclassical framework: in a competitive world where homogeneous goods are produced under conditions of constant or increasing costs and where developing countries' comparative advantage is determined in Heckscher–Ohlin fashion by relative factor endowments. Ironically, new approaches were emerging in trade theory at a time when the theoretical (and empirical arguments) for export promotion were gaining an ascendancy. From the late 1970s onwards trade models which emphasize imperfect competition, differentiated products and decreasing costs were emerging (e.g. Krugman, 1979; Lancaster, 1980). These were a response to the growing weight of empirical evidence about the importance of two-way

* I am grateful for helpful comments on an earlier draft of this paper from David Greenaway and participants of the conference.

trade between similar industrialized countries in similar products. The spectre of trade not being driven by comparative advantage and of trade and industrial interventions being used to give domestic firms a strategic advantage in home and export markets posed new challenges (see Krugman, 1986a) to the traditional postulates of commercial policy for those countries where the new framework was most appropriate, namely, the advanced industrial economies. However, given the tendency of policy-makers in developing countries (amongst others) to believe that the shift towards export promotion strategies was not so much about the replacement of 'mandarins by markets' but rather about the picking of a new breed of winners, then the implications of the 'new trade theories' for development strategies are bound to attract the attention of developing countries.

The aim of this paper is, therefore, to examine the implications of the 'new trade theories' for the role of trade and trade policy in economic development. The remainder of the paper is organized as follows. The nature of the 'new trade theory' is considered in Section II. This is followed in Section III by a brief review of the trade policy implications of these theories. Section IV then examines the scope for and appropriateness of strategic trade policies for developing countries. Implications for the design and conduct of trade strategy in developing countries are discussed in Section V. Finally, Section VI offers some conclusions.

II WHAT IS THE 'NEW TRADE THEORY'?

The 'new trade theory' is set against the backcloth of imperfectly competitive product markets where consumers have diverse preferences, and producers face increasing returns. Since this is an extension of the analysis of imperfectly competitive product markets in a closed-economy setting to an open-economy setting, the number of models of trade has proliferated. Given the range of possibilities of imperfect competition this is not surprising. The literature may be divided into two distinct categories, one which deals with 'large number cases' and one which focuses on 'small number cases'.

Large number cases have in common an explicit assumption of free entry into the market, and an assumption that consumer preferences are sufficiently diverse to ensure that a large number of single-product firms coexist in the final equilibrium. The treatment of consumer preferences differs from model to model, with in some cases consumers demanding a single horizontally differentiated variety (e.g. Lancaster, 1980) or demanding all available varieties (e.g. Krugman, 1979). What these models demonstrate is that where consumers have diverse preferences and decreasing costs prevail over the relevant range of output, trade can emerge and free entry ensures that a large number of producers coexist at home and abroad. Moreover, these models can be embedded in a general equilibrium setting which permits factor endowments to vary and allows for the simultaneous existence of inter- and intra-industry trade[1] (e.g. Helpman and Krugman, 1985). The importance of this development is not only in providing models where both types of trade coexist but also in providing models where the direction of trade is determinate. In fact, once differential factor endowments are incorporated, the predictions of these models have a familiar ring with the relatively capital-abundant country speicalizing to a greater extent in the capital-intensive, differentiated commodity.

The classic problems of interdependence and uncertainty which are associated with the interaction of a small number of firms in a market have always provided problems for the student of oligopoly. Because a variety of assumptions can be made regarding conjectural variation, equilibrium outcomes can be generated in a wide range of contexts. The literature exploring trade in an oligopolistic context has experimented with several assumptions regarding conjectural variation: the Cournot assumption of zero conjectural variation in a single-stage game or the Bertrand assumption in a multistage decision-making process (for a review of these, see Greenaway and Milner, 1986).

As well as differing in their treatment of conjectural variation these models also differ with regard to product type—identical products, horizontally differentiated products or vertically differentiated products being assumed—and entry conditions—some assume blocked entry, others free entry. Some generalizations can be made about this work, however. Preference diversity is again influential, although as Brander (1981) demonstrated it is not necessary for trade to emerge. Where preferences are diverse the amount of trade which occurs depends upon the distribution of income (in the case of vertically differentiated goods) and taste overlap (in the case of horizontally differentiated goods). Decreasing costs are again relevant although the emergence of (intra-industry) trade appears to be quite robust with regard to the specification of the production function. Results in particular models do seem to be sensitive with regard to the conjectural variation assumption, in particular where trade in identical commodities is concerned.

The 'new theory' does not constitute a single theory or paradigm that might be applied widely to trade flows among different types of economies and in different types of products. Rather, it is a diverse collection of specific models which can be applied separately to a specific type of international exchange. From such diversity comes considerable richness, but also complexity and potential confusion. On the one hand, from simple one-sector models it is possible to demonstrate how economies of scale can lead to arbitrary specialization by nations in products of (monopolistically competitive) industries that are subject to increasing returns. On the other hand, not all models are single-sector ones which exclude the possibility of other factors (such as factor endowments) simultaneously influencing comparative advantage and the division of labour between industries where increasing returns are an independent force and those where they are not. In any case, the theoretical possibility of arbitrary specialization and trade without comparative advantage does not mean that the model is empirically robust, because arbitrary international specialization is in fact pervasive. Economies of scale of some form are likely to be present in many activities, especially where trade in industrial goods is involved. This has long been recognized: it was a major theme in Ohlin's classic work, *International and Interregional Trade*. Decreasing-cost technologies are not necessarily ones where relative costs do not differ internationally (because of differences in relative factor endowments). There is a body of empirical evidence that trade patterns are influenced simultaneously by an amalgam of theories (see for instance, Hufbauer, 1970). Indeed, the 'paradoxical' results for the naive version of the Heckscher–Ohlin or factor endowments model have tended to be superseded by the more sophisticated tests of an extended model (e.g. Leamer, 1984), which find support for the factor endowments explanation of trade in broad aggregates of goods (or sectors). Within those broad aggregates, scale economies are likely to be an important, but not sole, determinant of international competitiveness. Even then it must be remembered that the presence of economies of scale is not necessary to generate trade; the scope for product differentiation, the degree of taste overlap between countries, the degree of market segmentation, the number of firms and the behaviour of firms all also influence the degree and nature of international exchange.

What then is new in the 'new' trade theories? There is probably not a lot that is new in terms of our understanding of the determinants of international trade. There are new analytical tools that the trade economist has to analyse different types of trade flows, but these are predominantly borrowed from the industrial economist. The most significant feature of the new trade models is the interventionist policy conclusion that might be drawn from them. Let us consider why and if the conclusion is justified.

III COMMERCIAL POLICY AND THE 'NEW TRADE THEORY'

The reasons for the rapidly growing literature on policy intervention are not difficult to fathom. The issue is essentially a second-best problem and the proliferation of models has fed the policy debate, with some conclusions appearing to run counter to conventional wisdom. Because of this there is understandable interest on the part of policy-makers in the results of some of these models. The resultant danger is that policy may be guided by what is 'special-case' analysis.

There are at least three substantive conclusions which can be adduced from the new literature.[2] First, there will be circumstances where intervention in imperfectly competitive domestic or international markets can raise welfare. Second, these circumstances may be more widespread than suggested by traditional neoclassical theory. Third, the widely held belief grounded in neoclassical theory, that some form of subsidy is superior to an import tariff, may not always hold. The first of these conclusions is not in itself insightful. After all, the analysis of trade interventions in the neoclassical context is replete with second-best arguments for intervention. What is new perhaps is the nature of the distortions discussed and the implication that the distortions may be widespread and may create more persuasive and more general arguments for welfare-improving intervention in industrialized economies.

Some of the arguments for welfare-improving intervention are idiosyncratic and difficult to take seriously (e.g. Lancaster, 1984). Others have been taken much more seriously, certainly by academics,[3] and seemingly by policy-makers. The two which have probably enjoyed widest currency are intervention to stimulate an increase in the scale of output of some domestic producer(s) (the 'consumption distortion' argument), and intervention to redistribute rents from foreign firms to the domestic government (the 'rent-snatching' argument).

The 'consumption distortion' argument relies upon a situation where a divergence exists between price and marginal cost. An import tariff can be introduced which leads the domestic firm(s) to increase their scale of output and thereby reduce the gap between price and marginal cost. Given an interdependence of cost functions between a domestic and overseas monopolist, it could even be the case that import protection results in export promotion, as in Krugman (1984). The central idea can be presented in various ways. Basically, however, the crucial element is the presence of decreasing costs over the relevant range of output. Given this fact it is fair to say that the central idea is not especially novel. Such economies of scale arguments have been around in the intervention literature in one form or another for some time.

Of course, the arguments might be particularly appealing if policy-makers were led to believe that the presence of economies of scale permits arbitrary specialization by countries. This would appear to give a new credence (although not necessarily with justification) to the infant industry argument for intervention in developing countries. Indeed, infant exporters may be supported by governments, especially if simultaneous import protection and export promotion appear to be on offer! (We return to this issue in sections IV and V.)

The 'rent-snatching' argument is more novel. If international oligopolists earn positive rents, then the distribution of these rents can be influenced by government policy (Brander and Spencer, 1985). The government can use import tariffs to capture rents from foreign firms and, since welfare is evaluated from a nationalistic perspective, welfare gains materialize. The argument is analogous to the classical optimum tariff case for intervention, where there is a large country influence in international markets.

How important are these arguments and how generally applicable are the circumstances in which they might be observed? A casual observer might be forgiven for equating journal space and importance. In fact, the results of most of these models are simply not robust. In many cases they are model-specific and depend upon model specification—the nature of entry conditions, the initial number of firms in the market, the presence or absence of scale economies over the relevant range of output, etc.—and in particular upon the assumption made regarding conjectural variation. In any case, the circumstances under which intervention is potentially beneficial are not necessarily more widespread than might be inferred from a traditional perspective. Nevertheless, the circumstances under which policy-makers may feel justified to intervene may be more widespread. Thus, for example, the potential for rent-snatching tariffs may be more widespread than those circumstances which facilitate an optimal tariff. The argument is not necessarily any more convincing, however. After all, rent snatching is still a 'beggar-thy-neighbour' policy and is subject to more convincing counter-arguments than the optimum tariff; specifically, it is a second-best policy (in the absence of a global anti-trust policy) and the probability of retaliation is arguably higher than in cases where an optimum tariff is levied. This being so, the main contribution of the intervention literature might lie in the support it provides for policy coordination.

IV   STRATEGIC TRADE POLICY AND DEVELOPING COUNTRIES

The term 'strategic trade policy' sounds very seductive: it appears to offer the opportunity of using trade policy selectively to encourage the development of strategically important industries or sectors. Given the apparent success of Japan and some of the other Asian newly industrializing countries (NICs) in using active trade and industrial policies to manage rapid growth and industrialization, the concept might appear to provide a rigorous theoretical basis for such an approach to development in general. This would be a misconception. The term 'strategic trade policy' could be defined narrowly to describe only the 'rent snatching' motive for intervention identified in the previous section: that is, to strategic behaviour in oligopolistic international markets (for activities which may or may not be viewed as strategically important). The example provided by the apparently intervention-led industrialization episodes referred to above would not then be relevant to the debate at hand. It should be evident from the previous section that the relevance of the rent-snatching argument to industrialized countries is very limited. It must be strongly doubted whether international markets are typically imperfectly competitive; it is certainly the case that strict duopoly is very rare. Admittedly there are a very small number of producers globally (though not two) in the case of the aircraft industry, used by Krugman to illustrate the argument, but this is not the typical case. In a large range of traded goods there are producers in North America, Europe, Japan, the NICs and many of the middle-income countries. The post-war period may have witnessed increasing domestic concentration in many industrial countries but there has also been intensified international competition. Even in those industries where there is significant global concentration, the case for intervention by industrial countries is unlikely to be strong. Given behaviour by oligopolists different from that assumed in the model, then intervention may not successfully shift rents. Even if it does, it does not follow that the national interest is served once the protected industry is placed in a multisector setting, where the general equilibrium implications of any intervention must be allowed for. This complication is compounded, of course, where inappropriate interventions are induced as a result of pressures from domestic interest groups. Finally, even if the above errors are avoided, it must be recognized that the rent-snatching argument is symmetrical between countries and the unilateral intervention story told by the proponents of the 'new international economies' lacks credibility. Both players will be faced with the same apparent opportunity for restricting imports in order to shift profits from foreign to domestic firms. This clearly makes trade wars/retaliation almost inevitable: the tariff-ridden solution is invariably inferior to reciprocated liberalization. (This argument is supported by the work of Conybeare (1987) on the theory and evidence of international commercial rivalry.)

Given the above evaluation of the robustness of the 'rent-snatching' argument in the context of industrial countries, it is hardly necessary to say that the argument is even less relevant to developing countries. All the

above arguments apply, but it is obvious that the minimum conditions—namely, that domestic firms have the potential to establish a
substantial position in world markets—are even less likely to be achieved in
the case of developing countries. There are few firms in developing
countries likely to have a significant international market share in the
foreseeable future, and few governments with the resources to pursue
credible strategic trade policy. The potential for and relevance of 'rent-
snatching' to developing countries is negligible.[4] A similar conclusion was
reached by Srinivasan (1986a):

> the exercise of an interventionist trade policy by developing countries, based
> on recent theories of oligopolistic competition and increasing returns, is
> unlikely to be beneficial.

By contrast, the avoidance of rent extraction by oligopolistic foreign
firms may well be of more relevance to developing countries. Srinivasan
(1986b) considered the optimal policy for a small developing country faced
by an oligopolistic foreign-owned firm with power to extract excess profits
from its domestic market. An optimal lump-sum tax on the foreign firm
combined with an optimal import subsidy can avoid this rent extraction—assuming of course that profitable entry of domestic firms is not
achievable. However, optimal tax/subsidy arrangements may be difficult
(for developing countries in particular) to design and implement, and they
are likely in any case to have less appeal to policy-makers in developing
countries than interventionist policies aimed at inducing local production
capabilities.

It is in the context of selectively intervening to promote industries or
activities of 'strategic importance' to economic (in particular industrial)
development that the term 'strategic trade policy' has received most popular
attention. The 'consumption distortion' argument—i.e. that economies may
be associated with increased scale (in the presence of high fixed costs)—and
'external economies' arguments are likely to be of more interest and
relevance to policy-makers in developing countries than the idea of a
strategic struggle for rents. Specific industries are often viewed rightly or
wrongly as being of strategic importance; R&D-intensive activities in
industrialized countries or new technology activities in developing countries
are often viewed (for a mixture of economic and non-economic reasons) as
being of greater importance or long-term value than less technologically
sophisticated activities.

Traditional trade theory does not ignore the issue of externalities. On the
contrary, optimal intervention analysis is embodied in the 'orthodox'
literature. It might be argued that models of imperfect competition do
greater justice to the likely sources of externality than models of perfect

competition can. For example, in the case of the very high fixed costs associated with high-technology/R&D-intensive activities, only small numbers of firms can be supported in an industry by the market. If an externality is induced by the inability of (any or all) firms to be profitable following expensive innovation, then beneficial intervention is clearly possible if the government induces R&D/innovation that had previously been blocked by the externality. Ironically this type of argument, which is only a variant of the traditional infant industry argument, has received intellectual support and has been widely propounded in industrial countries (in the high-technology sectors) at a time when the infant industry argument has been in retreat in developing countries. Should this new variant of an old argument halt or reverse this retreat?

It is certainly not the case that developing countries should view the location of high-technology industries as the product of arbitrary specialization—i.e. activity that could be located in developing countries—and that they should intervene to try to promote such activities. It is not in any case likely that the location of such activities in the industrial North is arbitrary—competitive high-technology firms cannot be acquired simply through a commitment to bear the initial fixed outlays on R&D! Even if it were, the arguments against the 'rent-snatching' version of strategic policy—retaliation, general equilibrium, political economy and the danger of non-optimal interventions—would apply equally in this case. Such arguments against selective interventionism have long been rehearsed against infant industry protection in developing countries. The infant industry argument as such is therefore not enhanced by this renewed interest in externalities. There is, however, a new version of the infant industry argument that has been given some apparent impetus by the new trade theory: namely, simultaneous import substitution and export promotion through support for infant export industries. In the standard, constant-returns model, a single instrument could import-substitute or export-promote but not both. With scale effects present, the possibility of pushing the home producer down his scale curve and the foreign producer up his curve, provides an opportunity for a tradeable (both importable and exportable) to be promoted through selective intervention. The specific result (Krugman, 1984) is not robust and is again based on a simple duopoly model which is not applicable to many developing countries. However, the idea does have rather more general appeal. It has been suggested, for example (Westphal, 1982; Pack and Westphal, 1986), that infant export promotion avoids the pitfalls of infant import protection—greater competition in export markets provides a stimulus to efficiency, while greater potential market size allows scale economies to be realized more rapidly. The cost and duration of infant export promotion could therefore be lower than was associated with the old version of the argument. However, the significance of this appealing result has to be weighed with some care. If, as this chapter has argued earlier, the location of production for specific activities is not arbitrary, then the government is still faced with the familiar problem of 'picking winners', and in the face of the usual political economy pressures which may result in the selection of powerful industries rather than genuine infant exporters. It is also the case that retaliation to export protection may be greater than to import protection. Industrial countries may have been willing to forsake uncertain export opportunities in the face of import substitution policies in developing countries. The 'fair-trade' calls from the US for instance in response to increased competitive challenges in the US market from the Asian NICs suggests that industrial countries are likely to be less willing to lose known jobs to subsidized exports from developing countries.

V THE IMPLICATIONS FOR TRADE STRATEGY

It is reassuring, no doubt, for the advocates of export promotion strategies in developing countries that there is little or nothing to emerge from this review of the trade policy implications of the incorporation of increasing returns and imperfect competition into trade theory that gives restored intellectual credibility to general import substitution strategies. As one of the main architects of the new international economies has argued (Krugman, 1986b):

> Import substituting industrialization looks even worse in the new theory than it does in the standard theory.

However, there are a number of apparent alternatives to general import substitution that are available (in principle at least) to a developing country:

(1) a general pro-export bias, with the effective exchange rate for exports (EER_x) consistently higher than for imports (EER_m);
(2) a pro-export bias in general, with the *average* EER_x greater than the *average* EER_m;
(3) a neutral trade or bias-free strategy *on average* (export promotion in the Bhagwati classification), i.e. average EER_x = average EER_m across tradeable goods sectors;
(4) a bias-free strategy through free trade.

It is doubtful in practice, however, whether all these options are available to developing countries. International obligations (e.g. GATT membership or regional trading groups) and the threat of protective measures in importing countries (typically industrial countries) reduce the feasibility of pursuing pro-export bias options (1) and (2). Given that export promotion measures tend to be fiscally depleting (in contrast to the scope for government revenue enhancement from import substitution measures), then there is also likely to be a domestic constraint on the adoption of options (1) and (2).

The current focus of debate is therefore on options (3) and (4), mixed strategies versus free trade. The idea of mixed strategies of selective import substitution and export promotion has received considerable support. The 'new trade theories', with their emphasis on market imperfections and externalities, give rise to some further interest in interventionist trade and industrial policies, but the mixed strategy approach is inspired mainly by the (revised) structuralist response (e.g. Singer, 1988; Evans, 1990) to the advocacy of more liberal trade policies by agencies such as the World Bank. But is the mixed strategy approach feasible or desirable?

A neutral trade regime could of course involve uniform (positive) nominal protection for both exportables and importables. However, the long-term general equilibrium implications of this for relative incentives (i.e. true protection) and the structure of production are identical to those of free trade.[5] There may nevertheless be short-term incentives for producers in all sectors to seek to increase nominal protection in order to gain transitory rents. Such rent-seeking activity may in turn reduce the general productive capacity of the economy. Alternatively, a neutral trade regime requires only that incentives are on average equal across the importables and exportables sector—a state of affairs, incidentally, that Bhagwati (1988) labels as 'export-promotion' because the structure of relative prices on average mimics free trade. This condition is consistent with substantial variation in nominal protection/incentives between in-dustries or products both within and between the importables sector. This provides a greater incentive for rent-seeking activity since rents can be more permanent (with resulting larger potential losses in general productive capacity), and provides a reason for anticipating that the selection of industries/activities for higher nominal protection will not be driven by efficiency considerations alone. However, even if selectivity is driven by considerations of efficiency (i.e. the reduction of distortions) and long-term comparative advantage (e.g. legitimate infant industry promotion), it is very difficult to set policy instruments appropriately where there are complex interindustry linkages and where interventions have general equilibrium consequences.

General equilibrium considerations are often overlooked in the debate about the selective use of commercial policy and mixed trade strategies. There are fundamental difficulties of designing consistent interven-tions—even if the appropriate industries for promotion can be identified.

The authorities are likely to be working with imperfect information (of a partial equilibrium nature) when setting nominal rates of subsidization. However, the true or relative rates of subsidization involved are determined by the overall structure of nominal subsidization and by endogenous economic characteristics (the substitution relationships within and between the traded and non-traded sectors of the economy). In a world of non-uniform nominal subsidization, of multiple sectors, of differing weights between sectors of protected and unprotected activities, and of differing substitution characteristics for protected and unprotected activities in the given sector, then the general equilibrium structure of protection will be even more difficult for the policy-maker to identify prior to intervention.

Although Krugman recognized this type of general equilibrium criticism of selective/strategic use of trade policy, even in the context of industrialized countries, he argues (Krugman, 1987, p. 141) that:

> To say that it is difficult to formulate the correct interventionist policy is not a defense of free trade, however.

However, when combined with political economy considerations—external policy responses and domestic pressure groups—and when considered in the context of developing countries (where information and policy management capacity is likely to be lower), general equilibrium considerations constitute a significant argument in practice (post-'new trade theory' and new structuralist thinking) for liberal trade policies in developing countries.

Many developing countries are in fact committed to trade policy reform programmes that involve substantial import liberalization: liberalization, that is, of the overt and narrowly defined instruments of trade policy such as import taxes and formal quantitative import restrictions. World Bank and IMF conditionality acts as a constraint on the reversal of this process in the case of many of the poorest or smallest developing countries. In the case of the larger or richer developing countries (newly industrializing and newly exporting countries), international obligations (e.g. GATT) and the threat of bilateral reciprocity (e.g. 'graduation' from preferences) may well act as a constraint on the growth of selective trade interventions (both for imports and exports) of the traditional form. This is also the case for overt export subsidization, not only because it too threatens reciprocal actions but also because of the fiscal constraints associated with explicit subsidization of exports that most governments in developing countries face. However, demonstration effects are significant in policy formulation in developing countries: the 'new protectionism' (the use of hidden non-tariff interventions) and 'administrative protectionism' of the industrialized countries are capable of replication in developing countries. Import rationalization and liberalization programmes have been accompanied in recent years by the introduction of anti-dumping legislation and standards 'control' mechanisms in many developing countries. It is just such instruments that are increasingly being used and threatened by the industrialized countries to protect their own industries, strategic or otherwise. Herein lies the danger that the strategic trade literature appears to provide a justification for the proliferation of policy instruments (and with it, increased blurring of the distinction between trade and industrial policy instruments) and for the greater selectivity that administrative protection permits. It is important, however, that the reality rather than the rhetoric of many of these interventionist pressures in the industrialized countries is exposed to policy-makers in developing countries. The so-called selective or strategic use of trade and industrial policies is often a useful mask for simple protectionism. When such a strategy is applied against its own exports to industrial countries, a developing country is usually keen to recognize it as such!

VI CONCLUSIONS

There has been significant trade liberalization in the last decade in developing countries, often sponsored by the World Bank as part of structural adjustment lending programmes. The successes of the more outward-oriented Asian NICs and dissatisfaction with the results of second-stage import substitution provided an environment within which liberal trade economists could promote their arguments. The last decade has, however, also witnessed the development of new trade theories, relating to conditions (imperfect competition and increasing returns) that are not typically used by liberal economists to promote the case for free or freer trade in developing countries. Since these new models provide an apparent rationale for interventionist trade and industrial policies, they may appear to offer development economists of the structuralist tendency with an alternative theoretical basis for justifying selective intervention in both the import substitution and export promotion sectors. The present review of the 'new trade theory', and its commercial policy implications, concludes that this interpretation is inappropriate. Although the term 'strategic trade policy' is likely to have a seductive appeal to policy-makers in developing countries, the scope for such policy is very restricted. As strictly defined, the strategic use of trade policy to redistribute rents ('rent-snatch') internationally is likely to be an option available to very few developing countries, and then only in a very narrow range of products. Where interventions are aimed at remedying domestic distortions associated with externalities and scale economies, then the ideas of the 'new international economies' are not so new. It has long been recognized in the theory of trade policy that intervention may be welfare raising and that trade interventions are invariably not first-best instruments. The fact that there are more models of trade which incorporate decreasing costs and imperfect competition, and that there may be a greater proportion of international trade where such models are appropriate, does not necessarily mean that international specialization is arbitrary or that the incidence of 'distortions' has increased. Even if the potential for *partial* welfare improvement through intervention has increased, it does not follow that developing countries should therefore be encouraged to believe that interventionist trade strategies should be pursued.[6] Recent structuralist authors have tended to respond to criticisms of general import substitution with arguments in favour of mixed strategies of selective import substitution and export promotion. Besides the usual international and domestic political economy concerns (retaliation and 'rent-seeking') about the likely effectiveness of widespread and selective interventions, this chapter has emphasized the information demands and resulting general equilibrium constraints on mixed strategies and selective intervention.

NOTES

1 'Inter-industry' trade refers to international exchange of the products of different industries, and 'intra-industry' trade to the exchange of similar products from within the same industry.
2 For popular reviews of the arguments, see Krugman (1987) and Bhagwati (1989).
3 The *Bulletin of the Centre for Economic Policy Research* (1986, p. 14 for instance) reports that: 'The case for import protection may be much stronger than conventional wisdom suggests according to CEPR Programme Director Alasdair Smith and Research Fellow Tony Venables . . .'.
4 Baldwin and Flam (1989) identified scope for profit-shifting strategic policy in the case of the international market for 30–40-seat commuter aircraft. This is a close to real counterpart to the strategic trade models of Brander and Spencer in which Brazil is a potential player in the game. This should be viewed as a special case, however, both in terms of the industry involved and the size of the developing country.
5 The relative or 'true protection' concept was introduced by Sjaastad (1980) and applied to developing countries by Greenaway and Milner (1987).
6 Interventionist policies have been used throughout to describe explicit and implicit producer subsidies (e.g. resulting from trade interventions). Minimalist government is not being advocated. There are many areas where governments in developing countries should seek to foster long-term development (e.g. support

for skills and management training) and to reduce rigidities in the functioning of domestic markets.

REFERENCES

Baldwin, R. and H. Flam (1989) 'Strategic Trade Policies in the Market for 30–40 Seat Commuter Aircraft', *Weltwirtschaftliches Archiv* **125**, 484–500.

Bhagwati, J. (1988) 'Export-Promoting Trade Strategy: Issues and Evidence', *World Bank Research Observer* **3**, 27–58 (reprinted in C. Milner (ed.) (1990) *Export Promotion Strategies: Theory and Evidence from Developing Countries*, Wheatsheaf, London).

Bhagwati, J. (1989) 'Is Free Trade Passé After All?' *Weltwirtschaftliches Archiv* **125**, 3–30.

Brander, J.A. (1981) 'Intra-Industry Trade in Identical Commodities', *Journal of International Economics* **11**, 1–4.

Brander, J.A. and B.J. Spencer (1985) 'Export Subsidies and International Market Share Rivalry', *Journal of International Economics* **18**, 83–100.

Conybeare, J.A.C. (1987) *Trade Wars: The Theory and Practice of International Commercial Rivalry*, Columbia University Press, New York.

Evans, D.H. (1990) 'Outward Orientation: An Assessment' in C. Milner (ed.), *Export Promotion Strategies: Theory and Evidence from Developing Countries*, Wheatsheaf, London.

Helpman, E. and P.R. Krugman (1985) *Market Structure and Foreign Trade*, MIT Press, Cambridge, MA.

Hufbauer, G.C. (1970) 'The Impact of National Characteristics and Technology on the Commodity Composition of Trade in Manufactured Goods' in R. Vernon (ed.), *The Technology Factor in International Trade*, Colombia University Press, New York.

Greenaway, D. and C.R. Milner (1986) *The Economics of Intra-Industry Trade*, Blackwell, Oxford.

Greenaway, D. and C.R. Milner (1987) 'True Protection: Concepts and Their Use in Evaluating Commercial Policy in Developing Countries', *Journal of Development Studies* **23**, 200–19.

Krugman, P.R. (1979) 'Increasing Returns, Monopolistic Competition and International Trade', *Journal of International Economics* **9**, 469–79.

Krugman, P.R. (1984) 'Import Protection as Export Promotion: International Competition in the Presence of Oligopoly and Economies of Scale' in H. Kierzkowski (ed.), *Monopolistic Competition and International Trade*, Oxford University Press, Oxford.

Krugman, P.R. (1986a) *Strategic Trade Policy and the New International Economics*, MIT Press, Cambridge, MA.

Krugman, P.R. (1986b) 'New Trade Theory and the Less Developed Countries', paper presented at the Carlos Diaz-Alejandro Memorial Conference, World Institute for Development Economics Research, Helsinki.

Krugman, P.R. (1987) 'Is Free Trade Passé?', *Journal of Economic Perspectives* **1**, 131–44.

Leamer, E.E. (1984) *Sources of International Comparative Advantage: Theory and Evidence*, MIT Press, Cambridge, MA.

Lancaster, K.J. (1980) 'Intra-Industry Trade under Perfect Monopolistic Competition', *Journal of International Economics* **10**, 151–75.

Lancaster, K.J. (1984) 'Protection and Product Differentiation' in H. Kierzkowski (ed.), *Monopolistic Competition and International Trade*, Oxford University Press, Oxford.

Pack, H. and L.E. Westphal (1986) 'Industrial Strategy and Technological Change: Theory and Evidence', *Journal of Development Economics* **22**, 87–128.

Riedel, J. (1991) 'Strategy Wars: The State of the Debate on Trade and Industrialisation in Developing Countries' in A. Koekkoek and L.B.M. Mennes (eds), *International Trade and Global Development*, Routledge, London.

Singer, H.W. (1988) 'The World Development Report 1987 on the Blessings of Outward Orientation: A Necessary Correction', *Journal of Development Studies* **24**, 232–6.

Sjaastad, L.A. (1980) 'Commercial Policy, True Tariffs and Relative Prices' in J. Black and B.V. Hindley (eds), *Current Issues in Commercial Policy and Diplomacy*, Macmillan, London.

Srinivasan, T.N. (1986a) 'Development Strategy: Is the Success of Outward Orientation at an End?' in S. Guhan and M. Schroff (eds), *Essays on Economic Progress and Welfare*, Oxford University Press, New Delhi.

Srinivasan, T.N. (1986b) 'Recent Theories of Imperfect Competition and International Trade: Any Implications for Development Strategy?', World Bank, mimeo.

Westphal, L.E. (1982) 'Fostering Technological Mastery by Means of Selective Infant Industry Protection' in M. Syrquin and S. Teitel (eds), *Trade, Stability, Technology and Equity in Latin America*, Academic Press, New York.

3 First World's Machines and Third World's Economic Development*

HOMI KATRAK

I INTRODUCTION

Developing countries recognize that they need to import machines and technological know-how from the industrially advanced countries in order to promote their economic growth, set up new industries and increase productivity and output in the existing ones. At the same time they are also concerned about a number of aspects of those imports. Questions are raised on account of both machines with embodied technologies and disembodied technological know-how.

Initially, the developing countries' concerns were that they had only a limited choice in their imports of machines from the economically advanced countries and that most of those machines were inappropriate to local economic conditions. More recently, there has also been concern about the high prices being charged for imported machines and about their contribution to the growth of output.

This paper discusses these concerns of the developing countries and considers some questions for further research. Section II discusses questions about limited choice and inappropriateness of imported machines, Sections III and IV examine questions about the price of those machines while Section V considers some factors that may influence their contribution to the growth of output and their benefit–cost ratio. Section VI summarizes the main points.

* Paper presented to the Conference on International Aspects of Economic Development, University of Surrey, 18 September 1991.

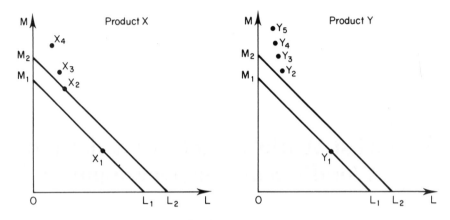

Figure 3.1 Allocations of expenditure on machines (M) and labour (L) for two products X and Y.

II LIMITED CHOICE AND INAPPROPRIATE MACHINES

Do the concerns about limited choice and inappropriateness of machines amount to the same thing? At first encounter it might seem that these two problems are interrelated. The developing countries' choices are limited since the range of machines that they can use is restricted mainly to those produced in the economically advanced countries. As the machines have been designed to suit the user requirements and economic conditions of the economically advanced countries, they are inappropriate to the factor prices and market size of the developing countries. But does this mean that there is a monotonic relationship between limited choice and inappropriateness? Does a decrease in the amount of choice increase the cost in terms of inappropriateness?

These questions may be examined with the help of Figure 3.1. M_1L_1 and M_2L_2 are iso-cost lines showing allocations of expenditure on two factors of production, machines and labour. The machinery expenditures are defined as the annual interest cost per unit of output, and depend on the rate of interest and the price of the machines.[1] The labour costs depend on the number of people employed and the wage rate, which is assumed to be independent of the type of machine used.

The points X_4, X_3 and X_2 show the cost combinations that would be required if a developing country were to make a product X, using machines imported from economically advanced countries. X_4 may pertain to a type of machine that is currently being used in, say, the USA, while X_3 and X_2

may pertain to machines from Germany and Spain. The developing country's choices are limited to these three machines. Each machine embodies a particular technology, so the terms 'machines' and 'technologies' will be interchangeable. If the developing country uses the Spanish machine, the unit cost of production, in terms of labour equivalent, will be OL_2. However, if a more appropriate machine, represented by the point X_1, had been available the cost of production would have been only OL_1. Thus the excess cost of having to use an inappropriate machine for the production of X is L_1L_2.

This may be compared with the situation for another product, Y. The choice of machines here is greater than for product X: there are four machines, as shown by the points Y_5, Y_4, Y_3 and Y_2. .However, the unit cost of production of the best available alternative would now be greater than OL_2. Further, if a more appropriate machine as shown by Y_1 had been available, the excess cost of having to use Y_2 would be greater than L_1L_2. Thus the cost of inappropriateness here is greater than for product X.

Admittedly, this is a highly simplified example. Nevertheless, it does help to show that the problems of limited choice and inappropriateness may not be the same. In fact, as the example shows, the excess cost of using inappropriate machines may be lower in a given industry X even though there is a narrower choice of machines. It may also be noted that the example need not be restricted to machines that are currently being produced in the economically advanced countries; it could include also machines of older vintages that may be available as second-hand machines.

The above example should not be taken to imply that limited choice *per se* does not matter. One reason for this is that inappropriateness is not a unidimensional problem: machines may be inappropriate with respect to diverse characteristics, such as factor prices, size of market, raw material requirements and so on. Some machines may be inappropriate in relation to factor prices, others in relation to market size. The greater the range of choice available, the greater the likelihood that some of the machines will be at least reasonably appropriate with respect to one of the characteristics and consequently the excess cost of using inappropriate machines will be less. Another reason why choice is important is that it may reflect the structure of the market for machines: if the design of particular machines is firm-specific, a wider choice of machines may reflect a larger number of alternative suppliers of machines. An increase in the number of suppliers may, in turn, enhance the bargaining power of the importer and hence lead to lower prices for the machines.

A fuller understanding and evaluation of the problems of limited choice and inappropriateness needs more detailed empirical information. There are at least four questions for empirical research:

(1) Does the range of choice differ between industries? Is the choice greater for, say, textile machines than for metal-working machines?

(2) If the range of choice does differ, do the industries with a greater range of choice also offer machines that are more appropriate? The answer may depend on two sets of influences. First, as suggested above, if inappropriateness has diverse characteristics, an increase in choice may make it more likely that some machines will be appropriate with respect to at least some of the desired characteristics. Second, the extent of inappropriateness may also depend on the costs of adapting the machines of the economically advanced countries to the conditions of the developing countries, but these costs may be unrelated to the choice of machines available.

(3) Do the developing countries undertake a detailed search for potential suppliers of machines and/or do the suppliers scan all the markets in the developing countries? Casual observation suggests that there is only limited search: most UK exports of machines are directed to those countries with which it has historical ties, and this also applies to Spain and France. Limited search is likely to make the developing countries' actual set of choices narrower than the potential choices.

(4) Is the developing countries' choice of machines restricted mainly to those that are being currently produced in the economically advanced countries (for machine users in those countries)? Or is there also a choice of second-hand machines, and/or of machines specially designed for the developing countries and also machines exported from the newly industrializing countries?

Empirical evidence pertaining to these questions would help to evaluate the developing countries' concerns about the limited choice and inappropriateness of imported machines.

III DEVELOPING COUNTRIES' CHOICE OF MACHINES

Given a range of choice, the type of machines actually purchased by a developing country will be influenced (at least partly) by the prices of those machines. In turn, the prices will be influenced by the bargaining power of the suppliers and purchasers. The role of bargaining and prices has been widely discussed in the literature on disembodied transfers of technology to developing countries by, among others, Chudnovsky (1981), Contractor (1981), Katrak (1990), Mytelka (1978) and Stewart (1990). However, rather surprisingly, the literature on the choice of machines (with embodied technology) has not given much attention to the price variable. This neglect of prices is a serious omission and, as is shown below, can lead to misleading conclusions and prescriptions.

For simplicity, the following analyses assume that technological know-how is entirely embodied in a machine, or is completely transferable. Each machine is sold with a set of blue-prints, or instructions which specify completely the operational procedures. The importer thus does not require any further know-how or technical assistance. It is also assumed that there are no maintenance requirements, breakdowns, etc. Finally, all products are assumed to produce the same quality of product.

Gouverneur (1971) analysed a simple model where a developing country has a choice between two types of machines:

(1) A vintage machine which was designed, say, 50 years ago for the market conditions of an economically advanced country. This machine has already been used in that country. It embodies old technology but may be appropriate for the present economic conditions of the developing countries.

(2) A new machine, recently designed for the market conditions of an advanced country. The machine embodies the most recent technology but may not be appropriate for the developing country.

I will refer to the above as used (U) and new (N) machines, respectively. There is also a third possibility: a new machine that embodies most recent technology and which would be designed specifically for a developing country. This type of machine is, however, not actually available and so may be thought of as an ideal (I) machine only.

Now although each of these machines embodies some specific technological know-how, Gouverneur suggests that all machines can be translated into a homogeneous and perfectly divisible primary factor, namely, capital. This capital is then combined with labour to produce some required level of output. Figure 3.2 is a slight modification of Gouverneur's analysis. The slopes of the lines C_1L_1 and C_2L_2 show the price of labour relative to capital in the developing country. Point U shows the (fixed-coefficient) amounts of capital and labour required to produce a unit of output with the used machine, N shows the corresponding amounts for the new machine and I for the ideal (but unavailable) machine.

There are two main conclusions from the analysis. The first pertains to the developing country's choice between U and N. The relative advantage of the former machine is that it is more labour-intensive, while the advantage of the latter is that it embodies more recent technological know-how. The choice between them will depend on (1) the factor-price ratio in the developing country, (2) the difference between the capital and labour intensities of the two machines, and (3) the 'technological gap' between them. As drawn in Figure 3.2, the impact of these three influences is such that

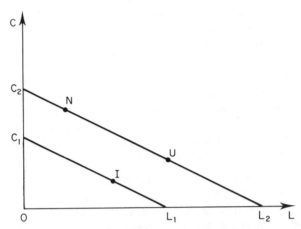

Figure 3.2 Inputs of capital (C) and labour (L) per unit of output (modified from Gouverneur, 1971).

U and N would entail the same unit cost of production in the developing country: the unit cost would be OL_2 in terms of labour equivalent.

The other conclusion of the analysis concerns the advantages of the ideal machine. If that machine were available, the unit cost of production would have been only OL_1. Machine I would thus have been preferable to each of the other two: it would have entailed a lower unit cost than U as it would have embodied more recent technological know-how, and it would also have entailed a lower cost than N because it would have been more appropriate to the factor prices of the developing country.

Unfortunately, however, this analysis is rather simplistic and misleading. It does not explicitly take account of the prices that the developing country would have to pay for the machines and consequently ignores the effect of those prices on the unit production cost of using those machines. As each machine is a durable input, the cost of using a machine will depend on its price and on the rate of interest (or the opportunity capital that is tied up when using the machine). The three machines will have the same unit production cost in use only if they all have the same price and face the same rate of interest.

IV MARKET STRUCTURE AND THE PRICE OF MACHINES

Is a developing country likely to face the same prices for used and new machines? What factors are likely to influence the relative profitability of those machines? An important consideration is likely to be the structure of the markets for those machines and the bargaining power of the purchasers vis-à-vis the suppliers. There may be a large number of alternative outcomes. In order to see this, consider a particular scenario. Following the 'small country' assumption of international trade models, let us suppose that a developing country is a price-taker for both used and new machines. This assumption helps to exclude many other possibilities but even in this scenario, the relative prices and profitability of used and new machines may depend on the nature of the market for those machines in the economically advanced country. This can be illustrated with reference to two polar cases: a perfectly competitive market, and a complete monopoly.

Suppose first that the market for both used and new machines is perfectly competitive. In this case a developing country will be faced with the same prices as those prevailing in the economically advanced country (abstracting from transport costs and import taxes). The question now is that of how those prices are determined. Consider briefly an approach that was analysed in an earlier paper (Katrak, 1991). Drawing on Salter's (1960) vintage-capital model, it was suggested that the relative prices of used and new machines facing a developing country may be determined by the profitability of those machines to their users in economically advanced countries. It was shown that if a user in an advanced country is indifferent between a new machine and an older one that is currently being used, the relative prices will be such that a developing country purchaser would always prefer the used machine.

This result is illustrated with the help of Figure 3.3 (an algebraic proof was given in the earlier paper). For expositional convenience it is assumed that the new machine is designed to produce the same level of output (and same quality of product) as the machine actually being used and that labour is the only variable input. The vertical axis measures the unit production costs of using the new machine. OV_n is the annual cost of the variable input in the economically advanced country and V_nF_n is the annual fixed cost (which is determined by the price of the machine and the rate of interest). The horizontal axis measures the unit production costs of operating a used machine. OV_u is the variable cost in the advanced country and, following Salter, is higher than for the new machine. The used machine may have been fully amortized. However, as long as it has some second-hand value (or even scrap value), its continued use will entail an opportunity cost. Let this opportunity cost per unit of output be V_uS_u.

Now a machine user in the economically advanced country will be indifferent between these two machines if $OF_n = OS_u$. In such a case, since $OV_n < OV_u$, we will have $V_nF_n > V_uS_u$, which means that the price of the

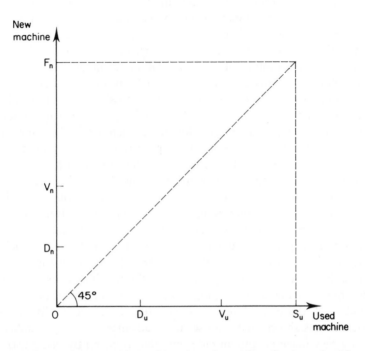

Figure 3.3 Costs of new (vertical axis) and used machines (horizontal axis) per unit of output.

new machine will exceed the second-hand value of the old one. Does this mean that it will be more profitable for a developing country purchaser to purchase the used machine? The answer for the perfectly competitive market is that it will. The reason is that the wage rate is lower in the developing country and the used machine entails a relatively greater labour input. In Figure 3.3 the unit variable costs in the developing country would be D_nV_n and D_uV_u for the new and old machines, respectively (such that $D_nV_n/OV_n = D_uV_u/OV_u$). Consequently, the average total cost for the new machine would be D_nF_n while that for the new one would be only D_uS_u.

The polar opposite case is that of a complete monopoly. There may be only one firm producing new machines in the economically advanced country and it may also be the sole buyer of second-hand machines. The firm would then be the sole exporter of machines to the developing country. In some cases its pricing policy would need to take account of the interdependence between the sales of the two types of machines. However, in some other situations, as suggested by Besanko *et al.* (1988), the firm may be able to separate out the various purchasers and sell them different machines. It may sell used machines to some buyers and new ones to others, or sell only one type of machine.

The monopolist's strategy may be analysed as follows. Suppose first that it sells, say, used machines only. It may charge a uniform price to all consumers or, if it can segregate the various purchasers, set discriminatory prices. Next it considers whether its profits can be further increased by selling only new, rather than used, machines to some of the buyers. This would bring a further increase in profits if:

$$d(TR_n - TC_n)/dQ_n > -[d(TR_u - TC_u)/dQ_u](dQ_u/dQ_n) \qquad (1)$$

where TR_n, TC_n and Q_n denote respectively the total costs, total revenue and quantities of the new machines, TR_u, TC_u and Q_u are the corresponding terms for the used machines and (dQ_u/dQ_n) is negatively signed.

This condition may be simplified by considering the effect of selling just one new machine, instead of a used one. In this case, $(dQ_u/dQ_n) = -1$ and the above inequality may be written as:

$$P_n - MC_n > P_u - MC_u \qquad (2)$$

where P_n and P_u are respectively the prices of the new and used machines that the monopolist would charge to the purchaser concerned, and MC_n and MC_u are the corresponding marginal costs to the monopolist of acquiring those machines.

The above condition tells whether or not the monopolist would want to sell a new machine instead of a used one. However, it is also necessary to examine whether a developing country enterprise would prefer to buy the new machine. The potential purchaser will consider the unit costs of production with the two types of machines and so will prefer a new machine if:

$$P_n R_d + L_n W_d < P_u R_d + L_u W_d \qquad (3)$$

where L_n and L_u are respectively the unit labour requirements for the new and used machines, R_d is the unit cost of capital that is tied up when using machines in the developing country, and W_d is the wage rate in the developing country.

Next, by combining the inequality conditions for the seller and the buyer and rearranging terms, it is found that both parties would prefer to transact in a new machine, rather than a used one, if:

$$(W_d/R_d)(L_u - L_n) > (P_n - P_u) > (MC_n - MC_u) \qquad (4)$$

So the monopoly case could result in the sale of a new machine even if more labour-intensive used ones were available.

The above outcome obviously contrasts with that obtained in the case of a perfectly competitive market. The reason for this may be seen as follows. In the competitive case, the prices of the two machines are determined by the condition that the machines be equally profitable to users in the economically advanced country. This condition may be written as:

$$P_nR_a + L_nW_a = P_uR_a + L_uW_a$$

or:

$$(W_a/R_a)(L_u - L_n) = (P_n - P_u) \tag{5}$$

where R_a is the unit cost of capital in the economically advanced country and W_a is the wage rate. Now if, as is very likely, $(W_a/R_a) > (W_d/R_d)$, and if equality (5) holds, then inequality (3) cannot be satisfied, i.e. the developing country will not prefer the new machine.

These two polar cases do not exhaust the range of possibilities. However, they do help to illustrate the general point that in order to analyse developing countries' purchases of used and new machines it is important to know something about the nature of the market for those machines and also the relative bargaining power of the sellers and buyers. Neglect of the market makes for an incomplete analysis and may lead to misleading conclusions.

The role of the market is also important when considering the ideal type of machine. These are machines that embody the most recent technological know-how and are designed for the economic conditions of the developing country. Gouverneur suggested that if such machines were available they would be preferable to both used and new machines. Would this always be the case? Engineers and technologists may well be able to design and produce such machines. But what about the costs of design and production and the prices charged to developing countries? As ideal machines would require different designs from those used to produce machines for the economically advanced countries, would be produced in relatively small lots for the limited markets of the developing countries and would be produced by only a few firms, it could well be that the prices charged to the developing countries would be higher than for other new machines and the higher price could more than offset the advantage of the more appropriate design of the ideal machine.

V   THE BENEFITS–COSTS OF IMPORTED MACHINES

In addition to the concerns about limited choice and the prices of imported machines there has recently also been concern that those machines have made only a limited contribution to the growth of output and welfare in the developing countries. This latter concern gains support from a recent study by UNCTAD (1988) which showed that during the period 1981–6 the developing countries' imports of machines accounted for only 17 per cent of the intercountry variation in growth of manufacturing value added *per capita*, and the 'marginal product' of the imported machines[2] was less than 0.2. This finding suggests that the benefit–cost ratio of imported machines was rather low in the years of the study.

The UNCTAD study raises a number of questions for further research:

(1) Were the findings particular to the years covered by the study? Would similar results be obtained for other periods?
(2) Was the benefit–cost ratio of the imported machines lower than that of other types of investment in the developing countries?
(3) Could the benefit–cost ratio of imported machines be enhanced by the developing countries undertaking a wider search for those machines and having a greater choice of machines?
(4) Has the benefit–cost ratio been dependent on the availability of domestic skills in management and in production and/or on some technical assistance from the machinery suppliers?

The above questions, like the UNCTAD study itself, concern mainly the private benefits–costs of imported machines. However, a more comprehensive assessment should also consider questions about the social benefits–costs. The social evaluation may differ from the private one for at least two reasons, namely, market distortions (including government-imposed ones) and inappropriability. The implications of inappropriability, though well known in the industrial economics literature, have not been discussed adequately in the context of developing countries.

An enterprise that installs an imported machine (or uses an imported technology) may not be able to appropriate all of the benefits of that machine. The private benefits will be less than the social benefits. Some of the inappropriated benefits will accrue to consumers. This raises at least two possibilities. First, a machine may not be imported because it is not privately profitable and yet the machine may enhance social welfare. Second, the private benefits may be greater for, say, used machines but the social benefits may be greater with new machines. The latter possibility arises because used machines have relatively lower fixed costs which enhance their private profitability relative to new machines, but the latter have lower variable costs which allow for a higher level of output and consequently increase the social (and private) benefit of those machines relative to that of used ones.

The former case is illustrated with the help of Figure 3.4. M_1C_1 and

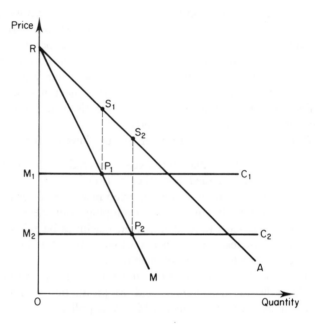

Figure 3.4 Marginal revenue (MR) and average revenue (AR) curves for new and used machines.

M_2C_2 show the variable costs of production with used and new machines, respectively. RM is the marginal revenue curve for products made with either type of machine: it incorporates the enterprise's conjectures about its rivals' responses to its own output changes. RA is the corresponding average revenue curve. The enterprise's operating profits (defined as the excess of revenue over variable costs) would be M_1RP_1 and M_2RP_2 with the used and new machines. The corresponding areas of consumer surplus are S_1RP_1 and S_2RP_2, respectively.

Now the used machines may be privately unprofitable but yet may be socially beneficial if:

$$M_1RP_1 < AFC_u < M_1RS_1P_1$$

where AFC_u (not shown in the figure) denotes the annual fixed costs of having the used machine. This outcome could also arise with the new machine; the required condition is:

$$M_2RP_2 < AFC_n < M_2RS_2P_2$$

where AFC_n (not shown in the figure) denotes the annual fixed cost of having the new machine. In such situations the enterprise concerned would decide not to import either machine and yet the imports would be socially beneficial.

The second of the possibilities mentioned above may also be illustrated with the help of Figure 3.4. The private benefits will be relatively greater with the used machine if:

$$(M_1RP_1 - AFC_u) > (M_2RP_2 - AFC_n) > 0$$

while the social benefits may be greater with the new machine if:

$$(M_2RS_2P_2 - AFC_n) > (M_1RS_1P_1 - AFC_u) > 0$$

Rearranging terms shows that both conditions will hold simultaneously if:

$$(M_2RP_2 - M_1RP_1) < (AFC_n - AFC_u) < (M_2RS_2P_2 - M_1RS_1P_1)$$

In such cases an enterprise would decide to buy the used machine but social considerations would indicate the import of the new machine.

In principle, the above problems could be resolved by giving enterprises a sales subsidy such as to make their marginal revenue schedule coincide with the consumers' marginal utility schedule. Each enterprise would then produce a level of output which would equate its marginal costs to the marginal utility and it could thereby appropriate all of the consumer surplus over that level of output. If enterprises knew *ex ante* that they would receive such a subsidy, they would choose the type of machine that would yield the greater level of social (and private) benefits. In practice, however, such a subsidy may raise two problems. First, the subsidy has to be financed and the income distribution problems associated with this may be undesirable. Second, as each enterprise's perceived marginal revenue incorporates its conjectures about its rivals' responses, the required level of subsidy and the conjectures may become interdependent.

The distinction between social and private benefits is important in another type of situation also. Suppose that a developing country has a choice of only one type of imported machine but that the level of demand facing the country is large enough to accommodate the output of two (or more) machines of that type. Suppose also that the country's enterprises are able to bargain with the machinery supplier over the prices of those machines. The question that arises here is whether the developing country will be better off with a single domestic enterprise, or should it have two (or more) competing enterprises?

The answer to this question depends on two opposing considerations. On the one hand, the larger the number of domestic enterprises, the smaller the machine capacity requirement of each enterprise and consequently the weaker its bargaining power vis-à-vis the machinery supplier: thus the price that must be paid for the machines (per unit of output) is likely to be higher. On the other hand, the larger the number of competing domestic enterprises, the lower the likely prices of products charged to domestic consumers. These two opposing effects are shown in Figure 3.5. The comparison is between a monopoly and a competing duopoly. PR is the average revenue curve facing the domestic industry. VC shows the variable costs of production with imported machines; these costs are assumed to be identical for each of the domestic enterprises and independent of their number. The monopolist's output is OQ_m and its price is OP_m, while the duopolists' combined output is OQ_d and price is OP_d. The fixed costs per unit of output are VF_m for the monopolist and VF_d for each of the duopolies; the former is relatively lower because the monopolist has greater bargaining power and will pay a lower price, per unit of output, for imported machines.

The social benefits under the two situations are as follows. In the monopoly case the social benefits are F_mPAB, of which P_mPA is the consumer surplus and F_mP_mAB the enterprise's profits. In the duopoly case

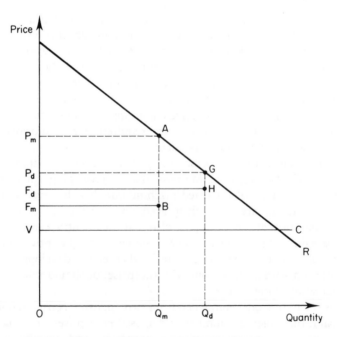

Figure 3.5 Purchase of a single type of imported machine according to whether the domestic market is monopolistic or duopolistic.

the benefits are F_dPGH, of which P_dPG is the consumer surplus and F_dP_dGH the profits. Thus the overall social benefits could be greater in the monopoly situation, even though the consumer surplus is greater under the duopoly.

Admittedly, the above example is rather simplified and abstracts from certain factors, such as organizational slack, which are more likely to arise under monopoly. Nevertheless, the example helps to show that the social (and private) benefits–costs of imported machines may depend on the bargaining power of domestic enterprises with the machinery suppliers as well as on the competition between those enterprises in the domestic market. These considerations may be important for policy-makers who want to decide on the optimum number of competing enterprises in an industry.

VI CONCLUSIONS

This chapter has discussed four reasons why the developing countries are concerned about their imports of machines from the economically advanced countries: these are the range of choice and appropriateness of the machines, the prices charged and the benefits–costs of the machines. It has been shown that limited choice and inappropriateness are not necessarily related: industries that have a relatively limited choice of machines need not be those where the cost of using inappropriate machines will be relatively high. Nevertheless, limited choice may be a cause of concern as it may reduce the developing countries' bargaining power vis-à-vis the machinery suppliers and so may result in high prices being charged for the machines.

The role of prices and choices has been examined in the framework of models of used and new machines. It has been shown that the relative profitability of such machines to the developing countries will depend on the structure of the markets involved. In particular, the outcome may depend on whether or not the importing countries are price-takers and also on the extent of competition amongst the suppliers of machines.

In considering the benefits–costs of imported machines it was suggested that inappropriability may cause the private profitability of those machines to be less than their social benefits. The consequences of this divergence were illustrated with reference to two examples: the social benefits could be relatively greater with a new machine and yet private profitability could be greater with a used machine; and an increase in the number of competing domestic users of a machine will decrease the private profitability of each enterprise but could either increase or decrease the social benefits.

NOTES

1 These expenditures arise because once the machines are purchased money is tied up and consequently the enterprise incurs an opportunity cost in terms of interest payments (or interest earnings foregone). The machinery expenditures are defined as annual costs so as to make them comparable to labour costs and other variable costs.

2 For a 53-country sample the study reports a regression equation:

$$V = 0.150 + 0.189G; \; R^2 = 0.17$$
$$(0.293) \quad (3.17)$$

where V denotes manufacturing value added growth rate *per capita*, G is capital goods imports growth rate and the figures in parentheses are the t-values.

REFERENCES

Besanko, D., S. Donnenfeld and L.J. White (1988) 'The Multiproduct Firm, Quality Choice and Regulation', *Journal of Industrial Economics* **XXXVI**, 411–429.

Chudnovsky, D. (1981) 'Regulating Technology Imports in Some Developing Countries', *Trade and Development* No. 3, 133–150.

Contractor, F.J. (1981) *International Technology Licensing*, D.C. Heath, Lexington.

Gouverneur, J. (1971) *Productivity and Factor Proportions in Less Developed Countries*, Oxford University Press, Oxford.

Katrak, H. (1990) 'Imports of Technology of the Newly Industrialising Countries: An Inter-Industry Analysis for Mexico and Pakistan', *Journal of International Development* **2**, 352–372.

Katrak, H. (1991) 'Market Rivalry, Government Policies and Multinational Enterprise in Developing Countries' in P.J. Buckley and J. Clegg (eds), *Multinational Enterprises in Less Developed Countries*, Macmillan, London.

Mytelka, L.K. (1978) 'Licensing and Technology Dependence in the Andean Group', *World Development* **6**, 447–460.

Salter, W.E.G. (1960) *Productivity and Technical Change*, Cambridge University Press, Cambridge.

Stewart, F. (1990) 'Technology Transfer for Development' in R.E. Evenson and G. Ranis (eds), *Science and Technology: Lessons for Development Policy*, Intermediate Technology Publications, London.

UNCTAD (1988) *Recent Trends in International Technology Flows and their Implications for Development*, UNCTAD, Geneva.

4 | Economic Development and the World Energy Market

PAUL STEVENS

I INTRODUCTION

This chapter concerns the serious incompatibilities which exist between the process of economic development in Third World countries and the world energy markets into which those countries are linked. These incompatibilities, unchecked, will probably become more problematical in the future. The purpose here is to explain the nature and causes of the incompatibilities, why they may worsen, and what possible means might exist to alleviate the negative consequences of their existence.

The chapter concentrates upon Third World countries which enter the World Bank's low-income and lower middle-income category. It is useful to distinguish between two types of country within these groups since the nature of the incompatibilities differs. There are net energy-importing countries, defined as countries whose energy imports constitute more than 10% of merchandise imports,[1] and net energy exporters, whose energy exports constitute more than 50% of total exports.[2] The world energy markets refers to the international trade in energy. For mainly technical reasons, this is confined almost entirely to trade in hydrocarbons—oil, coal and gas. Of these, the trade is dominated by oil.[3] The hypothesis presented here is that this international market has certain characteristics which are inimical to the process of development. Before considering these characteristics, it is necessary to explain why a link exists between Third World countries and the world energy market.

II   LINKS BETWEEN DEVELOPMENT AND ENERGY MARKETS

II.1   Exporters

For exporters, the link with the world energy market is the obvious one of supplier to market. The oil exporters find that they are highly dependent upon oil revenues for foreign exchange and government revenue. The most obvious example is provided by the OPEC countries where in 1980, on average, 94% of exports were in the form of oil (OPEC, 1984). Furthermore, oil accounts for a significant proportion of GDP both directly by the production and sale of oil and indirectly via the spending of oil revenues within the economy.[4]

II.2   Importers

There exists an extensive literature (Humphrey and Stanislaw, 1979; Pearson, 1988; Diwan, 1978; Rosenburg, 1980) which shows that commercial energy is a key input into the process of economic development whether defined as expanded output or in terms of improved quality of living. For example, between 1960 and 1973 based upon World Bank data (World Bank, 1976), the energy intensity[5] of low-income countries increased from 0.85 to 1.02. For the middle-income countries the rise was from 0.66 to 0.97. Equally, in many Third World countries, domestic production of crude oil is constrained. This occurs either because of unfavourable geology or, more commonly, because of severe financial and institutional constraints facing conversion of a resource base into productive capacity (Khan, 1987; Lambert and Fesharaki, 1990; Stevens, 1992). The result has been a significant growth of import dependence between large parts of the Third World and the world energy market, a process which began in the 1960s.

III   CHARACTERISTICS OF THE WORLD ENERGY MARKET RELEVANT TO DEVELOPMENT

The characteristics of the world energy market relevant to development can be divided into three areas—demand, supply and price. Supply is relevant for net energy importers, demand for net energy exporters and price for both.

III.1 Demand characteristics

The demand for oil has certain characteristics which are likely to have a negative impact upon Third World exporters. First, there are the well-known and much discussed development problems associated with other primary commodities. Demand is a derived quantity and hence at the whim of the level of economic activity in the industrialized countries. This leaves demand volatile. Also, technology is able to reduce the unit input for a given output, thereby presenting the supplier with a declining trend in demand. To a greater or lesser extent these arguments also apply to oil, although there has been much discussion over the extent to which the link between energy demand and economic growth has been broken in the OECD countries as a consequence of the oil price shocks of the 1970s (Hawdon, 1992; Stevens, 1987). The result is that export earnings, via volume fluctuations, are unstable. This, however, is true for many primary commodities and its effect upon development is much debated (Glezakos, 1973; Love, 1989; Macbean, 1966).

There is an important aspect of demand for oil which differentiates it from other commodities. Energy has been and will increasingly become a target for consumer government policy. During the decades of the 1970s and 1980s, this was in response to the perceived vulnerability arising from import dependence upon oil in general and Middle East oil in particular. Thus oil's strategic importance made it a policy target. This gave rise to a whole series of policy measures, often lumped together under a large, much publicized programme such as President Nixon's 'Project Independence' and President Carter's 'National Energy Plan'. The whole thrust of these policy measures was to reduce the oil intensity of the economy, a policy which definitely produced significant results for the OECD. Indeed, the fall in demand between 1979 and 1985 which was so crucial in the 1986 price collapse, can in large part be attributed to such policies.[6]

Policies to reduce unit energy input are likely to intensify during the 1990s. The strategic role of oil has not changed and if anything has been accentuated by the recent events in the Gulf. However, there is now an added driver to policy—namely, concern over global environmental issues, notably global warming. This is giving rise to serious discussion over the introduction of carbon taxes and other measures to encourage less use of hydrocarbons (Pearce, 1991; Pearce et al., 1989). How far this will translate into policy is uncertain. However, it will reinforce existing tendencies to see imported oil as something to be avoided if possible.[7] Strategic importance and environmental impact present a serious threat to the export markets of many of the countries of the Third World.

The result is that a Third World energy exporter faces double jeopardy. It faces the revenue volatility associated with being a primary exporter and it faces the market hostility associated with being a manufacturing exporter.

III.2   Supply characteristics

The first supply characteristic is that availability can be subject to politically induced interruption, leading to physical shortage and consequent reduction in output. The reasons for this are many and varied but among the most obvious is that a large amount of world traded supply[8] comes from a region—the Middle East—which is riven by conflict and strife. Thus the most obvious supply threats have stemmed from events in that region.[9]

Threats of supply disruption are unlikely to diminish. The tensions in the region will be worse following the Gulf War due to the effect it has had upon the process of radicalization in the region. Some oil producers such as Algeria face serious political pressures arising from the failure of their economic system. Other producers such as those in the Gulf Cooperation Council face serious political pressures associated with essentially feudal systems trying to come to terms with changing political expectations. Added to this is the relatively new dimension of upheavals in the Soviet Union: in 1990 the Soviet Union accounted for 10% of traded crude supplies and 12% of products (BP, 1991).

This creates an obvious problem for those dependent upon such supplies. The production process requires a continuous flow of energy. It is technically feasible to store oil and coal but this is expensive in terms of both the physical infrastructure required and the opportunity cost of tied-up capital. Storing gas in any quantity is not feasible. Thus physical interruption means that the country either does without and loses output, or it switches to alternatives which are much higher cost.[10]

The second supply characteristic which is inimical to development in certain circumstances, concerns the nature of the production function involved in processing crude oil and handling product distribution. Because oil is fluid and flows in three-dimensional space, activities of any sort associated with oil and its products attract huge economies of scale. Thus they tend to be associated with projects which are highly capital-intensive, involve relatively high levels of technology and are characterized by long lead times. All of these present problems to Third World countries.

This issue of economies of scale is of especial relevance for small Third World countries. Small markets often rule out domestic refining because the shape of the barrel required by the market (i.e. light, versus middle versus heavy products) is technically incompatible with refining techniques without resulting in product surpluses which have a limited market.[11]

Imported gas suffers from all of these scale problems and more besides. If the gas is imported by pipeline this often involves transit through a third country, which leaves both supplier and consumer very vulnerable to pressure over transit fees because of the sunk costs involved in the pipeline (Stevens, 1984). Importing LNG involves extremely complex technical problems and involves highly specific contracts which are likely to be overtaken by events, leading to damaging disputes.

The final supply characteristic concerns developments in the way in which oil and its products are traded internationally. Prior to the second oil shock of 1979–80, most crude was traded on the basis of long-term contracts. This was also true in the product market. There were spot markets but these were rather small (Roeber, 1979). Since the effective break-up of the vertically integrated oil industry as a result of the second oil shock, trading has moved rapidly towards either spot or very short-term contract purchases. At the same time this has become very 'high-tech' and increasingly involves sophisticated trading and hedging mechanisms.

Third World countries operating in such a world face very serious difficulties. An obvious starting point is the lack of skilled manpower in general. Furthermore, past experience is of limited value because of the rapid and dramatic changes in market structure which have taken place during the 1980s. A second problem concerns institutionally created rigidity in the decision process which leaves even the most competent trader constrained.[12] Thus the key requirement of successful operation in the market—quick response—is often impossible in Third World countries. These trading problems apply equally to many new oil exporters in the Third World although their inexperience can be offset in part where foreign oil companies are involved in joint ventures. However, the interest of the host government and its foreign oil companies may differ, leaving the country vulnerable.

It is legitimate to consider why oil in these respects is different from other commodities which have similar trading mechanisms. There are two differences. First, the other commodities have been traded in such a way for a long time, and this has allowed skills to be developed. In oil, such trading is new and is very rapidly changing, which precludes the possibility of learning by doing. Second, oil is all-pervasive in the economy, a crucial point to be developed below.

III.3 Price characteristics

At first sight, it might seem that the obvious characteristic of the oil price which makes it inimical to development is its volatility. This, however, does not fit the empirical evidence. In general, since 1960, international oil prices have proved to be significantly less volatile than many other commodity prices which in any case seem to have a strong tendency to move together

Table 4.1 The standard deviation of selected commodity prices 1960–89.

1960–9		1970–9		1980–9	
Crude oil	0.0	*Crude oil*	17.7	All non-fuel	11.9
All non-fuel	2.1	Metals	22.1	Food	14.5
Food	2.4	Copper	23.4	Wheat	15.6
Wheat	2.4	All non-fuel	24.9	*Crude oil*	25.0
Coffee	3.2	Food	26.5	Metals	25.7
Metals	5.8	Wheat	30.4	Coffee	28.7
Rice	14.2	Coffee	54.8	Copper	35.5
Copper	23.7	Rice	55.4	Rice	39.7

Source: computed from commodity price index data in *IFS Statistics*.

(Pindyck and Rotemberg, 1990). Table 4.1 attempts to quantify the point by taking the standard deviation of various commodity prices per decade. In the 1960s and 1970s, oil was the least volatile of the categories chosen although volatility did increase in the 1980s.

More significant than volatility are two features. First, oil's ability to exhibit one-off spectacular changes in price; and second, the large and pervasive role of oil in the economy. The oil market is characterized by very inelastic demand and supply. If this is linked to imperfect information then there exists a very wide range of price which could approximate to an equilibrium price. It is perfectly feasible for oil prices to be in a range in the short term from $10 to over $70[13] depending upon market expectations and the degree of control over supply.[14] For example, in 1974, the oil price index rose by 294%. No other commodity comes near such an increase. Thus although the unit price of oil is no more volatile than that of other commodities over time, it is capable of sudden huge changes. This has happened three times: in 1973–4, 1979–80 and 1986. It is perfectly plausible to argue that it could happen again. The characteristics which created the potential for huge price spikes remain. Indeed, it has been argued that modern systems of electronic trading make the potential greater than ever. The experience of the recent events in the Gulf has led to some complacency, on the grounds that markets coped and no price shock occurred. While this is true, it is also true that coincidental events and factors played a crucial role in avoiding a spike, not least the speed with which the military operations were conducted.[15]

The second factor which makes price important concerns the pervasiveness of oil. For the exporters, by definition, these price changes apply to at least 50% of export earnings and for many of the OPEC countries the figure exceeds 90%. For the importers, Table 4.2 shows the importance of the oil bill in total imports.

Thus, if the price of coffee or copper fluctuates, the few exporters are hurt and importers face some small changes in their bill. If the price of oil fluctuates, the majority of low- and lower middle-income countries are significantly affected. If this dominance of oil is added to oil price changes then volatility in import bills is very significant indeed. Figure 4.1 takes the weighting of food and fuel imports given in Table 4.2 and uses this to illustrate the range of potential volatility of the oil import bill compared to fuel based upon a ranking of annual percentage changes in oil and food prices between 1960 and 1989.

Such fluctuations carry severe negative implications for the process of development. For the exporters, there are all the problems associated with

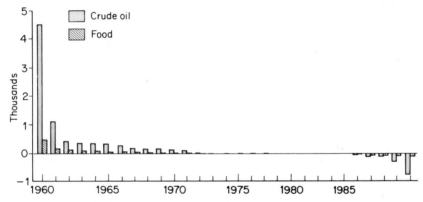

Figure 4.1 Volatility range of import components for low-income countries, showing ordered percentage annual changes in price 1960–89 times import weighting for 1988.

Table 4.2 Structure of oil-importing developing countries' imports in 1980 compared to 1988.

Countries	% Share of merchandise imports	
	Food	Fuel
1980		
Lower-income	11.4	28.8
Lower middle-income	10.9	24.0
1988		
Lower-income	6.0	15.3
Lower middle-income	11.0	19.1

Source: World Bank, *World Development Report.*

export instability already referred to. Equally, there are arguments which see the effect of large windfall profits from oil as detrimental to the country either through the mechanism of Dutch disease (Neary and Van Wijnbergen, 1986) or by its effect on government behaviour (Stevens, 1986). For the importers there are a host of negative effects which can be direct or indirect via the effect of the price shock on the general world level of economic activity (Pereira *et al.*, 1987; Corden, 1977; Rybczynski, 1976).

It is clear from the above analysis that the world energy markets have certain innate characteristics which are incompatible with the process of economic development. Furthermore, there are no signs that such characteristics are likely to diminish in the future and there are signs they could get worse. The final section of this chapter therefore considers some possible courses of action to reduce the negative effects on development.

IV POSSIBLE SOLUTIONS TO THE INCOMPATIBILITIES

IV.1 Net energy exporters

There are three possible options concerning net energy exporters. The first two—commodity stabilization and diversification—have been under discussion for a long time. The problems and limitations of various methods of commodity stabilization have a long literature (Caine, 1983; Finlayson and Zacher, 1990; Newbery and Stiglitz, 1981; McNicol, 1978). There is no obvious reason why oil should be any more or less amenable to such programmes than other commodities. On these grounds, the prospects for a solution via such a route are not encouraging. Diversification—especially via industrialization—equally has a long history of debate and discussion. At first sight, the oil exporters would have considerable advantages if they pursued such a path—very cheap raw material input from oil-associated gas plus the foreign exchange necessary to access the technology. However, the practical record has not been encouraging (Auty, 1990; Jazayeri, 1988) and again prospects for that route away from the incompatibilities are not encouraging.

A third option is cooperation with consumer countries. In October 1990, the Venezuelan President, Carlos Andre Perez, called for the creation of a 'new world energy order' from a dialogue between oil producers and consumers. Most oil producers and a few consumers (notably France) welcomed the proposal. However, the other main consumers (notably the United States) were openly hostile. At the start of July 1991, a two-day 'seminar', jointly hosted by France and Venezuela, was held in Paris between 25 governments, eight international organizations and one oil industry association. The agenda contained four topics: analysis of the petroleum market and energy policies, industrial cooperation, the function of the futures market, and the protection of the environment.[16]

In 1987 the Bruntland Report on 'Sustainable Development' had advocated a similar dialogue but received no response. The trigger to the interest evinced by Perez's call was the invasion of Kuwait in August 1990.

This generated three areas of concern. First, there were fears over the ability of market mechanisms to cope with the crisis without causing serious economic consequences. The volatility of oil prices up to and during the fighting fed those fears. Second, consumer governments had fears over security of supply if the Gulf were to experience major fighting. In particular, the effectiveness of the stock policy of the IEA countries, the main bulwark against such a crisis, attracted serious doubt. The stocks were largely in the form of crude rather than products. This caused concern because of the loss of Kuwaiti refinery capacity and the expectation that the crude to replace the 4 million barrels/day lost via United Nations' sanctions would be heavier and contain more sulphur. Stocks were also highly concentrated in a few industrialized countries. There was a consensus that in the event of real physical shortage, the IEA's sharing mechanism would have been swept away as countries with stocks saw to their own interests first. Third World governments felt even more vulnerable since they were not part of any IEA safety net and their stocks for the most part were low.

Finally, producer governments feared that consumer concern over security would trigger policy responses aimed at reducing the market for imported oil. This added to the fears developed before the crisis that the industrialized countries would use environmental concerns to reduce oil imports.

Coincidentally to the Gulf crisis, there were two additional reasons for the revival of interest in a producer–consumer dialogue. Prior to the crisis, there was a growing consensus in the international oil industry that the call upon OPEC production by consumers would rise through the 1990s. To meet this call, significant investment in additional capacity within OPEC would be required. The most commonly quoted figure in the year before the crisis was that $60 billion must be invested.[17] This led to fears that OPEC might be neither willing nor able to invest such sums without external assistance and assurances about market access. Secondly, the apparent end of the Cold War led to much talk of a 'new world order' based upon cooperation rather than conflict. This led to talk of reviving the abortive North–South dialogue of 1975–6. The cornerstone of that dialogue was discussion between OPEC and the industrialized world.

Those who favoured the dialogue expressed their desire to see protection from long-term disruptions plus mechanisms to smooth short-term fluctuations. This translated into a desire for transparency, stability and crisis management. However, the three sets of participants—consumers, producers and the oil companies—each had their own interests. The consumers were concerned to ensure stable oil supplies and also to ensure access to these supplies at 'affordable' prices. The main concern of producers was to secure markets. They sought to restrain consumer governments from using energy policy to reduce oil demand in response to security or environmental issues. Indeed, at the Paris meeting, the producers' main attack was aimed at European and Japanese energy pricing policies. The Saudi Oil Minister Hisham Nazer explicitly rejected any form of discriminatory measures against oil. Also, as part of securing markets, the producers wanted to gain downstream access in the consumer countries to pursue their attempted recreation of the vertical integration of the industry. The producers were also interested in trying to stabilize oil revenues but (for many) at price levels somewhat above the official OPEC target of $21 per barrel. Finally, producers wanted help to secure finance to expand their capacity and help to secure access to oil technology.[18]

Three areas meant that any dialogue would face serious difficulties in producing anything of significance. The first concerned politics. Many of the consumer governments had fundamental ideological objections to interference with markets. In May 1991, President Bush specifically rejected the idea of any dialogue over prices precisely because it would interfere with the market process. This ideological split was reflected in the attendance at the Paris seminar, despite the explicit exclusion from the agenda of prices or production levels.[19]

Another politically based obstacle was the danger of widening focus. It would be almost inevitable that such a dialogue would spread into wider areas of political division between the parties. This was reinforced by the political aftermath of the Gulf crisis. Some claimed that this could be avoided by restricting meetings to technocrats who could rise above such political squabbling. Indeed, the objectives of Paris were claimed by some participants to be no more than to build 'a network of confidence'. This, however, ignored the fact that ultimately, the issues under discussion required an input from the politicians.

The second set of obstacles were the fundamental conflicts between what the different parties wanted. Consumers' supply security means diversification of energy supplies. This inevitably means reducing dependence on oil imports. The official OPEC line prior to Paris (*OPEC Bulletin*, March 1991) argued that 'OPEC is willing to discuss . . . but it takes two to tango'. In the same paragraph it dismissed consumer fears over supply security as 'bogus'. Such divisions were exemplified by the negotiations conducted between the United States and various countries in the 2 years prior to the Gulf crisis over the possibility of leasing oil supplies to supplement the Strategic Petroleum Reserve. The sticking points were price and guarantees. While both sides may have espoused a desire for stable prices, the producers sought stability at the higher end of a range and the consumers at the lower end. Even among the same side there were divisions. At the Paris meeting, the US delegate claimed further meetings would be of value only if there was greater involvement by the oil companies. The French promptly rejected any such proposal. The fundamental divisions within OPEC need little elaboration.

The talks also faced practical problems. The fears which pushed the dialogue up the political agenda had receded. Many in the consuming countries argued with hindsight that during the crisis the market worked. The crisis came and went and there was no re-run of the second oil shock with its catastrophic results. A second practical problem was the difficulty of ensuring that any agreement from such a dialogue would actually survive the very crisis which it was supposed to manage. The sort of political crises which tend to generate oil market disruptions often remove the very signatories to the agreement who are replaced by less than sympathetic alternatives.[20]

The obstacles outlined above suggest that probability favours the failure of any producer–consumer dialogue to provide any solution to the problems facing Third World exporters in the world energy markets. The outcome of the Paris seminar supports this rather negative conclusion. The seminar suggested a meeting of experts in autumn 1991 hosted by the IEA and (more vaguely) a politically oriented meeting in 1992 hosted by Norway and Egypt. These may well take place. However, as the memory of the Gulf crisis fades and the obstacles to progress remain, such meetings are unlikely to produce anything other than more meetings. The problems with the possible solutions to the dichotomy between energy markets and development for the energy exporters outlined above present a rather gloomy view of the future.

IV.2 Net energy importers

The net energy importers obviously face a different menu of possible solutions. Three will be considered: autarky, diversification and cooperation.

Autarky

An obvious possibility for importers is to remove the link with world energy markets by pursuing a policy aimed at reducing energy imports. This could be done by developing indigenous energy supplies or by reducing demand, or both. Expansion of domestic supplies faces two problems. First, the geology may be unfavourable. If nature provides no hydrocarbons, there is no resource base to develop. However, the general consensus is that many parts of the Third World do possess undeveloped hydrocarbons (Smith, 1984; World Energy Conference, 1974). The greater problem lies with the constraints provided by finance, technology and the institutional context (Davison *et al.*, 1988; Stevens, 1992; Khan, 1987). Nonetheless, many energy-importing Third World countries are currently developing indigenous energy supplies. The second option of reducing demand provides enormous potential in the Third World and many would regard investment in energy conservation as the most attractive possible energy investment in a Third World country (Munasinghe and Schramm, 1983). While this is undoubtedly true in terms of reducing the unit energy input, the fact remains that more development requires more inputs of commercial energy even allowing for greater efficiency.

For this reason, a policy of autarky in most cases is feasible only if the supply side is developed. This then raises serious questions about the optimal use of resources. This debate has a history going back into the 1960s (Tanzer, 1969, Chap. 10). It revolves around the fact that hydrocarbon exploration is very high-cost and involves a very high foreign exchange input and very high risk. Whether such exploration should be carried out by governments alone is extremely debatable, although to this author's knowledge no thorough cost–benefit analysis of such a project has been undertaken. In the past, foreign company involvement has been at fairly low levels. However, there are signs that this will improve during the 1990s (Stevens, 1992) and this could well provide a significant impetus to helping many Third World energy importers to a reduced dependence upon imported energy.

Diversification

A policy of moving away from dependence upon a single source of energy and a few suppliers of that source could well reduce the risks of supply disruptions.[21] Furthermore, it is plausible to pursue such a policy as part of a policy of autarky as described above. Certainly it is a policy being pursued by many countries.

There are, however, a number of problems. First is again the issue of optimal use of resources. Switching to another fuel can be expensive and if energy markets change, the viability of the new projects also changes. Furthermore, once the switch has been made there is the danger of dependence upon the new source, either for reasons of technology or because the new source has its own political lobby. Second, while diversification may be a real prospect for a large country, it may be much less feasible for small countries. As explained earlier, oil and its products have significant advantages over other energy sources when it comes to trade. For a small country,[22] often importing oil is the only economic possibility even when externalities such as supply security are considered. Importing oil does not *per se* rule out one form of diversification—namely, buying from multiple sources. However, for small countries this option is often not realistic. First there are the limitations imposed by economies of scale outlined earlier. Secondly, the sellers of products[23] do not find small markets attractive since overheads tend to eat into margins. Thus while a supplier may be willing to supply to a small market, they are unlikely to be willing to sell to only part of that market. This would be reinforced if there were any tendency for suppliers in a particular region to come to informal arrangements. Thus the solution of diversification is feasible for large countries but much less practical for smaller less developed countries and this includes much of Black Africa.

Cooperation with neighbouring importers

It could well be that for smaller Third World energy importers, cooperation with neighbouring importers is the only means by which they can mitigate the incompatibilities between development and the world energy markets. There are two aspects. The first is on the supply side. There is the possibility for neighbours to get together in a common approach to secure foreign company involvement in exploring for and developing hydrocarbons. Geology is no respecter of international boundaries. The prospect of a deposit lying across a frontier often inhibits exploration (Valencia, 1990) since oil and gas can flow. This is more likely between small countries for obvious reasons of geographical proximity. A joint approach would mean that acreage could be offered to foreign companies by two or more countries with agreement that any finds be developed jointly. This may reduce the competitive pressures upon host governments which create a rush to offer better terms to attract the investment, thereby reducing the government's benefits. Such a joint approach would also give the foreign companies more confidence, since a government might be less likely to renege upon agreement terms if the beneficiary would be its neighbour.[24] Similar arguments could be applied in the electricity sector, where the very smallness of the countries overcomes the major problem facing electricity trade—namely, distribution losses over distance.

A second area for cooperation on the supply side would involve joint purchase arrangements between a number of countries.[25] A number of scale advantages would follow. The removal of duplication of buying teams would allow more resources to be spent on upgrading one joint negotiating administration. A single team placing a significantly larger order than the individual country orders would have much greater bargaining power in the market (Broadman and Wilson, 1987). The success of such schemes could well encourage moves downstream into refining, although this begins to raise difficult and sensitive issues concerning location which do not apply to exploration or joint purchase.

There are also possible benefits on the demand side. Close neighbours might be logically expected to face similar conditions and problems with respect to energy use and conservation. A joint search for solutions would thus remove duplication of effort. Also important is that pricing policies designed to encourage conservation would be less constrained by the threat of smuggling if all neighbours pursued a common pricing policy.

V CONCLUSIONS

This chapter draws three broad conclusions. First, for Third World countries, operating in the world energy market produces negative effects upon the development process. Second, these negative effects arise from characteristics of the energy market which will not go away. Indeed, the paper suggests they may get worse as environmental concerns drive energy policy, as the Middle East experiences processes of radicalization and as the trading mechanisms become ever more sophisticated. Finally, the solutions which might mitigate these negative effects provide a long and depressing list of good reasons why they may be ineffective. The only solution which offers some degree of hope and has hardly been considered is cooperation between small neighbouring energy importers.

NOTES

1 In 1988, based upon data from the *World Development Report 1990*, this covered 15 out of the 42 lower-income countries, accounting for 44% of lower-income population, and 16 out of 37 lower middle-income countries, accounting for 35% of lower middle-income population.
2 According to the *IMF Annual Review*, 18 developing countries fall into this category. There are two low-income energy exporters based upon the IMF definition, accounting for 10% of the lower-income population. There are four in the lower middle-income category, accounting for 13% of the lower middle-income population. Thus of the 37 countries in the lower middle-income category, 20 face significant relations with the world energy market either as exporters or importers. However, in that group there are another six or seven

countries, such as Egypt, Colombia, Syria, Yemen, etc., where oil exports play a central role in the acquisition of foreign exchange. If other categories of Third World countries were included, this would add six importers and 10 exporters to the list.

3 This arises because of two characteristics of oil. First, the fluidity of oil and its products enables very low-cost handling, a characteristic coal does not have. Second, oil has a very high energy content per unit of volume, a characteristic which gas does not have: a cubic metre of oil contains 950 times as much energy as a cubic metre of gas. In 1990, 23.85 million barrels per day of crude were exported and 7.59 million barrels per day of products. Together these accounted for 50% of world consumption (BP, 1991). The trade in international coal was only about 15% of the oil trade (computed from BP, 1991). In 1990, only 8% of international gas by pipeline came from the Third World and only 2% was imported by Third World Countries (BP, 1991). LNG trade saw 93% of exports emanate from the Third World and only 5.7% go to the Third World. However, LNG accounts for only 24% of traded gas which in turn is a negligible proportion of oil traded: in 1990, it was 0.05% of crude and product exports.

4 There is a strong element of double counting in oil-exporting countries' estimates of GDP (Al-Sadik, 1985).

5 Defined as commercial energy input (tonnes of oil equivalent) per thousand dollars of GDP (1972 dollars).

6 This is true even if the policy was simply to let higher prices do their work.

7 Peter Pearson in his chapter reports on a study which indicates just how badly hurt the oil exporters might be by carbon taxes, which would have very significant negative effects on their growth.

8 In 1990, the Middle East accounted for 51% of world traded crude and 28% of world traded products (BP, 1991).

9 The list of disruptions is depressingly long. In 1967 there was an attempted oil embargo following the Six Day War. In 1973, there was the Arab Oil Embargo. In 1978–9, there were supply disruptions following the Iranian Revolution. In 1980, the start of the Gulf War reduced supplies from both Iraq and Iran. During that war there were periodic threats to supplies via threats to close the Straits of Hormuz and from the Tanker War which developed. Finally, in 1990, supplies were threatened by the Iraqi invasion of Kuwait and its aftermath.

10 Often the higher cost is incurred because of the speed involved in the switching.

11 Most Third World countries are characterized by a rapidly growing demand for middle distillates. This leaves the heavy fuel oil with no market. The fuel oil can be reprocessed to produce yet more middle distillates but only by installing very expensive and technically complex upgrading refining equiment: again, an activity not especially compatible with many Third World countries.

12 Broadman and Wilson (1987) cite the case of a country where a crucial crude procurement contract was almost lost because the Chairman of the Central Bank was out of the country and only he could sign off the $25 million payment.

13 If that seems excessive it is worth remembering that in 1979, spot prices of crude were exceeding $40 per barrel. $40 per barrel in 1979 is roughly equivalent to more than $70 in 1991.

14 For a more detailed explanation of how oil prices are set, see Stevens (1991).

15 When the Allies opened their air attack, only the Far Eastern markets were trading. Within 2 hours of the hostilities becoming public via the CNN reporters in Baghdad, the oil price rose from around $25 to over $40. However, the official reports which emerged several hours later implied the war was virtually over bar the shouting, with the result that the price collapsed back to $25 per barrel. This was helped by announced stock releases from the IEA. It is unlikely that any other commodity could exhibit such volatility.

16 At the time of writing, nothing has been published on this revival of the producer–consumer dialogue outside of the trade press. What follows is based upon that source together with private conversations.

17 This number was almost certainly an overstatement but gained credibility by much repetition in the trade press.

18 Oil companies were also interested in the dialogue. For many, their strategy for the 1990s hinged upon 'frontier exploration'. Thus, there was considerable interest in gaining upstream access in OPEC countries which a dialogue might assist. Another common strand of corporate strategy was to look to the development of alliances in the international market. The OPEC countries with their huge reserves were seen as potential partners.

19 The ministers of the producers met often very junior officials from the consumers. The United States actually sent a *Deputy Assistant* Secretary for Economic Affairs!

20 In the leasing debate mentioned above, one option seriously considered by the US was to lease crude oil in the actual reservoirs to ensure against politically induced supply interruption. The main candidate considered for such an agreement was Kuwait!

21 The ability of such a policy to reduce the impact of price shocks is less obvious since there is a certain tendency for energy prices to track each other, although this is increasingly a controversial view.

22 What follows applies very much to the countries of West Africa, Central America and the Caribbean.

23 It is reasonable to assume that small Third World countries would be forced to import products because of the prohibitive cost of domestic refining.

24 The foreign company could withdraw (leaving the reneging government trying to produce from the wells on its side of the frontier) and drill more wells in the neighbouring country.

25 There have been some attempts at this in the South Pacific (Broadman and Wilson, 1987).

REFERENCES

Al-Sadik, A.T. (1985) 'National Accounting and the Income Illusion of Petroleum Exports: The Case of the Arab Gulf Cooperation Council Members' in T. Niblock and R. Lawless (eds), *Prospects for the World Oil Industry*, Croom Helm, London.

Auty, R.M. (1990) *Resource Based Industrialization: Sowing the Oil in Eight Developing Countries*, Clarendon Press, Oxford.

BP (1991) *Statistical Review of World Energy*, British Petroleum, London.

Broadman, H.G. and E.J. Wilson III (1987) 'Trials and Tribulations of Third World Petroleum Development: Lessons and Advice for Prospective Producers' in K.I.F. Khan (ed.), *Petroleum Resources and Development*, Belhaven Press, London.

Caine, S. (1983) *The Price of Stability. Hobart Paper 97*, Institute of Economic Affairs, London.

Corden, W.M. (1977) *Inflation, Exchange Rates and the World Economy*, Clarendon Press, Oxford.

Davison, A., C. Hurst and R. Mabro (1988) *Natural Gas: Governments and Oil Companies in the Third World*, Oxford University Press, Oxford.

Diwan, R. (1978) 'Energy Implications of Indian Economic Development: Decade of 1960–70 and After', *Journal of Energy and Development* 3, 318–37.

Finlayson, J.A. and M.Z. Zacher (1990) 'International Competition and Commodity Market Management: The Politics of the International Sugar Agreements' in D.C. Pirages and C. Sylvester (eds), *Transformations in the Global Political Economy*, Macmillan, London.

Glezakos, C. (1973) 'Export Instability and Economic Growth: A Statistical Verification', *Economic Development and Cultural Change* 21, 670–8.

Hawdon, D. (1992) *Energy Demand—Evidence and Expectations*, Academic Press, London.

Humphrey, W. and J. Stanislaw (1979) 'Economic Growth and Energy Consumption in the UK 1700–1975', *Energy Policy* 7, 29–42.

Jazayeri, A. (1988) *Economic Adjustment in Oil-Based Economies*, Avebury, Aldershot.

Khan, K.I.F. (ed.) (1987) *Petroleum Resources and Development*, Belhaven Press, London.

Lambert, J.D. and F. Fesharaki (eds) (1990) *Economic and Political Incentives to Petroleum Exploration: Developments in the Asia Pacific Region*, International Law Institute, Washington, DC.

Love, J. (1989) 'Export Instability in LDCs: Consequences and Causes', *Journal of Development Studies* 25, 183–191.

Macbean, A.I. (1966) *Export Instability and Economic Development*, Allen & Unwin, London.

McNicol, D.L. (1978) *Commodity Agreements and Price Stabilization*, Lexington Books, Lexington.

Munasinghe, M. and M. Schramm (1983) *Energy Economics, Demand Management and Conservation Policy*, Van Nostrand Reinhold, Amsterdam.

Neary, J.P. and S. Van Wijnbergen (1986) *Natural Resources and the Macroeconomy*, Blackwell, Oxford.

Newbery, D.M.G. and J. Stiglitz (1981) *The Theory of Commodity Price Stabilization: A Study in the Economics of Risk*, Clarendon Press, Oxford.

OPEC (1984) *Annual Statistical Bulletin*, OPEC, Vienna.

Pearce, D. (1991) 'The Role of Carbon Taxes in Adjusting to Global Warming', *Economic Journal* 101, 938–48.

Pearce, D., A. Markandya and E.B. Barbier (1989) *Blueprint for a Green Economy*, Earthscan Publications, London.

Pearson, P.J.G. (1988) *Energy Transitions in Less Developed Countries: Analytical Frameworks for Practical Understanding. CERG Energy Discussion Paper*, Cambridge Energy Research Group, Cambridge.

Pereira, A., A. Ulph and W. Tims (1987) *Socio-Economic and Policy Implications of Energy Price Increases*, Gower, Aldershot.

Pindyck, R.S. and J.J. Rotemberg (1990) 'The Excess Co-Movement of Commodity Prices', *Economic Journal* 100, 1173–89.

Roeber, J. (1979) 'The Rotterdam Oil Market', *Petroleum Economist (London)*.

Rosenburg, N. (1980) 'Historical Relations Between Energy and Economic Growth' in Dunkerley (ed.), *International Energy Strategies*, Oelgeschlager, Gunn & Hain, Cambridge, MA.

Rybczynski, T.M. (1976) *The Economics of the Oil Crisis*, Macmillan, London.

Smith, S.R. (1984) 'Energy Supply Management' in *Energy Planning in Developing Countries, Division of Natural Resources and Energy Technical Cooperation for Development*, Oxford University Press, Oxford.

Stevens, P. (1984) 'The Economics of Hydrocarbon Pipelines in the 21st Century', *Pipes and Pipelines International* (Sept–Oct 1984).

Stevens, P. (1986) 'The Impact of Oil on the Role of the State in Economic Development: A Case Study of the Arab World', *Arab Affairs* 1, 87–101.

Stevens, P. (ed.) (1987) *Energy Demand: Prospects and Trends*, Macmillan, London.

Stevens, P. (1991) 'Oil Prices—An Economic Framework for Analysis' in G. Bird and H. Bird (eds), *Contemporary Issues in Applied Economics*, Edward Elgar, Aldershot.

Stevens, P. (1992) 'Contemporary Oil Exploration Policies in the Gulf Region' in R. Schofield (ed.), *The Territorial Foundations of the Gulf States* (forthcoming).

Tanzer, M. (1969) *The Political Economy of International Oil and the Underdeveloped Countries*, Temple Smith, London.

Valencia, M.J. (1990) 'Joint Development of Petroleum Resources in Overlapping Claim Areas' in J.D. Lambert and F. Fesharaki (eds), *Economic and Political Incentives to Petroleum Exploration: Developments in the Asia Pacific Region*, International Law Institute, Washington, DC.

World Bank (1976) *Energy and Petroleum in Non-OPEC Developing Countries. Bank Staff Working Paper 229*, World Bank, Washington, DC.

World Energy Conference (1974) *World Energy Conference Survey of Energy Resources*, US National Committee of the World Energy Conference, Washington, DC.

5 | North–South Interaction: Retrospect and Prospect

S. MANSOOB MURSHED*

I INTRODUCTION

As the twentieth century draws to a close, international interdependence is becoming of paramount importance. This chapter focuses on macro-economic interaction between North and South at an analytical level. Interaction between North and South is asymmetrical as it is the North which wields the greater economic power. Thus macroeconomic conditions in the South are influenced to a very large extent by events in the North; and Northern macroeconomic policies have substantial spillover effects on the South. To analyse North–South interaction a structuralist North–South model is employed where the North exhibits fix-price characteristics and the South flex-price features. The analysis is extended to cover protectionism, the debt crisis and the environment, as well as long-term North–South terms of trade.

There is currently a renewed interest in growth theory amongst theoretical macroeconomists. In this respect analytical macroeconomics has come full circle in the last quarter of a century. Lucas (1991) attempted to analyse why growth rates differ amongst different countries. Lucas's views regarding growth and development are very much in keeping with the spirit of our times—pessimistic, as far as the poorer nations of the world are concerned. Growth and development could be a zero-sum game. Moreover, there is no necessary tendency for *per capita* income levels in poorer developing countries to approach (let alone converge to) the levels of the richer developed countries: that would require a growth miracle. While the

* I am indebted to Somnath Sen for introducing me to the subject and for providing concrete suggestions and ideas over the years.

search for explanations for divergences in the long-term growth rates of economically successful and unsuccessful countries continues in earnest, related to factors such as differences in human capital, the importance of shorter-term macroeconomic interaction as a contributory factor to longer-term growth rates remains.

This is because short-term macroeconomic interactions between North and South help to explain the impact of shocks upon factors such as the terms of trade and the international indebtedness position of the South, as well as the ability of the South to access markets in the North. These variables, in turn, have a profound impact on the South's overall ability to grow and develop. It is with these very short- to medium-term macroeconomic interactions between North and South that this chapter is concerned.

The rapid and accelerating rate of global economic interdependence and integration implies, among other things, that macroeconomic policies pursued in the North will have major, even painful, spillover effects on Southern macroeconomies, even when these Northern policies are meant only to redress (or address) problems in a domestic Northern macro-economy or intra-Northern context. In this respect macroeconomic interaction between North and South is asymmetrical, as events in the North can, and do, have major consequences for the South; the converse is, however, generally not the case.

Asymmetrical North–South models have a long history, harking back to the celebrated work of Prebisch (1950) and Singer (1950). Findlay's (1980) growth-theoretical North–South model, for example, makes the Southern growth rate depend directly on the Northern profit rate. The tradition of modelling macroeconomic interactions between North and South is more recent, even if it is implicit in the earlier writings of Prebisch and Singer. Kaldor (1976) outlined a heuristic model of North–South interaction, where rising prices of Southern goods could contribute to Northern inflation rates via real wage resistance in the North (a price–wage–price spiral); and recession in the North (caused in some cases by anti-inflationary policies) could hurt the South through declining export demand. Kanbur and Vines (1986) formalized some of Kaldor's ideas and showed that commodity price stabilization was in Northern interests, inasmuch as it helps to combat Northern inflationary tendencies working via real wage rigidity. Murshed and Sen (1989) formulated a dynamic model of North–South interaction where excess demand for Southern goods (reminiscent of the oil price increases of the 1970s) leads to global inflation, and once again real wage rigidity in the North plays an important role. Attempts to control Northern inflation would then plunge the world into recession; however, the North could pass on a great deal of the burden of disinflation to the South, via falling commodity prices in the South. This was, perhaps, the central theme of macroeconomic interaction between North and South in the 1980s. The empirical work of Beckerman and Jenkinson (1986) suggested that a major role was played by falling commodity prices in the Northern anti-inflation successes of the early 1980s; much less of the fall in inflation was due to weakening of real wage rigidity.

If falling commodity prices (Southern terms of trade) were related to Northern policies to combat inflation, these very same policies provided the macroeconomic backdrop to the emergence of the debt crisis. Whilst the roles of Southern (domestic) macroeconomic policies and the actions of Northern commercial banks cannot be discounted in the events that led to the debt crisis, it is clear that the macroeconomic environment in the major OECD economy—the United States—contributed to rising interest rates and created an intolerable burden of debt servicing for the heavily indebted countries of the South. Two, perhaps three, events are of significance here. First are the contractionary monetary policies used in the North during the early 1980s to combat inflation. Second is the huge military expenditure programme in the US during the Reagan administration, one which was financed not by taxation but by borrowing, reflected in a budget deficit of gargantuan proportions. Both these policies served to raise world interest rates. The US, the richest nation in the globe, found itself running the world's largest balance of payments deficit. It became the absorber of much of the world's surplus savings. Meanwhile, as the decade progressed, the heavily indebted countries because of their burden of debt servicing received net *negative* transfers: the poorer nations appeared to be subsidizing the richer countries of the world! Third is the related issue of growing protectionism in the North towards Southern goods. This makes debt servicing more difficult and requires a further decline in Southern terms of trade to keep up exports. All in all, the 1980s have been described as the 'lost decade' for Africa and Latin America, where the debt problem is most acute. Table 5.1 attests to this fact, showing the poor growth performances of the heavily indebted countries during the 1980s. The burden of debt servicing was as high as 5% of GDP for many countries, which represents a significant transfer of resources from a poor economy.

Protectionism in the North towards the exports of the South has grown significantly since the early 1970s. A great deal of this protectionism is directed towards manufactured goods, as pointed out by Singh (1989). These are in areas where the North is rapidly losing its competitiveness compared to the South and has yielded to domestic protectionist lobbies, with suspension of the free market and the principle of comparative advantage, often in favour of various 'regulatory' arguments. Protectionism is probably one of the factors most inimical to Southern growth prospects and it also serves to increase the burden of debt servicing.

Table 5.1 GDP growth rates (annual average) in developing countries 1965–87.

Region	1965–80	1980–7
Sub-Saharan Africa	5.1%	0.4%
East Asia	7.2%	8.0%
South Asia	3.8%	4.8%
Latin American and Carribean	6.0%	1.4%
17 Highly indebted countries	6.1%	1.1%

Source: World Bank, *World Development Report* (1989).

The central focus of North–South interaction continues to be on the terms of trade. Here the statistical debate on whether or not there is a secular tendency for the prices of primary goods to fall relative to those of manufactured goods lingers on (the Prebisch–Singer hypothesis). More recently, Sarkar and Singer (1991) argued that more relevant are the *North–South terms of trade*, given the growing importance of the South as an exporter of manufactured goods. Statistical debates aside, the Prebisch–Singer hypothesis requires a firm analytical underpinning. One possibility is to relate it to Northern aggregate supply features (real wage rigidity) to demonstrate a long-term decline in Southern terms of trade relative to the North. This is done later in this chapter.

In most areas of North–South interaction the interdependence between North and South is non-reciprocal because of the greater economic power of the North. There is, however, one exception, and this concerns environmental issues: many issues such as global warming, involving the emission of greenhouse gases, have reciprocal · (negative externality) dimensions. Thus in these areas the North cannot ignore the South, even if in other areas the South has become effectively decoupled from the world system. Thus progress on environmental issues will require North–South cooperation and its ultimate success will rest on linkages to other issues. These could include offsetting debt in return for environmental conservation and the relaxation of Northern protectionism. Here it must be remembered that the North's historical contribution to the stock of pollutants is much higher than that of the South and this continues to be the case. Thus, having made a large contribution to atmospheric pollutants, the North owes a large 'debt to nature', just as the South is heavily indebted to commercial banks and other institutions in the North.

The plan of the rest of this chapter is as follows. Section II presents an analytical macro-model of North–South interaction. The inspiration for all structuralist macroeconomic models of North–South interaction is the seminal work of Taylor (1983), and the present model is no exception. The model is then used as a basis for the examination of some topical issues of North–South interaction. Section III examines protectionism; Section IV analyses the emergence of the debt crisis; Section V considers environmental issues surrounding the use of tradeable permits to emit greenhouse gases; and Section VI examines long-term North–South terms of trade, including the secular decline of Southern terms of trade. Section VII is by way of conclusion—retrospect and prospect.

II THE MODEL

As indicated above, the North–South model employed here is of the macro-structuralist variety and is based on the pioneering work of Taylor (1983). These models, in common with more trade/growth-theoretical models (e.g. Findlay, 1980), emphasize asymmetries between North and South. Where structuralist macro-models differ is in the fix-price and flex-price distinction they make between North and South, respectively. These distinctions are due originally to Hicks (1965).

The North is characterized as a fix-price economy. This means that quantities adjust to discrepancies between aggregate demand and supply, rising when there is excess demand and *vice versa*. Prices, on the other hand, respond to changes in cost conditions governed by aggregate supply considerations. Unlike trade-theoretical models, the assumption of full employment in the North is dropped. This makes the North akin to a fix-price *Keynesian* economy with excess capacity. Two of the major innovations in the model adopted in this paper are:

(1) the notion of balanced trade in equilibrium is dropped; this is because trade between the two regions is unbalanced, the imbalance being financed by capital flows; and

(2) in analysing real wages from the point of view of workers, the real consumption wage is related to a price index which is a weighted average for the two types of goods consumed, i.e. of Northern and Southern origin, and not just a single good, as in trade-theoretical models.

For the South, the market clearing mechanism proposed is of the Walrasian flex-price variety. In other words, excess demand for Southern goods causes the price—the Southern terms of trade—to increase. Excess supply has the converse effect. A linear expenditure system is employed for the South. This makes total consumption and its division between home and imported goods proportionate to income. This results in the major asymmetry of the model—Northern demand for Southern goods determines the equilibrium terms of trade. Another asymmetry is that the South, unlike the North, does not benefit from an export multiplier (as it is not a Keynesian-type economy). Following Kanbur and Vines (1986), the model postulates the following equilibrium relation for the South:

$$Q_S = c_S P_S Q_S + P_S S(.) - c_S(1 - v_S)P_S Q_S \tag{1}$$

where Q_S denotes Southern output or aggregate supply, P_S the price of the Southern goods, c_S the fixed consumption or absorption propensity in the South, v_S the expenditure share of home goods, $1 - v_S$ the share of imported (Northern) goods in total consumption, and S exports to the North. The last two terms on the right-hand side of equation (1) represent the South's trade balance. Cancelling terms and nomalizing by P_S gives:

$$Q_S = c_S v_S Q_S(.) \tag{2}$$

Let Southern output be an increasing function of P_S, or of $\sigma = P_S/P_N$, the North–South ratio of terms of trade:

$$Q_S = F(\sigma), \ F_1 > 0 \tag{3}$$

where F_1 denotes the first derivative of F. Substitution of equation (3) into (2) yields:

$$F(\sigma) = c_S v_S F(\sigma) + S(.) \tag{4}$$

As far as the (Keynesian) North is concerned, the equilibrium relation for aggregate demand (expenditure) equal to aggregate supply (income) is:

$$Q_N = A(Q_N, \sigma) + c_S(1 - v_S)\sigma F(\sigma) - \sigma S(Q_N, \sigma) + G \tag{5}$$

where Q_N denotes output in the North, A denotes absorption in the North, $c_S(1 - v_S)\sigma F$ denotes the exports of the North, S the imports of the North, G refers to autonomous expenditure in the North, and $\sigma = P_S/P_N$ is the North–South ratio of terms of trade. Note that equation (5) has been normalized by P_N. The partial derivatives in (5) are of the following order:

$$A_1 > 0; \ S_1 > 0; \ S_2 < 0$$

As far as the North is concerned a standard open-economy macroeconomic formulation is employed, and this differs from Kanbur and Vines (1986).

It is of interest that Northern absorption (A) is a function of both income (Q_N) and the terms of trade (σ). The inclusion of the latter is dictated by the presence of the Laursen–Metzler effect (for a detailed derivation, see Laursen and Metzler, 1950; Dornbusch, 1980). This effect relies on a concept of real income and real absorption obtained by deflating their nominal counterparts by a price index, which is a weighted sum of the expenditure shares of the prices of the (two) goods which enter the Northern consumption (or absorption) basket:

$$P = P_N^\beta P_S^{1-\beta} \tag{6}$$

where β and $1-\beta$ are the shares of home and Southern goods, respectively. A deterioration of Northern terms of trade, i.e. a rise in σ, implies that real income $(P_N Q_N/P)$ declines. Real absorption (consumption, $P_N A/P$) will also fall *but less than real income*, as the marginal propensity to absorb is less than unity. This, in turn, implies excess aggregate demand as absorption in nominal terms increases—a beneficial aggregate demand effect for the North.

By including the Laursen–Metzler effect the terms of trade are brought firmly into the centre of the model by giving them due emphasis in the Northern component instead of letting them influence solely the South, as in most of the literature. More importantly, the inclusion of this effect provides a novel channel of North–South interdependence by letting the terms of trade directly affect Northern aggregate demand. Furthermore, the inclusion of the Laursen–Metzler effect is apposite for our open Keynesian (Northern) economy. In the standard Keynesian model, absorption is usually a function of income only, as the prices of the goods in question are fixed. This practice needs to be modified when at least one of the goods absorbed is flex-price. Formally, the Laursen–Metzler effect in equation (5) is $A_2 = S(1 - \epsilon)$, where ϵ is the elasticity of absorption with respect to real income, $A_2 > 0$.

III PROTECTIONISM

The issue of Northern protectionism towards Southern exports, particularly of manufactured goods, is becoming a matter for grave concern. Much of this tendency is due to declining competitiveness in the North. A good example of protectionist legislation is the Super 301 legislation in the US which confers wide protective powers on the authorities. The decline of manufacturing sector competitiveness is related in no small degree to the volatility of the dollar exchange rate in the 1980s, which in turn is related largely to contractionary monetary and expansionary fiscal policies in the US (Bhagwati, 1988). The US should not be singled out as the only source of protectionism in the North—these tendencies are just as manifest in the EEC, especially as it crawls forward to the goal of a single market. It should be borne in mind that various product cycle theories (e.g. Krugman, 1979) predict that the South will gradually gain competitiveness in old (vintage) goods, and it is in these areas such as textiles, covered by the Multi-Fibre Agreement (MFA), where protectionism is likely to be strongest.

The motivation behind this protectionism is to boost output and employment in flagging Northern industries. It is not solely to improve the terms of trade (the optimum tariff argument of neoclassical trade theory). Thus the objective behind Northern protectionism is macroeconomic. A related question concerns the extent to which a country or region can gain by employing macro-commercial policy. Mundell's (1961) analysis for a small open economy under flexible exchange rates suggested unambiguously that there are no gains from such a policy. This is because the exchange rate appreciation that follows imposition of a tariff will negate any initial beneficial effects of the tariff. Ford and Sen (1985) demonstrated that this result, however, need not necessarily hold under all circumstances and parameter values. The model presented below demonstrates that for a large economy such as the North operating under flexible real exchange rates (North–South terms of trade are variable), the North can gain from macro-commercial policy (for a detailed analysis, see Murshed, 1991).

Concerning the magnitude of gains to the North, commercial policy is unlikely to have the same effect as fiscal or monetary policy. However, it is an eminently feasible option given the weak bargaining power of the South and its inability to retaliate effectively. These dangers of retaliation, however, are considerable in an intra-Northern context. Consumers in the North would lose from such a policy as they would pay more for imported goods, while the producers in the competing import sector would gain. Even though the latter group is smaller than the former (consumers), its bargaining power and lobbying position are stronger.

The present analysis is confined to an *ad valorem* tariff (a similar analysis in the case of VERS can be found in Murshed, 1992). Equation (5) for the North must be rewritten as:

$$Q_N = A(Q_N + \tau\sigma S; \sigma(1+\tau)) + c_S(1-v_S)\sigma F(\sigma) - \sigma S(Q_N + \tau\sigma S; \sigma(1+\tau)(1+\tau)) + G \qquad (7)$$

where τ is the *ad valorem* tariff rate and $\tau\sigma S$ is the tariff revenue which is redistributed back to the public in a lump-sum fashion, enhancing disposable income. The equation for the South stays similar to equation (4) with the additional arguments included in the $S(.)$ function.

The tariff has two aggregate effects in the North: one, directly, on absorption and the other, indirectly, via the trade balance. On impact the tariff raises the domestic price of importables, which causes a switch of expenditure away from imports towards home goods and a resulting beneficial impact on absorption. Another beneficial impact upon absorption occurs via the Laursen–Metzler effect $(A_2 > 0)$. Against these two beneficial absorption effects there will be a negative impact on aggregate demand, of increased imports (as absorption rises, so too will imports).

Secondly, the tariff has trade balance effects. The tariff tends to depress Southern prices and terms of trade. This lowers Southern income and thus Southern imports from the North. This will have a negative export multiplier effect on the North. On balance, if the first effect dominates the second, Northern income will rise, and *vice versa*.

These results can be depicted diagrammatically. In Figure 5.1, the lines NN depict equilibrium in the Northern goods market, and the lines SS equilibrium in the Southern goods market, both in Q_N versus σ space. Both sets of lines are upward-sloping, as at a higher income Q_N in the North, the demand for Southern goods (imports) is higher and hence pushes up the Southern price P_S and hence σ. In Figure 5.1, the initial equilibrium is given by point A. Imposition of a tariff shifts the SS lines downwards and the NN lines rightwards. The case where the North's income rises is depicted at point B; the contractionary possibility is represented by point C. The South is disadvantaged in both cases, evidenced by falling terms of trade at both points B and C.

If the Northern labour market exhibited real wage rigidity, the beneficial

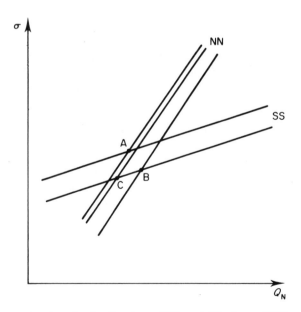

Figure 5.1 Equilibrium in the Southern (SS) and Northern (NN) goods markets under conditions of protectionism. Q_N, Northern output; σ, terms of trade.

impact of tariffs would be greatly diminished, due to the adverse aggregate supply consequences (see Murshed, 1991). If VERs were employed there would be greater income spillovers to the South and its terms of trade could rise (see Murshed, 1992).

IV THE DEBT CRISIS

The problems of the debt crisis have existed since 1982, when Mexico was about to default on its international payments (oddly, Poland's default in 1981 created less of a stir). The origins of the debt crisis are deeply embedded in the macroeconomic interaction between North and South, notwithstanding domestic policies in the heavily indebted countries. In macroeconomic terms the debt crisis is akin to a transfer from the South (some of whom pay up to 5% of GDP) to the North. It is reminiscent of the German reparation problem as analysed by Keynes (1929) and Naoroji's (1901) argument that India's current account surplus with Britain at that time drained India of valuable investable funds.

We begin by introducing the role of interest rates, r:

$$r = r(G,H) \qquad (8)$$

and

$$dr = r_1 dG + r_2 dH; \quad r_1 > 0, \; r_2 < 0 \qquad (9)$$

where G represents fiscal policy and H monetary policy. Expansionary fiscal policy and contractionary monetary policy in the North will raise (world) interest rates (which are relevant to debt). The equilibrium relation for the North becomes:

$$Q_N = A(Q_N + T + rD; \; \sigma(1+\tau); \; r) + G + \sigma c_S(1-v_S)(Q_S - rD) - \sigma S(.) \qquad (10)$$

where $T = \tau \sigma S$ represents tariff revenue and D represents the stock of debt. Observe that debt servicing increases the disposable income of the North by rD and lowers the disposable income of the South.

The balance of payments (current account) for the North, B, is:

$$B = \sigma c_S(1-v_S)(Q_S - rD) + rD - \sigma S(.) \qquad (11)$$

This includes debt servicing (rD). The *flow* current account deficit of the South will represent the change in the *stock* of debt. In other words:

$$\left. \begin{array}{l} dD = B \\ dB = B - B_0 \end{array} \right\} \qquad (12)$$

where B_0 is some initial value of the current account. If $B_0 = 0$, then:

$$dD = dB \tag{13}$$

Note that B is the Northern (Southern) current account surplus (deficit).
Turning now to the South:

$$Q_S = c_S(Q_S - (rD/\sigma)) + S(.) - c_S(1-v_S)(Q_S - (rD/\sigma)) \tag{14}$$

or:

$$Q_S = c_S v_S(Q_S - (rD/\sigma)) + S(.) \tag{15}$$

into which equation (3) can be substituted for Southern output supply.

On the basis of this model, expansionary fiscal policy, contractionary
monetary policy and protectionism will exacerbate a debt problem, turning
it into a debt crisis as well as leading to a decline in terms of trade (for full
details, see Murshed, 1990a, 1992). These conclusions fit the facts of the
1980s. The emergence of a debt crisis is shown diagrammatically in Figure
5.2, which relates debt (D) to terms of trade (σ). The $\dot{D} = 0$ lines are
upward-sloping as increased debt payments (transfers) to the North worsen
the North's current account (a stability condition). The $\dot{\sigma}/\sigma = 0$ lines are

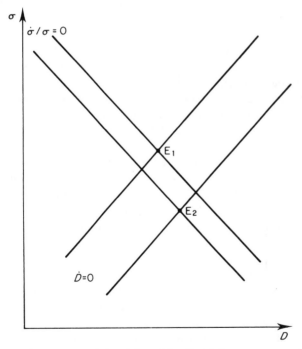

Figure 5.2 Emergence of the debt crisis. D, Debt; σ, terms of trade.

downward-sloping as an increase in debt and debt repayment lowers Southern disposable income, and excess supply in that region leads to declining prices and terms of trade. Also, debt servicing requires increased exports by the South to the North, which also causes Southern terms of trade to decline. The protectionist policies mentioned above cause σ to decline from the initial equilibrium at E_1 towards a new $\dot{\sigma}/\sigma = 0$ line which shifts downwards. Meanwhile, the $\dot{D} = 0$ line shifts to the right. The stock of Southern indebtedness gradually increases and the rising pressure of debt servicing causes the terms of trade to decline even further as the new equilibrium point E_2 is reached.

Note that the transfer from the South to the North should increase the latter's demand for the former's goods, but the rise in Northern expenditure on Southern goods is less than proportionate to the transfer—the transfer is undereffected. This poses an additional burden on the South, and ensures that its terms of trade have to fall.

V THE ENVIRONMENT

If protectionism and the debt crisis are undirectional negative externalities from North to South, and refer to areas of North–South interaction where the South is powerless to arrest the spillover effects in any meaningful fashion, environmental issues are one area in which the South does have some bargaining power: the externalities here are largely reciprocal. The problem has international dimensions, and progress towards its resolution will require international cooperation in a multilateral framework. It also offers the South some bargaining power: restriction of greenhouse gases (GHGs) and chlorinated fluorocarbons (CFCs) could be linked to debt relief and relaxation of protectionism.

Concern about the environment is at three levels. The environment can be viewed as having use value, existence value and option value. With regard to the first, it can be viewed as forming part of the natural capital stock in addition to physical and human capital. Depreciation or irreversible depletion of this natural capital stock needs to be accounted for in national income accounts, a process which has not yet entered into the conventions of GNP accounting. As Pearce and Maler (1991) pointed out, once these practices are followed, growth figures could look less impressive. A related concept is that of sustainable growth or development. Growth which does not repair environmental damage or which harms the environment irreversibly is unsustainable. At the very least, environmental degradation should be matched by substantial accretions to the physical and human capital stock. If damage to the environment is a result of production or consumption, it represents a negative externality arising from these processes which may be unidirectional or reciprocal (if it affects polluter and polluted alike). Secondly, the environment has existence value. For example, residents of the North could derive utility from the (undefiled) preservation of tropical forests and wildlife, even though these are located in the South and have no direct use value. Thirdly, the environment can be said to have option value, arising from uncertainty and the irreversibility of many types of environmental damage. When an action (environmental damage in this case) is irreversible it is prudent to avoid excess even if the immediate (known) effects appear to be minimal.

What should be done to reduce levels of environmental damage? One option is direct regulation of pollution. Other solutions are market-based and rely on economic incentives. The latter solutions are more in conformity with the spirit of our times. The ultra-market-based solution (the Coasean solution) relies on well-defined property rights: the owner of the property rights would either be paid by others for the privilege of polluting or would pay them to desist from polluting, as the case might be. Such solutions are difficult given the presence of transaction costs and asymmetrical bargaining power. In an international context they are, however, less far-fetched than might first appear: the notion of transfers from the North to the South not to emit GHGs constitutes a Coasean solution.

The alternative to the above is the Pigovian solution of a tax which the polluter pays—a carbon tax. Pearce (1991) listed the advantages of such a tax, including its double dividend property, as it allows other taxes to be reduced while correcting distortions and encouraging the use of cleaner technologies. Perhaps the greatest advantage of a carbon tax is its flexibility: it allows pollluters with a high abatement cost not to reduce emission levels but simply pay the tax. However, this could mean that in the presence of uncertainty about demand elasticities, the tax could fail to achieve the desired reduction in the emission of GHGs.

Agreement about the imposition of a carbon tax is unlikely in a North–South context. What is more likely to succeed is a system of tradeable permits which puts an upper limit on the quantity of GHG emissions, unlike a carbon tax which affects the price or cost of emissions. Tradeable permits are similar to quotas, whereas carbon taxes are akin to tariffs. Once the upper emission limit has been decided on, permits to emit are granted on the basis of some agreed criterion. Thereafter permit-holders are free to buy and sell permits to emit GHGs at the market-determined (competitive) price.

In a North–South context, tradeable permit schemes could be the most feasible way forward to environmental control. The cooperation of the

South could be induced via side payments taking the form of overissuing tradeable permits which they could then sell back to the North. There are elements of a Coasean solution here: countries vested with property rights to their part of the atmosphere would be paid to reduce emission. These side payments are, therefore, *economically efficient*.

An international scheme of tradeable permits would have to reach agreement about the upper levels of emission, which would be a Herculean task. Secondly, permits once acquired could give rise to rent-seeking behaviour among permit-holders, which could render the market for tradeable permits uncompetitive. These problems could be avoided by staggering, withdrawing and reissuing permits. The greatest problem with a scheme of tradeable permits embracing North and South would be the initial allocation of permits. One proposal is to relate allocation to GNP or income—such a scheme would clearly favour the richer North. The other is to make it proportional to population. Some proponents of tradeable permits such as Grubb (1989) strongly favour this approach, as it invests in every human being an equal right to the atmosphere, making the proposal attractive on *equity* grounds. Assigning emission permits on this basis (population) would clearly favour the more populous South. An additional (equity) argument for a population-based scheme is embedded in the North's historical responsibility for having polluted more in the past (it still continues to emit vastly more GHGs on a *per capita* basis, although the emission growth rate is faster in the South). This is the *natural debt* argument elucidated by authors such as Smith (1991), where the advanced countries in the North owe a debt to the rest of the world because of their high historical levels of GHG emission. The natural debt argument is all the stronger because the greenhouse effect depends heavily on the accumulated stock of GHGs and the time these have remained in the atmosphere.

If a population-based permit allocation scheme favours the South, such transfers can be justified on efficiency grounds as they induce participation; and on the equity side, there is Grubb's argument of equal rights to the atmosphere for each human being, as well as the argument of debt to nature. The North, in its own early stages of economic development, treated environmental quality in a cavalier fashion; it seems a lot to expect poorer and developing nations to care equally about the environment as the (currently) rich North without some compensation and/or transfer of resources.

Despite the major difficulties facing a system of tradeable permits in GHG emissions, it remains, arguably, the most fruitful route for making progress in GHG emission abatement on a global (North–South) basis. The rest of this Section extends the macro-model of North–South interaction outlined in Section II to analyse a tradeable permit scheme. It is assumed, for the sake of simplicity, that emission of GHGs is related only to production and not to consumption. Once the scheme is introduced, each unit of output will have associated with it emission of GHGs which will have to be paid for, to the amount of the price of the tradeable permit. This will lower the value of aggregate supply by the extent of this tax. Against this will be offset each country's share of the revenues raised from the sale of tradeable permits. Since the *ex ante* allocation of permits and revenue shares from their sales do not necessarily coincide with the *ex post* use of tradeable permits, there is a possibility of transfers from one region to another. Since *ex post* use of tradeable permits depends on actual output produced, permits can be bought for this purpose, but *ex ante* permit/ revenue allocation is a policy decision: a transfer occurs from the region which uses less permits than its initial allocation to the region which requires more than its *ex ante* allocation.

It is assumed that the price of the tradeable permits is market-determined. For the South, the equilibrium relation becomes:

$$Q_S(1-te_S/\sigma)) = c_S v_S(Y_S) + S(.) \tag{16}$$

where t is the price of the tradeable permit, denominated in Northern currency units, e_S is the GHG emission/output ratio ($e_S = E_S/Q_S$) assumed to be fixed exogenously in the short term, and Y_S represents disposable income in the South. Disposable income is:

$$Y_S = Q_S - te_S Q_S + t\alpha_S \bar{E} - rD \tag{17}$$

where $te_S Q_S$ is payment for tradeable permits, $t\alpha_S\bar{E}$ the South's share of total revenues received from the scheme, decided *ex ante*, and rD represents debt servicing. In equilibrium, if equation (17) is positive the South receives net transfers from the North.

As far as the North is concerned:

$$Q_N(1-te_N) = A(Y_N;\sigma) + G + \sigma c_S(1-v_S)(Y_S) - \sigma S(.) \tag{18}$$

where e_N represents the emission/output ratio in the North ($e_N = E_N/Q_N$). Disposable income Y_N in the North is:

$$Y_N = Q_N - te_N Q_N + t(1 - \alpha_S)\bar{E} + rD \tag{19}$$

where $t(1-\alpha_S)\bar{E}$ represents the North's share of revenues. $\bar{E}$ represents total emissions, calculated from permit use in the two regions:

$$t\bar{E} = te_N Q_N + te_S Q_S \tag{20}$$

A more detailed analysis is contained in Murshed (1992). An increase in emission efficiency in the South—a fall in e_S—induced by technological changes or as a condition of aid would lower Southern terms of trade. However, this policy, if combined with increased net transfers to the South, could benefit the South via improved terms of trade. Increased transfers could be achieved through reduction of existing debt or by giving the South a greater share of the revenues from the sale of tradeable permits. This would make a policy-induced increase in emission efficiency more palatable and acceptable.

A properly designed combination of these policies could benefit both regions, as shown in Figure 5.3. Starting from initial equilibrium at point A, the NN lines could shift rightwards and SS upwards, to a new equilibrium at point B with higher income in the North and improved Southern terms of trade.

VI   REAL WAGE RESISTANCE IN THE NORTH AND THE TERMS OF TRADE

Thus far we have concentrated on short-term macroeconomic interaction between North and South. What of the long term? The key variable in the

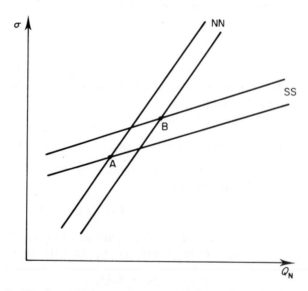

Figure 5.3 Equilibrium in the Southern (SS) and Northern (NN) goods markets under a system of tradeable GHG emission permits. Q_N, Northern output; σ, terms of trade.

long term remains North–South terms of trade. Here aggregate supply features in the North play a crucial role and the model presented below provides an additional analytical underpinning for the famous Prebisch–Singer hypothesis regarding the secular trend of decline in the South's terms of trade.

The phenomenon of real wage rigidity in Northern labour markets has been gradually gathering momentum since the 1960s (see Branson and Rotemberg, 1980). This tendency is far stronger in the Western European segment of the North compared to the US. The idea of introducing union militancy into the determination of North–South terms of trade goes back to Prebisch (1950), although Kaldor (1976) spoke more explicitly about real wage resistance. Real wage resistance is taken to imply that workers seek to preserve, and succeed in maintaining, a particular level or growth rate of their standard of living. The growing literature in insider–outsider models of unemployment suggests that insiders maximize their living standards subject to the continual employment of insiders only. Unemployment has an insignificant effect on real wages. By the same token, on the other side of the fence, firms seek to preserve profit margins. Whereas in the short term the share of real wages relative to profits in national income may behave cyclically, in the long term in the North these shares remain fairly constant. The upshot as regards North–South terms of trade is that a conflict between wages (workers) and profits (capitalists) in the North can be resolved if workers are compensated for falling money wage growth rates by a decline in the overall cost of living, induced by falling prices of consumption goods supplied by the South. This helps to keep the relative income shares of various classes in the North constant. The North's greater market power means that Northern demand plays a major role in determining the North–South terms of trade. The South is disadvantaged by falling terms of trade and in the limit may become effectively decoupled from the international economic system, as the model below demonstrates.

We begin by postulating an equation which determines Northern prices following Dornbusch (1980) and in the spirit of a fix-price (cost mark-up pricing) mechanism:

$$P_N = aW(1 + x) \tag{21}$$

where P_N is the Northern price, representing a mark-up on wage costs (capital costs are ignored for the sake of analytical tractability), W denotes the money wage, x is the mark-up factor, and $a = Q_N/L$, the output–labour ratio; a is hence the inverse of labour productivity. Equation (21) can also be interpreted as the supply function for Northern output: an increase in aggregate demand will be supplied only if the real product wage W declines relative to P_N.

As far as workers as consumers are concerned, they consume both Northern and Southern goods, and their cost of living can be measured by the price index in equation (6) where β and $1-\beta$ are the shares of home and imported goods in the consumption basket. Hence the real wage w is:

$$w = W/P \qquad (22)$$

Substitution of equation (6) into (22), and then into (21), gives:

$$\bar{\sigma} = [(1 + x)aw]^{-1/(1-\beta)} \qquad (23)$$

Note that $\sigma = P_S/P_N$, the ratio of North–South terms of trade, is a *required* factor which must hold *in equilibrium* to be consistent with the objectives of Northern firms and workers regarding profit rates and living standards. Thus equation (23) determines the equilibrium terms of trade and Southern supply behaviour is *redundant*: the South becomes effectively decoupled from the world trading system, although it continues to supply goods passively to the North at going prices.

The problem remains of closing the model. It has already been noted that the equilibrium terms of trade must be consistent with the objectives of Northern firms and workers. These Northern supply considerations in equation (23), together with the market equilibrium level of Northern goods in equation (5), jointly yield equilibrium values of Q_N and σ. Consequently, there remain three equations in two unknowns, Q_N and σ, so a third variable is needed to close the model. A plausible candidate for this role could be some Southern variable such as residual expenditure in the South (R). Another possibility is to cast autonomous expenditure in the North (G) into this role. An endogenous G would imply that benevolent Northern governments pick up the slack whenever there is excess supply in the South, and conversely reduce G whenever there is excess demand in the South. Kanbur and Vines (1986), for example, considered the latter case only, i.e. Northern governments reduce G whenever there is excess demand for Southern goods, putting upward pressure on the terms of trade. They do this because a rise in the terms of trade, via its adverse effect on Northern cost of living, has inflationary consequences for the North. However, G is not increased to eliminate excess supply in the South in the Kanbur and Vines model, precisely because it is unreasonable to expect Northern governments to intervene to counter a fall in Northern costs of living.

Given that the problem of closure arises from the fact that once the equilibrium levels of Q_N and σ are determined in the model the situation could still remain where the Southern market is not cleared, the choice of the Southern variable R allows a symmetrical closure to the model. In other words, R rises (falls) whenever there is excess supply (demand) in the South (for a more detailed analysis, see Murshed, 1990b, 1992). The market clearing relation for the South becomes:

$$R = (1-c_S v_S)Q_S - S(.) \tag{24}$$

The results are illustrated in Figure 5.4. The AD lines are similar to the NN lines in Figures 5.1 and 5.3. The RWR lines resemble the aggregate supply curve for the North, whose negative slope can be explained best by a rise in G.

The effect of an increase in autonomous expenditure G in the North is to boost aggregate demand in that region. This excess demand, however, will be supplied by firms in the North only if the real product wage to them falls, i.e. if P_N rises relative to W (from equations (23) and (21)): workers will resist a decline in their living standards. They can be compensated for any rise in P_N required by Northern firms, by a decline in Southern prices P_S so as to keep their living standards intact. Hence the equilibrium terms of trade (σ) decline, as more output (Q_N) is supplied in the North. Residual

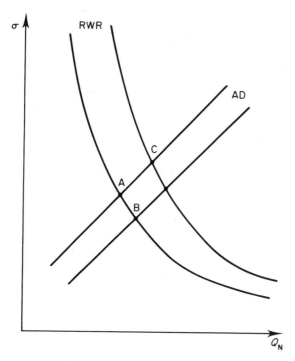

Figure 5.4 Real wage resistance in the North. Q_N, Northern output; σ, terms of trade.

expenditure in the South will have declined and the South unambiguously loses, just as the North unambiguously gains. Output and employment decline in the South, and the reverse occurs in the North. Northern workers are better off, as more of them are employed at the fixed real wage; while employment declines in the South, in addition to a decline in residual expenditure on investment and basic needs. Thus, there is a complete absence of worker solidarity across North and South in this case. In terms of Figure 5.4 the increase in Northern output shifts the AD curve to the right along the RWR curve. The new equilibrium is at point B, which when compared to A shows a higher Q_N and lower σ.

The North has been able to benefit from unprecedented growth rates in standard of living in the post-war era. Expansion in the North in this manner has also managed to avoid class conflict: the conflicting objectives of workers and capitalists have been reconciled aided by the flexibility of the South (as long as Southern terms of trade adjust downwards). The greater economic power of the North, and its ability to influence Southern terms of trade (via demand), ensure the continuation of this most important aspect of 'unequal exchange' between North and South.

It is interesting to note that in the absence of real wage resistance in the North, say if the North had fixed money wages, expansion of autonomous demand would benefit the South via improved terms of trade. 'Global Keynesianism' as suggested by the Brandt Commission of 1980 could have worked in the absence of real wage resistance, as both regions would have gained. Productivity improvements in either region lead to results similar to those postulated by Prebisch (1950). Point C in Figure 5.4 reflects a decline in real wage resistance in the North.

VII CONCLUSIONS

The prefactory remarks to this chapter spoke of a renewed interest in growth theory. This new interest is equally about the causes of lack of growth, or why lagging regions remain behind. It has been maintained that part of the explanation may lie in the macroeconomic interaction between the two regions, both in the short and in the long term. To this end, Section II outlined a structuralist macroeconomic model of North–South interaction which was then applied to recent events and concerns: protectionism, the debt crisis and the environment.

Protectionism in the North towards Southern goods has been growing as the North loses competitiveness in many areas to the South, as pointed out by Singh (1989). This has created conflict and competitive interests between the two regions. Given the power and influence of protectionist lobbies in the North and the weak position of the South in the international trading system, protectionism vis à vis the South is a relatively easy option for the North. Given the rampant regionalism in the world economy and the floundering GATT negotiations in the Uruguay Round, protectionism is likely to grow. The present model demonstrates that it is possible for the North to gain at the expense of the South by pursuing macro-commercial policy, contrary to the findings of Mundell (1961) for small open economies.

The debt crisis of the 1980s meant a lost decade for many heavily indebted countries in the South. Their growth rates were severely curtailed, investment remains low, and many of them transfer nearly 5% of GDP in the form of debt servicing to the North. This transfer burden is larger than the proportion of German national income paid out in reparation payments during the Weimar republic, recalls the latter's catastrophic political consequences. Notwithstanding domestic factors, the debt crisis is to a great extent a painful spillover of Northern macroeconomic policies—contractionary monetary policies and fiscal deficits fuelled by military expenditure, as well as protectionism.

With regard to environmental issues, the South has slightly more room for manoeuvre. This is because in this respect the North cannot fully disregard the South. Here there is a question of both efficient and equitable burden sharing between North and South, bearing in mind the North's current and historically higher levels of *per capita* pollution. A system of tradeable permits in greenhouse gas emission, despite the difficulties associated with it, seems to be the best policy option in the North–South context. The scheme would have to contain an element of transfer to the South (which could take the form of debt relief or trade concessions), but this is justifiable on both efficiency and equity grounds.

Lastly, the long-term nature of North–South macroeconomic interaction must be considered. Northern real wage resistance and the greater economic power of the North can make Southern terms of trade bear a major part of the burden of adjustment to shocks. The South can become effectively decoupled from the international trading system, as its terms of trade have to conform in long-term equilibrium to the objectives of Northern workers and capitalists. This can be the case even though the South participates fully in the international trading system: it merely supplies the Northern market passively at the required terms of trade. This is the real source of unequal exchange (see Emmanuel, 1972; Bacha, 1978).

What of the future prospects for North–South interaction? The last two decades have witnessed the decline of the familiar pattern of North–South interaction. The old pattern cast the South as the supplier of raw materials and the North as the producer of manufactured goods. There was a high degree of mutual interdependence, albeit asymmetrical as the South provided an important market for Northern goods. Moreover, the South provided an important source of investment for Northern surplus savings. The South has ceased to be (on the whole) central to supplies of Northern primary products (as European food surpluses testify). Moreover, deficit regions in the North such as the US, and the united Germany, coupled with the demands of Eastern Europe, mean that surpluses are being diverted to uses in the North, given the current overconsumption patterns in that region. The debt crisis has ensured that the flow of funds from developed to developing regions has greatly diminished, in contrast to earlier periods where the South provided a vent for surplus Northern capital. Competing interests between North and South, and regionalism within the North (competing economic blocks), are likely to foster growing protectionism towards the South.

The North, in contrast to its position in the immediate post-war era characterized by a single dominant world economic power (pax Americana), has ceased to be an engine of growth for the South. The virtuous cycle of mutually beneficial economic interaction appears to have been broken, evidenced by ever more competitive international interests. Growth in one region (the North) appears to be at the expense of the other (the South). Despite localized exceptions as in East Asia, the South is unable to extricate itself from the unequalizing spiral of interaction with the North, given the importance of Northern markets. The end of the Cold War and ever-accelerating regionalism in the North will further disadvantage the South. The prospects for successful North–South cooperation look bleaker than ever. Among the few meaningful bargaining chips left to the South are the environmental issue and Northern fears of migration from Southern countries. The current international climate militates so greatly against (most of the) South's growth prospects and the possibility of the South catching up with Northern living standards, that the term 'development economics' could be excised from the lexicon of economics and replaced instead by a corpus examining the causes of underdevelopment, at least until the next long wave in economic interaction between regions.

REFERENCES

Bacha, E.L. (1978) 'An Interpretation of Unequal Exchange from Prebisch–Singer to Emmanuel', *Journal of Development Economics* 5, 319–30.

Beckerman, W.J. and T. Jenkinson (1986) 'What Stopped the Inflation? Unemployment or Commodity Prices', *Economic Journal* 96, 39–54.

Bhagwati, J. (1988) *Protectionism*, MIT Press, Cambridge, MA.

Branson, W.J. and J. Rotemberg (1980) 'International Adjustment with Wage Rigidity', *European Economic Review* 13, 309–22.

Dornbusch, R. (1980) *Open Economy Macroeconomics*, Basic Books, New York.

Emmanuel, A. (1972) *Unequal Exchange: A Study of the Imperialism of Trade*, Monthly Review Press, New York.

Findlay, R. (1980) 'The Terms of Trade and Equilibrium Growth in the World Economy', *American Economic Review* **70**, 191–9.

Ford, J.L. and S. Sen (1985) *Protectionism, Exchange Rates and the Macroeconomy*, Blackwell, Oxford.

Grubb, M. (1989) *The Greenhouse Effect: Negotiation Targets*, Royal Institute for International Affairs, London.

Hicks, J.R. (1965) *Capital and Growth*, Oxford University Press, Oxford.

Kaldor, N. (1976) 'Inflation and Recession in a World Economy', *Economic Journal* **86**, 703–14.

Kanbur, R. and D. Vines (1986) 'North–South Interaction and Commodity Control', *Journal of Development Economics* **23**, 371–87.

Keynes, J.M. (1929) 'The German Transfer Problem', *Economic Journal* **39**, 1–7.

Krugman, P. (1979) 'A Model of Innovation, Technology Transfer, and the World Distribution of Income', *Journal of Political Economy* **87**, 253–66.

Laursen, S. and L.A. Metzler (1950) 'Flexible Exchange Rates and the Theory of Employment', *Review of Economics and Statistics* **32**, 281–99.

Lucas, R.E., Jr (1991) 'Making a Miracle', Lecture given to Econometric Society's European Meeting at Cambridge, Sept. 1991.

Mundell, R.A. (1961) 'Flexible Exchange Rates and Employment Policy', *Canadian Journal of Economics and Political Science* **27**, 509–17.

Murshed, S.M. and S. Sen (1989) 'Inflation and Macroeconomic Adjustments in a North–South Model', *Greek Economic Review* **11**, 95–118.

Murshed, S.M. (1990a) 'Stabilisation Policy, Commercial Policy and Debt in a North–South Framework' in G. Bird (ed.), *The International Financial Regime*, Academic Press, London.

Murshed, S.M. (1990b) 'Unequal Exchange and North–South Unemployment', *Journal fur Entwickslungs Politik* **6**, 45–60.

Murshed, S.M. (1991) 'Macro-Commercial Policy Revisited: A Global North–South Analysis', *Greek Economic Review* (forthcoming).

Murshed, S.M. (1992) *Economic Aspects of North–South Interaction*, Academic Press (forthcoming).

Naoroji, D. (1901) *Poverty and Un-British Rule in India*, Swan Sonnenschein, London.

Pearce, D. (1991) 'The Role of Carbon Taxes in Adjusting to Global Warming', *Economic Journal* **101**, 938–48.

Pearce, D. and K.G. Maler (1991) 'Environmental Economics and the Developing World', *Ambio* **20**, 55–8.

Prebisch, R. (1950) *The Economic Development of Latin America and its Principal Problems*, United Nations, New York.

Sarkar, P. and H.W. Singer (1991) 'Manufactured Exports of Developing Countries and their Terms of Trade since 1965', *World Development* **19**, 333–40.

Singer, H. (1950) 'The Distribution of Gains between Borrowing and Investing Countries', *American Economic Review* **40**, 473–85.

Singh, A. (1989) 'Third World Competition and Deindustrialisation in Advanced Countries', *Cambridge Journal of Economics* **13**, 103–20.

Smith, K.R. (1991) 'Natural Debt Index', *Ambio* **20**, 95–6.

Taylor, L. (1983) *Structuralist Macroeconomics*, Basic Books, New York.

6 | Greenhouse Gas Scenarios and Global Warming: The Role of Third World Countries

PETER J.G. PEARSON

I INTRODUCTION

Environmental issues, especially those related to energy, are once more on the international policy agenda. This chapter focuses on the enhanced greenhouse effect and global warming. This is not to imply that other environmental problems that are faced by Third World countries are less serious than global warming: for example, the problems of natural resource degradation and the ways in which they can be exacerbated by external pressures of trade and debt are fairly well known.[1] However, this chapter concentrates on a new element in outside pressures on Third World countries—the control of greenhouse gases (GHGs) in general and of carbon dioxide (CO_2) in particular.

If Third World countries are to develop, their use of energy and consequent pollutant emissions will increase—particularly the use of fossil fuels and the emission of damaging pollutants such as carbon monoxide (CO), CO_2, nitrogen oxides (NO_x), sulphur dioxide (SO_2) and hydrocarbons. Moreover, for those countries that fail to develop, there are usually serious environmental problems of another kind, associated with traditional forms of biomass energy and deforestation. Quite apart from the need to address their purely domestic environmental problems, Third World countries will play an increasingly prominent part in contributing to, and perhaps cooperating in the resolution of, the enhanced greenhouse effect and global warming. International cooperation is necessary if GHG emissions are to be controlled—as this chapter shows, given the projected rapid increase in the share of Third World countries in global emissions, abatement by industrialized countries will be ineffectual if Third World countries do not also participate.

A number of the poorest developing countries might be very hard hit during the next century by the impacts of global warming. However, the present costs of reducing emissions related to fossil fuels and adapting to expected climatic and environmental changes imply some painful trade-offs (for example, loss of gross domestic product). Given the uncertainties and the long time scale, many Third World countries will be tempted to lean towards an optimistic assessment of the damage that may be caused by global warming. For a number of reasons (including strategic bargaining), they will tend to set lower targets for emission control than the developed, industrialized countries (Pearson, 1991b).

As Third World representatives have often emphasized, because of their currently low levels of *per capita* income and energy consumption, and their development aspirations, the participation of Third World countries in global GHG emission limitation agreements cannot be taken for granted. Furthermore, when control measures (such as carbon taxes, tradeable permits or quotas) which would ration the use of the atmosphere are proposed, Third World countries tend to counter with the argument that while *their* economies were maturing the industrialized countries treated the atmosphere as an open-access resource, using it as a free waste-sink for long-lived GHGs.[2] So it seems that Third World countries are likely to cooperate with the industrialized countries only at a price—if they are compensated, whether financially or through the transfer of energy- and pollution-efficient technology, or both. Of course, part of the problem of Third World participation is that richer countries would like poorer countries to take the decisions and make the trade-offs that make sense to richer countries—in particular, to control the growth of greenhouse gas emissions directly and to have the smaller families that would limit population growth and hence the future demand for energy. This is not necessarily to suggest that Third World policy-makers take the threat of global warming lightly. Rather, it is to emphasize the severity of the difficulties and constraints that poorer countries face when deciding which energy and environmental pathways to follow.

The aim of this chapter is to examine what is known about the greenhouse effect and global warming, and then to relate this to the future role that Third World countries might play in contributing to, suffering from and possibly participating in the limitation of GHG emissions. The following Sections examine the nature of the enhanced greenhouse effect and global warming, the role of anthropogenic emissions of GHGs (particularly CO_2), and the present and future role of Third World countries in global emissions. Later Sections deal with the factors behind the GHG scenarios, projections of energy consumption, Third World vulnerability to the effects of climate change, GHG emission control costs and damage costs, the economic impacts of GHG limitation strategies and Third World participation in such strategies.

II THE GREENHOUSE EFFECT

Current models of global climate change are descended from the work of Manabe (the 'godfather' of climate modelling) and Wetherald in the 1960s. According to Gribbin (1990a, p. 126):

> They developed the idea of a global energy balance between the amount of heat reaching the Earth from the Sun, the amount being radiated from the ground, the amount being trapped in the atmosphere and the amount finally escaping into space. In equilibrium the amount arriving from the Sun and the amount escaping from the top of the atmosphere are in balance, but atmospheric feedbacks make the surface of the planet warmer than it would be if the planet had no atmosphere.

Thus the earth is heated by energy from the sun, mainly visible radiation plus some shorter-wave radiation. The earth emits long-wave thermal radiation, some of which is absorbed and reflected back by the GHGs. This 'greenhouse effect' makes the earth's surface about 30°C warmer than it would otherwise be. The processes are complex, with much interaction and feedback.[3] Moreover, the moderating effect of the oceans (thermal inertia) causes a lag of the order of 50 years between a given level of warming becoming inevitable and its happening (Allen and Christensen, 1990, p. 19). Consequently, the observed warming at any point (the transient warming) can lag 50 years behind the steady-state warming.

It is important, however, to stress that while the general principles underlying the greenhouse effect are well understood, there is still much uncertainty in the science. Of particular concern, of course, is the role of anthropogenic emissions of GHGs. These emissions have been growing at increasing rates since the industrial revolution, and have the potential to create an 'enhanced greenhouse effect' and thus raise global temperatures. The work of the Intergovernmental Panel on Climate Change (IPCC), discussed below, has represented one attempt to address the concerns associated with the enhanced greenhouse effect.

III   THE ENHANCED GREENHOUSE EFFECT AND GLOBAL WARMING: THE IPCC REPORTS

The IPCC was established in November 1988 by UNEP (United Nations Environment Programme) and WMO (World Meteorological Organization) with the task of reporting on global warming to the Second World Climate Change Conference in Geneva in November 1990.[4] It had three Working Groups: Group 1 on the Scientific Assessment of Climate Change (Houghton *et al.*, 1990); Group 2 on the Impact of Climate Change; and Group 3 on Strategies to Combat Climate Change.[5]

III.1   The scientific assessment of climate change: IPCC Working Group 1

IPCC Working Group 1 published its first *Assessment Report* in August 1990. Its conclusions included the following points:

(1)   There is an enhanced greenhouse effect: a natural greenhouse effect is being enhanced by anthropogenic emissions of gases—principally CO_2, methane (CH_4), the chlorofluorocarbons (CFCs) and nitrous oxide (N_2O). The main greenhouse gas, water vapour, will increase in response to global warming and enhance it. CO_2 has been responsible for more than 50% of the enhanced greenhouse effect in the past and is likely to remain so.

(2)   Continued emissions of the long-lived gases (CO_2, N_2O and the CFCs) would commit us to increased concentrations for decades. Immediate reductions of anthropogenic emissions of more than 60% would be needed to stabilize concentrations of these gases at 1990 levels (Table 6.1 provides estimates of the relative effectiveness ('global warming power') of various GHGs, their present concentrations and growth rates, their atmospheric lifetimes, and the expected relative contribution of 1990 emissions over the succeeding 100 years).

(3)   Under the IPCC's 'business-as-usual' scenario, global mean temperature could rise by 0.3°C per decade during the 21st century. On present trends, an increase of 3°C above the present level by the year 2100 could occur, unless emissions are cut. There could be a global mean sea-level rise of 6 cm per decade during the 21st century, mainly the result of thermal expansion of the oceans and the melting of some land ice. A rise of about 65 cm could occur by 2100.

(4)   The observed warming during the last century, of 0.3–0.6°C, with a global sea level rise of 10–20 cm, is of the same magnitude as natural

Table 6.1 Role of the different greenhouse gases.

Greenhouse gas	CO_2	CH_4	CFC_{11}	CFC_{12}	N_2O	Others[a]
Warming power (GWP)[b]	1	21	3 500	7 300	290	Various
Present concentration (ppmv)[c]	353	1.72	0.00028	0.00048	0.31	Various
Annual growth rate	0.5%	0.9%	4%	4%	0.25%	Various
Atmospheric lifetime (years)	50–200[d]	10	65	130	150	Various
Relative contribution over 100 years	61%	15%	11.5%	11.5%	4%	8.5%

Source: OECD/IEA (1991, Table 1.1, p. 14). Data from *IPCC Policymakers' Summary of the Scientific Assessment of Climate Change* (June 1990).
[a] Includes a number of gases, such as O_3. The effects of NO_x and CO are included in this table through their influence on the formation and destruction of CH_4 and O_3.
[b] The warming effect of an emission of 1 kg of each gas relative to that of CO_2. These figures are best estimates calculated on the basis of present-day atmospheric composition, integrated over a 100-year time period.
[c] ppmv = parts per million by volume.
[d] The way in which CO_2 is absorbed by the oceans and biosphere is not simple and a single value cannot be given.

climate variability. This increase could be ascribed to natural fluctuations; alternatively, the natural variations could have offset an even larger anthropogenic warming effect. Furthermore, it is expected to take at least another 15 years for the unequivocal detection of the enhanced greenhouse effect, for a proper understanding of the climate-related processes (especially clouds, oceans and the carbon cycle), and for the development of global data and better models[6] of the earth's climate system.

How has the report of Working Group 1 been received? The editor of a recent special issue of the journal *Energy Policy*, devoted to global warming, gave this view (Skea, 1991, p. 90):

> . . . IPCC scientists have succeeded in drawing robust conclusions which, at the same time, acknowledge limitations and identify areas in which further work would be fruitful. The report's authors declare themselves certain that the greenhouse effect is real, confident that anthropogenic greenhouse gas emissions are adding to this effect, and predict, within a large band of uncertainty, the temperature increases and sea level rises which may be expected over the coming decades.
>
> So, although climatologists will not put their hands on their hearts and declare that recent weather records prove beyond all doubt that climate change is under way, analyses they have made using sophisticated computer models which simulate the world's climate system have removed all but the last vestiges of uncertainty.

There seems, therefore, to be a broad consensus in the scientific community that, if present trends in the emission of greenhouse gases continue, global mean temperatures could rise substantially compared with observed historic changes. However, there have been a few notable dissenting voices. For example, work emanating from the George C. Marshall Institute in Washington has questioned the likelihood of global warming and is said to have influenced President Bush and US attitudes to policy responses to the threat of global warming.[7] Furthermore, as will be seen below, and as Skea confirms (Skea, 1991, p. 90), if the output of Working Group 1 was the product of broad agreement, the same cannot be said for the reports of Groups 2 and 3 which considered, respectively, climate change impacts and policy responses.

III.2   Sources of GHG emissions: CO_2, fossil fuels and deforestation

Before considering the impacts of climate change and policy responses to it, however, it is helpful briefly to consider the underlying sources of GHG emissions. Table 6.2 presents a list of GHGs and their main anthropogenic

Table 6.2 Greenhouse gases and their main anthropogenic sources.

Gas	Sources
Carbon dioxide (CO_2)	Fossil fuel burning Deforestation and land use change Cement manufacture
Methane (CH_4)	Rice paddy cultivation Ruminants (e.g. cows, sheep) Biomass (wood, wastes, etc.) burning and decay Releases from fossil fuel production
Chlorofluorocarbons (CFCs)	Manufactured for solvents, refrigerants, aerosol spray propellants, foam packaging, etc.
Nitrous oxide (N_2O)	Fertilizers Fossil fuel burning Land conversion for agriculture
Precursor gases (involved in ozone and methane chemistry):	
Nitrogen oxides (NO_x)	Fossil fuel burning
Non-methane hydrocarbons	Evaporation of liquid fuels and solvents
Carbon monoxide (CO)	Fossil fuel and biomass burning

Source: Grubb (1989, Table 1, p. 6).

source activities. All of these activities occur in both industrialized and Third World countries, although in differing proportions in different countries. However, fossil fuel burning, deforestation and land use change are associated in particular with CO_2 emissions, and these activities are expected to increase more quickly in the Third World than in industrialized countries over the next few decades.

When considering CO_2 emissions, in particular, it is important to be aware of the different levels of carbon emissions of different fuels. Because fuels have differing ratios of carbon to hydrogen, combustion emits different amounts of CO_2 for a given amount of thermal energy released. Thus, on this basis, coal tends to release more CO_2 than oil or biomass fuels, both of which release more than natural gas (OECD/IEA, 1991, p. 15).[8] This is one of the reasons why fuel-switching away from coal and oil towards gas is often recommended as a way of limiting CO_2 emissions.

Figure 6.1 presents estimates of global CO_2 production from various fossil fuels for the period 1950–86, as estimated by Marland (1989). The figures indicate a rise in CO_2 emissions from these sources of almost 240% over this period, with solid fuels and then liquid fuels as the major contributors.

As Table 6.2 indicates, although fossil fuels are the major anthropogenic

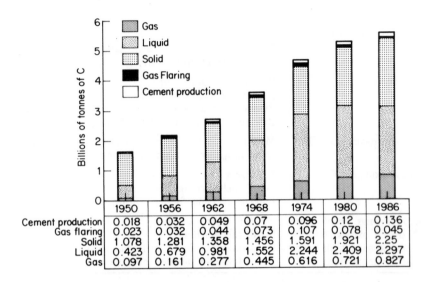

Figure 6.1 Global CO_2 production from fossil fuels (OECD/IEA, 1991, Fig. 3, p. 17; data from Marland, 1989).

source of CO_2 emissions, deforestation and land use change also play a part (Touche Ross, 1991, p. 92):

> Deforestation is second only to the burning of fossil fuels as a human source of atmospheric carbon dioxide. Since replenishment rates match deforestation rates in temperate regions, almost all future growth in greenhouse gas emissions resulting from deforestation will originate from tropical forests.

What sort of processes are involved? OECD/IEA (1991, p. 16) describe what happens when forests are converted to farmland. Three phenomena occur with additive effects: the soil's organic matter is oxidized and emitted as CO_2; the wood and organic forest material are also transformed into CO_2 through burning or other biochemical processes; and forest clearing eliminates a reservoir in which CO_2 could be absorbed and stored through photosynthesis.

Measurement of the contribution of deforestation to total CO_2 emissions (and absorption) is especially problematic, for both conceptual and practical reasons. The precise role of deforestation in GHG emissions and absorption is not yet fully understood and there are many problems of data coverage and interpretation.[9] According to the US Office of Technology Assessment

(OTA, 1991, p. 17), estimates of CO_2 emissions from tropical deforestation differ by a factor of 4. Thus by various estimates, deforestation could be the source of roughly 7–35% of total annual emissions of CO_2.[10] Such a high level of uncertainty about the absolute and relative contributions of deforestation obviously poses serious problems for policy-making.

The scientific assessment of global warming is only part of the issue, and part of the IPCC's work. The following Section considers the potential impacts of climate change, the responsibility of IPCC's Working Group 2.

III.3   The potential impacts of climate change: IPCC Working Group 2

There are three key effects of climate change: temperature rise, shifting rainfall patterns and sea-level rise (Touche Ross, 1991, p. 12). The conclusions of Working Group 2 included the following points:

(1)   Climate and sea level changes could be so rapid that in many cases adaptation of the natural environment will not occur quickly enough.
(2)   Northern forests could be severely affected. Deserts are expected to advance and droughts to increase in the USA, Central America, South East Asia and especially Africa, notably the Sahel countries. Parts of the northern hemisphere could benefit by being able to produce grain in areas that were once too cold.
(3)   The most serious effects of climate change may be those on human migration as millions of people could be displaced by shoreline erosion, coastal flooding and agricultural disruption. For example, 8–10 million people live within 1 metre of high tide in each of the unprotected river deltas of Bangladesh, Egypt and Vietnam. Island nations are under threat, as are the coastal areas of industrialized nations.[11]
(4)   Severe weather patterns, such as tropical cyclones, are likely to become more widespread and frequent, disrupting human settlements and industry.
(5)   Drinking-water supplies could be disrupted, and air pollution could increase, especially in cities.

III.4   Policy responses to climate change: IPCC Working Group 3

Before considering the output of Working Group 3 of the IPCC, it is worth summarizing the possible policy responses to the threat of global warming and the policy instruments that might be employed to promote them. The policy responses include:

(1)   Do nothing now and adapt only when the impacts arise.
(2)   Invest in anticipatory *adaptive* measures before the full equilibrium

impacts happen (for example, build sea-walls, invest in adapting agriculture to a changing climate, encourage migration from threatened coastal areas).

(3) Implement *preventive* measures by reducing or slowing projected changes in the level and pattern of GHG emissions, especially CO_2. For example:

   (a) Reduce the carbon intensity of energy use, by switching to less carbon-intensive fossil fuels (e.g. from coal and oil to gas) and by switching away from fossil fuels towards nuclear power or renewables such as solar, wind, tidal or biomass-derived fuels.

   (b) Use less GHG-emitting energy than otherwise, through stimulating greater energy efficiency.

   (c) Reduce the rate of deforestation and biomass burning.

   (d) Aim to sequester carbon through reforestation programmes.

   (e) Remove CO_2 from the exhaust gases of combustion plants (potentially feasible but as yet fairly costly).[12]

   (f) Attempt to remove CO_2 from the atmosphere (for example, by pumping it into deep oceans or into empty oil and gas reservoirs beneath the earth's surface).[13]

   (g) Phase out CFCs *and* replace them with greenhouse-friendly substitutes.

The key policy issue here for governments is to what extent they should try either to take action now in the absence of scientific certainty and precision about the timing, scale and location of effects, and so risk buying 'too much' insurance, or postpone action and risk greater (and partly irreversible) damage as a result, thus paying 'too much' in the future (in terms of the social costs of experiencing and reacting to the effects of global warming). As Nordhaus (1991a, p. 925) put it:

> The fundamental policy question involves how much reduction in consumption society should incur today to slow the consumption damages from climate change in the future.

This is an issue to which I return later, in discussing Nordhaus' estimates of damage costs and control costs.

The policy instruments that might be used to implement proactive policy responses could include command and control regulation or market-based instruments such as carbon taxes and tradeable permits. Economists tend to praise the static and dynamic efficiency features of market-based instruments.[14] However, it seems increasingly possible that if there is to be an international GHG-limiting agreement, a quota approach followed by various deals and side-payments could be adopted, even though this might imply considerable efficiency losses.

IPCC Working Group 3 proposed a global climate change convention and called for national plans to evaluate measures to control GHG emissions and to adapt to the potential impacts of global climate change. It did not, however, recommend any *specific* set of policy responses by governments. According to one report, the group was dominated by politicians rather than scientists and by the United States and Japan. The report emphasized uncertainties over the level and pace of climate change and the costs of reducing the consumption of fossil fuels. Although the group had been asked to produce targets for stabilizing and reducing emissions, it said that '. . . it was not possible to complete such an analysis by the time of this report's publication'. The report suggested that Western Europe would be able to stabilize emission rates in 10 years and Eastern Europe in 20 years, while developing countries could cut their increases by 1% and North American and Pacific nations '. . . may be able to slow the growth'.[15]

At the final Working Group meeting, disagreements are said to have emerged between governments over the agenda for the November 1990 World Climate Change Conference: the USA, Japan, USSR, China and Saudi Arabia argued that they could not meet early targets to cut greenhouse gases, while several Western European and Scandinavian countries wanted to proceed immediately towards agreements for global cuts. Saudi Arabia's reluctance was interpreted by some to reflect anxieties among oil exporters about the potential impacts on world oil demand. The Chinese delegation is reported to have said that '. . . if we stabilize emissions, that means we cannot develop the Chinese economy'.[16]

The meeting recommended that the November 1990 Conference should include a call for governments to '. . . take steps now to limit, stabilize or reduce the emissions of energy-related greenhouse gases'.[17] Moreover, market-based policy instruments such as carbon taxes were suggested, together with longer-term strategies such as increasing the share of non-fossil fuels. The report was much criticized by environmental groups.

III.5 The 1990 Second World Climate Change Conference in Geneva

The IPCC Working Group reports were an input into the Second World Climate Conference in November 1990. The Conference reached an agreement which was signed by Ministers from 137 countries. It was reported that the scientific case that the rate of climate change will prove unprecedented and threatens the sustainable development of some areas in the world, was accepted by all governments. The agreement provided the initial basis for the negotiation of an eventual world convention that *might* result in industrialized countries agreeing to cut CO_2 emissions and to participate in the provision of financial assistance and technology transfer that might both encourage and enable Third World countries to control the growth of their emissions.

It was agreed to start negotiations to outline a legal convention for the United Nations-sponsored conference to be held in Rio de Janeiro in June 1992: this is UNCED, the UN Conference on Environment and Development, also known as the Earth Summit. Interested parties are currently jockeying for position in attempts to influence the agenda and its outcomes. A preparatory conference meeting was held in Washington in February 1991, again attended by delegates from more than 130 countries. The meeting agreed that future talks should concentrate on identifying 'appropriate commitments' to reduce GHG emissions and to provide aid to Third World countries to facilitate the development of less-polluting industries. According to one report:[18]

> At the conclusion of the meeting, little progress had been made beyond agreeing procedural rules and setting up two working parties. Several delegations, including that from Britain, expressed disappointment at the slowness of the progress. The UK and other European countries came out in favour of setting strict targets on emissions of carbon dioxide, methane and nitrous oxides. The continuing reluctance of the US Administration to agree to any specific targets on emissions or Third World aid was identified as the principal brake on progress.

It remains to be seen whether any clear positive agreement on GHG emission limitation and compensatory financing will be reached at UNCED in 1992.

IV SCENARIOS FOR GHG SHARES

This Section focuses on the role of Third World countries in global emissions because it is the evolution of this role that explains why the industrialized countries have a strong interest in seeking Third World cooperation in strategies for global emission limitation. Figure 6.2 illustrates the EC's recent scenario for 1987–2010 and shows the evolution of estimated shares in global CO_2 emissions over this period. In particular, the pie charts at the top of the Figure indicate that while in 1987 the Third World's share (comprising China and the rest of the world) was 30%, the EC scenario suggests that by 2010 it could rise by more than one-third to 41%. The bar chart at the bottom of the Figure shows the striking differences in CO_2 emissions *per capita* (measured in tonnes of carbon per inhabitant) in 1987 between the Third World on the one hand and the industrialized countries and Eastern Europe on the other. In particular, Third World emissions are about one-tenth those in the USA.

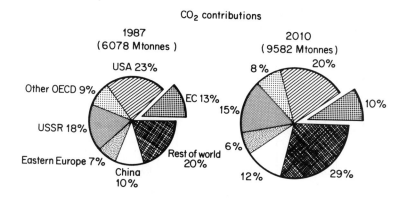

CO₂ contributions

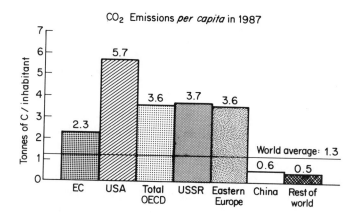

Figure 6.2 Evolution of estimated shares in CO_2 emissions 1987–2010 and *per capita* data for 1987 (CEC, 1990, Fig. 4.8, p. 81).

Extending the time horizon 15 years beyond that of the EC's scenario, Working Group 3 of the IPCC produced a scenario where Third World emissions grow from 26% of the global total in 1985 to 44% by 2025 (OTA, 1991, pp. 16 and 131), while other forecasts suggest that the Third World's share in global CO_2 will have risen to more than 50% by 2030.

Figure 6.3 shows regional and sectoral contributions to projected increases in annual GHG emission rates (excluding CFCs), based on estimates by the US Environmental Protection Agency and the IPCC. Note the especially rapid increases projected for Eastern Europe and the USSR, as well as for Central Asia, Latin America and South and East Asia. Also,

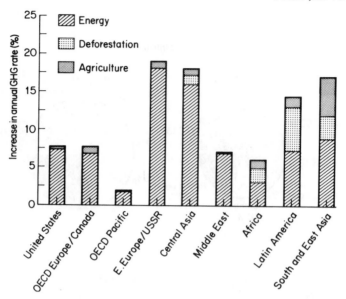

Figure 6.3 Regional and sectoral contributions to the annual increase in GHG
emission rates (excluding CFCs) 1986–2025 (data expressed as CO_2
equivalents) (Touche Ross, 1991, Fig. III.6, p. 95; data from USAID
(1990) and IPCC reports).

energy is the major contributor to each region's increases. However,
deforestation is estimated to be significant, particularly in Latin America (as
would be expected) but also in Africa and to a lesser extent in South and
East Asia, where agriculture is second to energy.

A view of the Third World's shares in global CO_2 emissions over an even
longer time horizon is provided by the modelling work done by Manne and
Richels (1991). Figure 6.4 shows their unconstrained carbon emissions
scenario for the years 1990 and 2100. Thus while in 1990 the Third World's
share (China plus the rest of the world) amounts to 29%, by 2100 it rises to
a dominant global share of 57%.

V   THE FACTORS THAT LIE BEHIND THE GHG SCENARIOS

What lies behind the above GHG scenarios? They are essentially the
outcome of relatively rapid Third World growth rates in population, gross
domestic product and energy use, as Table 6.3 indicates. These data are
taken from the OECD/IEA rising oil price scenario, and they show much
faster rates of growth in each of these variables in the developing countries

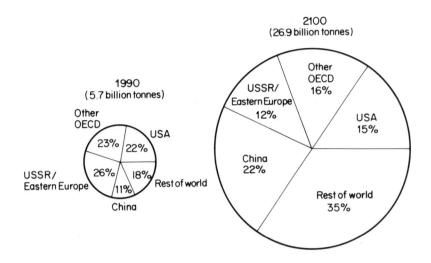

Figure 6.4 Unconstrained carbon emissions scenario (Manne and Richels, 1991, Fig. 3, p. 98).

Table 6.3 Comparative average annual growth rates (%) of economies, energy and greenhouse gas emissions[a] 1987–2005, with rising oil prices.

	OECD	Centrally planned economies	Developing countries	World
Population	0.5	0.6	1.9	1.3
GDP	2.7	2.7	3.8	—[b]
TPER[c]	1.3	2.9	3.8	2.4
CO_2	1.2	2.6	3.7	2.3
CH_4	0.7	2.4	2.1	1.8
NO_x[d]	−0.4	2.7	4.3	1.9
CO	−3.2	2.1	2.1	0.4

Source: OECD/IEA (1991, Table 3.1a, p. 45).
[a] CO_2 and CH_4 are both direct greenhouse gases. NO_x and CO influence climate change as precursors of O_3, and CO influences the concentrations of CH_4 in the atmosphere. Therefore, they are included as greenhouse gases by the IPCC and this study.
[b] Due to lack of comparability of economic data, exchange rates, etc., neither a value for world GDP, nor for growth rates of world GDP, has been calculated.
[c] Total primary energy requirements.
[d] For the period 1986–2005.

compared with the OECD countries in particular, but also with the centrally planned economies (China is classed as such by the OECD in this table).

Table 6.4 Average annual percentage rate of change in factors that contributed to global growth in carbon dioxide emissions, 1973–87.

Factor	Rate of change (%)
Population	+1.74
GDP *per capita*	+0.99
Energy/GDP ratio	−0.59
CO_2/energy ratio	−0.39
CO_2	+1.75

Source: Darmstadter (1991, p. 7). Data from Ogawa (1991).

Table 6.4 shows Darmstadter's (1991) results for the average annual percentage rate of change in factors that contributed to global growth in CO_2 emissions for 1973–1987, based on a study by Ogawa (1991). According to Ogawa's estimates, downward trends in the intensity of energy use (the energy/GDP ratio) and in the carbon content of the fuel mix (the CO_2/energy ratio) were not sufficient to outweigh the effects of upward trends in population and, to a lesser extent, in GDP *per capita* on the rate of growth of CO_2 emissions. As Darmstadter stated:

> This suggests that even with some future deceleration of population increase, if growth of CO_2 emissions is to be significantly slowed (let alone reduced) and economic growth (especially in the less developed countries) is to continue at an adequate rate, a heavy burden would be placed on declining intensity of energy use and increasing recourse to noncarbon fuels. Thus, almost by definition, studies of the cost of mitigating CO_2 emissions focus, explicitly or implicitly, on one or both of these two factors as critical to the success of any CO_2 abatement effort.

It is the relatively rapid increases in Third World commercial energy use, mostly fossil fuel consumption, that are driving up the GHG projections (and the CO_2 projections in particular). For example, OTA (1991, p. 9) cites an analysis of 100 different projections of global energy consumption which concluded that the share of Third World countries in global commercial energy consumption would rise from less than one-quarter in 1985 to more than one-third by 2010, reflecting an increase of 250% in commercial energy use (Manne and Schrattenholzer, 1989). Table 6.5 gives more details of these projections. The differences between the annual average rates of growth of commercial energy consumption for the developing countries and for the OECD are particularly striking, as is China's prominent role.

Over a slightly longer period, Figure 6.5 shows the Third World's share

Table 6.5 Commercial energy consumption in 1985 and projections for 2010 (EJ=exajoules).

	Consumption, 1985 (EJ)	Share of total (%)	Consumption, 2010 (EJ)	Share of total (%)	Average annual growth rate, 1985–2010 (%)	Increase in consumption, 1985–2010 (EJ)	Share of increase (%)
Developing countries	69.26	23.3	175.56	34.5	3.8	106.30	50.2
China	21.91	7.4	59.54	11.7	4.1	37.63	17.8
OPEC	11.65	3.9	28.91	5.7	2.5	17.26	8.1
Non-OPEC developing countries	35.70	12.0	87.11	17.1	3.6	51.41	24.3
OECD	155.83	52.4	215.03	42.2	1.3	59.20	27.9
United States	73.87	24.8	98.47	19.3	1.2	24.60	11.6
USSR and Eastern Europe	72.32	24.3	118.66	23.3	2.0	46.34	21.9
Total	297.41	100.0	509.25	100.0	2.3	211.85	100.0

Source: OTA (1991, Table 2.2, p. 35). Taken from Manne and Schrattenholzer (1989).

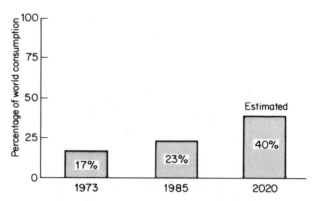

Figure 6.5 Commercial energy consumption, 1973, 1985 and 2020: energy demand
of developing countries as a percentage of world total (OTA, 1991,
Fig. 1.3, p. 10; data from *Global Energy Perspectives 2000–2020*, 14th
Congress of the World Energy Conference, Montreal, 1989).

in commercial energy consumption rising from 17% in 1973 to 23% in 1985
and then to an estimated 40% by 2020 (with an implicit 300% rise in
commercial fuel consumption between 1985 and 2020), according to World
Energy Conference figures.[19] Figure 6.6 emphasizes that despite the
expected increases in the Third World's share in total consumption, much
of the great inequality between developed and developing regions in *per
capita* commercial energy consumption is expected to persist well into the
next century. It is this inequality which explains the Third World's current
minor share in global energy consumption, despite its dominant share (more
than 75%) of world population. Moreover, quite apart from the influence of
expected population growth on commercial energy demand,[20] to the extent
that a significant gap in *per capita* consumption remains to be narrowed in the
future, it signals a potentially massive pent-up demand for commercial energy
in the Third World. It is, therefore, not surprising that an emission scenario
report for the IPCC suggests that, over a wide range of scenarios, the Third
World's share is envisaged to increase from the 1985 reference level of 23% of
global energy consumption to 40–60% by 2100. During this period the Third
World could be responsible for 60–80% of incremental global energy
consumption. Moreover, developments in the Third World account for a large
part of the difference between the low- and high-growth scenarios.[21]

VI   THE UNEVEN DISTRIBUTION OF THIRD
WORLD ENERGY CONSUMPTION

Energy consumption is not only unevenly distributed between industrialized countries and the Third World, it is also very unevenly

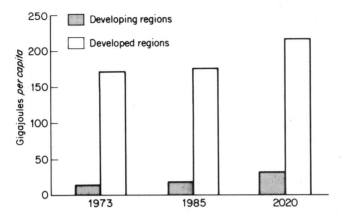

Figure 6.6 Commercial energy consumption *per capita*, 1973, 1985 and 2020 (OTA, 1991, Fig. 1.4, p. 10; data from *Global Energy Perspectives 2000–2020*, 14th Congress of the World Energy Conference, Montreal, 1989).

distributed between different Third World countries. This, of course, carries potentially significant implications for the nature—and the negotiation—of global CO_2 reduction strategies. In terms of the distribution between individual Third World countries, China, India and Brazil account for about 45% of total Third World consumption of commercial and traditional energy, while these three countries plus another four—Indonesia, Mexico, Korea and Venezuela—account for 57% of the total. At the other end of the scale, however, the 50 countries of Africa used less than 3% of the Third World's estimated 23% of 1985 global commercial energy consumption (OTA, 1991, p. 8). Table 6.6 shows OTA estimates, based on UN data, of the total and *per capita* commercial energy consumption of the 20 largest consumers in 1987. The variations in the *per capita* levels between industrialized and Third World countries are even more evident than in the much more highly aggregated data of Figure 6.6 above. Table 6.6 also ranks separately the 10 largest Third World consumers. Even for this set of countries the differences in *per capita* consumption are striking.

VII THE NATURE AND FEASIBILITY OF PROJECTED GROWTH IN THIRD WORLD ENERGY CONSUMPTION

The feasibility of the projections of rapid growth in Third World energy consumption, of the sort discussed earlier, has often been questioned.[22] In particular, it is clear that the funding of both energy imports and investments in domestic energy infrastructure has in the recent past caused

Table 6.6 Largest energy consumers in 1987.

Rank	Country	Total commercial energy consumption (exajoules)	Per capita commercial energy consumption (gigajoules)
20 largest commercial energy consumers			
1	United States	68.1	280
2	USSR	54.7	194
3	China	23.5	22
4	Japan	13.4	110
5	West Germany	10.0	165
6	United Kingdom	8.5	150
7	Canada	7.5	291
8	India	6.5	8
9	France	6.1	109
10	Italy	6.0	105
11	Poland	5.3	141
12	Mexico	4.1	50
13	East Germany	3.8	231
14	Australia	3.2	201
15	Brazil	3.2	22
16	South Africa	3.2	83
17	Romania	3.1	136
18	Netherlands	3.1	213
19	Czechoslovakia	2.9	185
20	Spain	2.4	147
10 largest developing country energy consumers			
1	China	23.5	22
2	India	6.5	8
3	Mexico	4.1	50
4	Brazil	3.2	22
5	South Africa	3.2	83
6	South Korea	2.2	52
7	Argentina	1.7	56
8	Venezuela	1.6	88
9	Indonesia	1.4	8
10	Egypt	1.0	20

Source: OTA (1991, Table 1.4, p. 9). Data from United Nations Secretariat. Data for the top 10 developing country energy consumers include only countries listed in Appendix 1A of OTA (1991).

major difficulties for many Third World countries. Energy supply, particularly for petroleum-importing countries (about three-quarters of all Third World countries), is highly intensive of capital and foreign exchange.

In the 1980s, investments in energy supply (electricity, coal, oil and gas) amounted to more than 30% of public investment budgets in a wide range of Third World countries, with electricity dominating (OTA, Table 1.8, p. 14). Not only is electricity of major significance in the growth of CO_2 emissions (when generation uses fossil fuels), it is also essential for economic development, as Munasinghe (1992) stressed:

> Electric power has a vital role to play in the development process, with future prospects for economic growth being closely linked to the provision of adequate and reliable electricity supplies . . . Based on the OECD example, energy efficiency improvements will continue to reduce the growth of demand for commercial energy in the developing world. However, the 1979–90 trend for electricity demand in the LDCs, and the inability of the OECD countries to significantly decouple electricity use from GDP in the past, suggest that the growth-related power needs of the LDCs will increase rapidly in the future . . .
>
> In the medium term, assuming no drastic changes in past trends with respect to demand management and conservation, the World Bank's most recent projections indicate that the demand for electricity in LDCs will grow at an average annual rate of 6.6% during the period 1989–99 . . . This compares with actual growth rates of 10% and 7% in the seventies and eighties, respectively . . .
>
> In comparison with the total projected annual requirement for LDCs of $75 billion, the present annual rate of investment in developing countries is only around $50 billion. Even this present rate is proving difficult to maintain. Developing country debt which averaged 23% of GNP in 1981, increased dramatically to 42% in 1987 and has not declined significantly since then. Capital-intensive power sector developments have played a major role in the growth of national debt.

In the light of this, it is clearly necessary to look very carefully at the plausibility of the Third World energy developments that underly the GHG emission scenarios that are being constructed.[23]

Even if actual electricity growth rates do turn out to be lower than projected, this does not, however, necessarily imply that Third World policy-makers will select electricity generation options that minimize CO_2 emissions, particularly where such options significantly increase generation costs and/or foreign exchange requirements. For example, coal is the major domestic energy resource in China, the world's third largest energy consumer and producer, and is expected to remain the dominant fuel well into the next century;[24] coal is also India's major domestic energy resource and figures largely in scenarios to 2030.[25] As Munasinghe (1992) suggested, the combination of the high priority accorded to increasing electricity supplies and a shortage of investment resources is likely to mean that there will be difficulties in allocating resources to environmental programmes, including CO_2 abatement.

VIII   GHG EMISSIONS IN SPECIFIC COUNTRIES

This Section considers current and future GHG emissions in specific Third World countries. There is a fairly broad set of available data relating to existing GHG emissions at the country level. For example, the World Resources Institute (WRI, 1991) presented data on sources of current anthropogenic GHG emissions and on estimated net additions to the greenhouse heating effect in 1986 or 1987 (for CO_2, methane and CFCs) for more than 100 countries (although, of course, there are gaps in some cases).[26] As an example, Table 6.7 shows data for the top 20 countries in the World Resources 'Greenhouse Index' for 1987. The Index combines each country's annual emissions of CO_2, methane, CFC_{11} and CFC_{12} into an aggregate score, with each gas weighted according to its estimated contribution to global warming. The top 20 countries include eight Third World countries, of which three—Brazil, China and India—are ranked in the top five (the others are Indonesia, Mexico, Burma, Colombia and Thailand).

It is important to note, however, that data on GHG emissions in the Third World are both uncertain and contentious. For example, the WRI CO_2 data for Brazil are dominated by estimates of the contribution from deforestation, which are acknowledged to vary strikingly from year to year and according to estimation methodology.[27] Moreover, both WRI's estimation methods and the interpretation of the results have been challenged (Agarwal and Narain, 1991; McCully, 1991). McCully suggested that the estimates are particularly unfavourable to Third World countries by exaggerating their responsibility for contributions to global emissions, thus making it possible to claim that the industrialized countries and the Third World share this responsibility equally; and that WRI's claim that their index is particularly suitable for diplomatic purposes and could form the basis for international agreements[28] is specious. McCully criticized the way in which WRI deals with the problem of deciding the time scale over which the contribution of each GHG to global warming is estimated.[29] He also claimed that combining each country's emissions of each GHG into a single measure in the index helps to put the emphasis for international negotiation on a 'comprehensive approach' to GHG emission limitation (favoured by the

Table 6.7 Top 20 countries in the WRI Greenhouse Index for 1987.

Country	Greenhouse Index rank	Greenhouse gases[a]			Total	Percentage of total	Per capita emissions
		CO_2	CH_4	CFCs			
United States	1	540 000	130 000	350 000	1 000 000	17.6	4.2
USSR	2	450 000	60 000	180 000	690 000	12.0	2.5
Brazil	3	560 000	28 000	16 000	610 000	10.5	4.3
China	4	260 000	90 000	32 000	380 000	6.6	0.3
India	5	130 000	98 000	700	230 000	3.9	0.3
Japan	6	110 000	12 000	100 000	220 000	3.9	1.8
West Germany	7	79 000	8 000	75 000	160 000	2.8	2.7
United Kingdom	8	69 000	14 000	71 000	150 000	2.7	2.7
Indonesia	9	110 000	19 000	9 500	140 000	2.4	0.8
France	10	41 000	13 000	69 000	120 000	2.1	2.2
Italy	11	45 000	5 800	71 000	120 000	2.1	2.1
Canada	12	48 000	33 000	36 000	120 000	2.0	4.5
Mexico	13	49 000	20 000	9 100	78 000	1.4	0.9
Myanmar (Burma)	14	68 000	9 000	0	77 000	1.3	2.0
Poland	15	56 000	7 400	13 000	76 000	1.3	2.0
Spain	16	21 000	4 200	48 000	73 000	1.3	1.9
Colombia	17	60 000	4 100	5 200	69 000	1.2	2.3
Thailand	18	48 000	16 000	3 500	67 000	1.2	1.2
Australia	19	28 000	14 000	21 000	63 000	1.1	3.9
East Germany	20	39 000	2 100	20 000	62 000	1.1	3.7

Source: McCully (1991, Table 1, p. 158). Data from 'Climate Change: A Global Concern' in *World Resources, 1990–91*, World Resources Institute, Washington, DC (1990). The emission figures are not the actual amounts emitted but 'net' emissions as calculated by WRI. WRI do not give *per capita* figures in the same table.

[a] CO_2 heating equivalents (thousand tonnes of carbon).

US, and which would permit increases in CO_2 to be offset by already agreed decreases in CFCs), rather than on a convention which deals separately with each gas (favoured by the EC and a number of other countries).[30]

The controversy aroused by the WRI index of current emissions brings into relief the political importance that attaches to estimates of GHG emissions, particularly those of Third World countries. However, although aggregate scenarios have been prepared, as yet there are no available comprehensive estimates of *future* individual country contributions to match the WRI current emissions data.[31] The existence of such estimates matters, both at national and international levels, because it is hard to see how sensible emission limitation strategies can be prepared without them.

There are, however, a limited number of country-level emission case studies available, including that of Sathaye and Ketoff (1991) for nine countries plus the six member countries of the Gulf Cooperation Council, that of Ledic (1991) for China, and that of Mathur (1991) for India. For example, Table 6.8 shows the carbon emission estimates reported by Sathaye and Ketoff for nine countries for a base year (1985) and for two 2025 scenarios ('high emissions' and 'low emissions'—the latter's purpose is to examine how far CO_2 emissions could reasonably be lowered in a world where global warming was accepted as a major problem).[32] In both scenarios industry is the main contributor to carbon emissions, then transport and the residential sector. Residential sector emissions increase fastest as people switch from biomass to modern fuels.

Partly because of the highly skewed nature of the distribution of Third

Table 6.8 Carbon emissions by country (million tonnes of carbon).

	1985	2025	
China	480	1700	1370
India	115	700	615
Mexico	80	230	160
Brazil	45	140	70
Korea	45	170	110
Indonesia	25	130	105
Venezuela	25	110	85
Argentina	25	40	30
Nigeria	10	50	40
Total	845	3275	2570

Source: Sathaye and Ketoff (1991, Table 17, p. 193).

World GHG emissions, such studies confirm that significant reductions in the overall rate of growth of these emissions could result from reductions by a small number of major emitters and by concentrating on particular sectors. For example (Touche Ross, 1991, p. 67):

> There are particular countries (notably China, India and Brazil) and sectors (particularly electricity generation, industrial energy users and deforestation) which can be targeted to achieve a large proportion of the potential reductions.

In Sathaye and Ketoff's study, the transport sector displayed the biggest relative potential for carbon reductions but the authors pointed out that the promising sectors for reducing carbon intensity and/or switching fuels vary across countries, depending on the growth rate and potential for reducing fuel use in each sector. In their view (Sathaye and Ketoff, 1991, p. 195):

> The primary avenue for the reduction of carbon emissions in the developing countries will be through improvements of energy efficiency, and only to a minor extent through fuel switching. Of the 23% reduction in carbon emissions between the HE and LE scenarios by 2025, 19% is because of efficiency improvement and only 4% because of fuel switching.

Thus it is evident that to make major cuts in the growth rate of Third World emissions, it would be sufficient to have a few key countries taking action. However, while only a few large countries are likely to be major players in terms of controlling emissions, many other Third World countries have an interest in the benefits of limiting global warming and, therefore, a desire to have control strategies implemented. There is, therefore, a significant asymmetry which is likely to influence the conduct and outcomes of international negotiations, both at UNCED in 1992 and beyond.

The next Section considers briefly this question of the vulnerability of different Third World countries and regions to the effects of climate change. GHG control costs and their implications for Third World countries are then considered.

IX THIRD WORLD VULNERABILITY TO THE IMPACTS OF CLIMATE CHANGE

The industrialized countries are motivated to act on the threat of global warming because a high level of environmental concern has become a part of their policy environment and they have the resources to translate that concern into some form of action—even if they are not yet sure how much insurance it makes sense to obtain, or who will pay. When considering how Third World countries could be affected by and respond to the impacts of climate change, the particularly vulnerable regions include parts of the semi-arid tropics, some humid tropical and equatorial regions, and delta regions and islands (Touche Ross, 1991, p. 15). Third World countries can undertake a variety of adaptive measures to cushion them from the adverse effects of climate change. Responses will be needed in the three key areas: temperature rise, shifting rainfall patterns and sea-level rise. The main sectors of concern are agriculture, forestry, buildings and construction. Table 6.9 summarizes the impacts and opportunities for adaptation in five major regions.

Figure 6.7 represents a way of classifying countries according to their degree of vulnerability to adverse socioeconomic effects resulting from climate change (vertical axis) and the size of their contribution to GHG emissions (horizontal axis). Note the position of India and China in the southeast quadrant. Touche Ross (1991, p. 14) draw this conclusion:

> The analysis highlights that few of the developing countries which contribute most to greenhouse gas are also those which are most vulnerable. There is

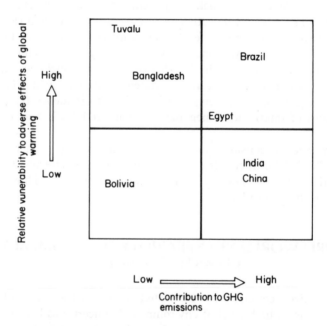

Figure 6.7 Vulnerability to climate change and contribution to GHG emissions (Touche Ross, 1991, Fig. 4.1, p. 14).

therefore little external pressure on significant GHG emitters arising from local adaptation problems. External incentives may be required.

It follows that for industrialized countries seeking the cooperation of major Third World emitters, the problem lies particularly with countries that combine high GHG emissions with relatively low vulnerability. It is this type of country that is likely to seek substantial assistance, both financial and technical, before it agrees to initiate a programme to slow the growth in emissions. Such a country will tend to argue that the present value of the control costs will otherwise substantially outweigh the benefits it may experience from reduced damage.

Part of the difficulty here, of course, is that so far there have been few attempts to undertake the challenging task of estimating the value of the damage from global warming, even for industrialized countries. At a grander level, however, Nordhaus (1991a) produced an 'order-of-magnitude estimate' of the impacts of global warming on the world economy. He estimated damage costs for a doubling of CO_2-equivalent concentrations and a 3°C rise in global mean surface temperature and associated climate changes. He based his estimates on data for the USA and then extrapolated to the rest of the world, to produce global estimates for 2050.[33] These estimates suggest that the flow of damages amounts to about 0.25% of current US national income, while unmeasured and unmeasurable impacts could increase this to 1% or at most 2% of total global output, although the latter figures are 'no more than an informed hunch'. Nordhaus (1991a, p. 930) noted that:

A full assessment of the impact of greenhouse warming must, of course, include regions outside the United States. To date, studies for other countries are fragmentary, and it is not possible to make any firm conclusions at this time. A preliminary reading of the evidence is that other advanced industrial countries will experience modest impacts similar to those of the United States. On the other hand, small and poor countries, particularly ones with low population mobility in narrowly restricted climatic zones, may be severely affected. Much more work on the potential impact of climate change on developing countries needs to be done.

As noted earlier, it is clear that the current international discussions are being conducted against a backdrop of woefully incomplete data on anticipated future emissions levels and damage costs.

After this short discussion of the damage associated with climate change (and thus the benefits from avoiding this damage), the next Section turns briefly to the other side of the calculation, i.e. to some recent estimates of the costs of slowing climate change. It then brings the cost and benefit estimates together to look at efficient policies for GHG emission reductions.

Table 6.9 Third World country adaption: climate change concerns by region.

Major climatic impacts	Regional significance					Opportunities for adaptation
	Sub-Saharan Africa	Indian subcontinent	South East Asia	Mediterranean	Indian Ocean, Caribbean and Pacific Islands	
Average rainfall (could be positive or negative)	xxxx Rain crucial to agriculture and water supply, especially in semi-arid areas	xxxx As in Africa	xx More diversified economies than Africa/Asia	xxx Water supply a major concern (e.g. Malta)	xx Fresh water supply often a concern	Improved water storage/supply/distribution systems; genotype shifts in crops, livestock and forests; erosion control and watershed management
Higher temperature	xx Increased evaporation loss; spread of tropical diseases	xx As in Sub-Saharan Africa	x As in Sub-Saharan Africa	x Some impact on tourism and water supply	x As in Sub-Saharan Africa and the Mediterranean	Irrigation efficiency; improved pest and disease control (man, crops, livestock)
Frequency of drought	xxxx Especially in semi-arid areas	xxxx In rain-fed agricultural areas	xx As in the Indian subcontinent	xx Domestic water supplies	xx As in the Mediterranean	Improved natural national/international food security measures; shift of international agricultural research to semi-arid tropics

Other aspects of variability (frequency of river flood)	x	xxxx Critical for Indus/Ganges basin	xxx Mekong and tributaries	xx Nile floods	x Flash floods on larger islands	Improved disaster preparedness systems; expanded credit/savings facilities for rural poor; housing design; infrastructre works (?)—but often massive changes required
Lower frequency of frost	x Cash crops in cool highlands					
Greater intensity of tropical storms	xx Indian Ocean coast	xxxx Cyclones in Bay of Bengal	xxx Typhoons	x	xxxx Hurricane intensity	International cyclone early warning systems; improved designs for buildings and construction
Sea level rise	xx Some delta regions, mangroves and coral reefs affected	xxxx Ganges and Indus delta especially	xx Vulnerable areas in Indo China, Malaysia, Indonesia	xxxx Nile delta; also recreation, beaches and tourism	xxxx Maldives, Pacific atolls, etc.	Infrastructure works; migration; control of related hazards: health, salinity, etc.

Source: Touche Ross (1991, Fig. 4.2, p. 17). Data adapted from Commonwealth Secretariat. *Key:* **xxxx**, priority concern; **xxx**, substantial concern; **xx**, concern; **x**, lesser concern. The classification is based on highly speculative guesses as to impacts and to their weighting. The severity of concern reflects several factors: the likelihood of change taking place; the importance of climate-sensitive activities in the region concerned; and their capacity to adjust (hence the poorest countries have obviously greater levels of concern for a given change).

X   CONTROL COSTS FOR REDUCING GHG EMISSIONS

The estimation of GHG emission control costs is not a simple matter. For several reasons estimates are both uncertain and subject to revision over time. Nevertheless, some figures are beginning to appear and Nordhaus (1991b)[34] reviewed a number of studies and used a variety of data to produce estimates of the marginal and average costs of reducing GHG emissions. As Nordhaus noted, the underlying 'GHG-reduction cost function' would include the cost of changing from fossil to non-fossil fuels, the substitution of different substances for CFCs, or the costs of removing CO_2 by growing trees. Nordhaus provided estimates of the costs of reducing CFC and CO_2 emissions and enquired into the costs of using forestry options to remove CO_2 from the atmosphere.

Nordhaus began with CO_2 and showed the marginal cost of reducing emissions as a function of the percentage reduction from a baseline path (this relationship is also the same as the relationship between a uniform carbon tax and CO_2 reduction).[35] He obtained his 'consensus' estimate by fitting an equation to a range of cost estimates from a set of nine econometric and mathematical programming studies. CFC mitigation cost estimates were derived from a range of proxy price elasticities of demand for CFCs. Nordhaus also developed estimates for various forestry options, including (a) 'tree bounty' (subsidies to encourage tree harvesting) and (b) 'tree pickling' programmes to sequester carbon, and (c) programmes to afforest or reforest open areas. Significantly, however, Nordhaus offered no cost estimates relating to reductions in tropical deforestation, although he acknowledged the scale of deforestation's contribution to CO_2 emissions. Noting that much tropical deforestation is thought to be uneconomic without invoking climatic impacts, he suggested that the stopping of uneconomical deforestation could 'significantly and inexpensively' slow greenhouse warming.

Figure 6.8 illustrates Nordhaus' estimates of the marginal and total costs of percentage reductions of total GHGs.[36] It shows marginal cost curves for the three reduction options and an 'all-GHG' marginal cost curve representing the most efficient combination of the three options. The cost estimates of marginal and total costs suggest that while a small reduction in GHG emissions is obtainable at relatively low cost, so that a 10% reduction comes at a marginal cost of less than $10 per tonne of CO_2-equivalent and a total cost of $2.2 billion, the costs then begin to rise sharply. Thus a 50% reduction has marginal costs of $120 per tonne and a total cost of almost $200 billion per year in 1989 dollars, or around 1% of 1989 world output.[37]

Armed with estimates of both the marginal damage from GHG emissions

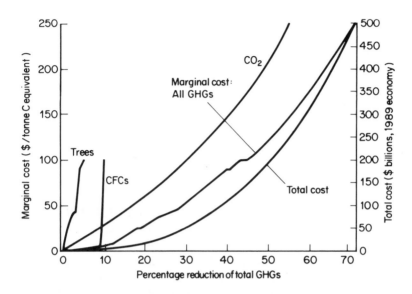

Figure 6.8 Marginal and total costs of GHG reduction (Nordhaus, 1991a, Fig. 2, p. 929).

and the marginal costs of reducing them, Nordhaus was then able to explore policies for GHG reduction that are efficient, in the sense that marginal damage equals marginal cost. For the three damage estimates mentioned earlier he estimated the efficient policy and derived the associated percentage GHG reduction. He summarized his findings as follows (Nordhaus, 1991a, p. 936):

> For the low damage function, which includes only identified costs and uses a middle discount rate, we estimate the marginal damage of greenhouse gases to be about \$1.83 per tonne of C in CO_2 equivalent, which suggests very little CO_2 abatement. For the medium damage function, which assumes damage from greenhouse warming of 1% of GNP, the cost is reckoned at \$7.33 per tonne carbon; in this case, the efficient reduction is 11% of total GHG emissions. In this case, CFC emissions are substantially reduced, and CO_2 emissions are reduced by about 2%. In the high damage case, with damages taken to be 2% of total output and with no discounting, GHG emissions are reduced by about one-third.

For all their acknowledged simplifications and shortcomings, Nordhaus' estimates are interesting in the context of the position of Third World countries. Firstly, if the low-damage estimate were to be accepted as the basis for action, then the industrialized countries would be much less concerned about cooperation from the major Third World emitters than they would need to be in the case of the high-damage estimate. Secondly, Nordhaus' exclusion of the costs of slowing tropical deforestation from his GHG reduction cost estimates is a gap that is potentially significant both for the size of his estimates and for the participation in climate conventions of Third World countries with high rates of deforestation.

The next Section considers studies that have estimated the economic impacts of particular types of control policy and levels of control on groups of countries. Such studies provide some insights into the willingness of Third World countries to participate in different types of GHG control strategies.

XI   ESTIMATED IMPACTS OF GHG CONTROL STRATEGIES

In a recent paper, Manne and Richels (1991) examined how the costs of a CO_2 emissions limit might vary among regions between 1990 and 2100. They used a model, Global 2100, based on parallel estimates for five groups of countries: the USA, other OECD countries (OECD), the USSR and Eastern Europe, China, and the rest of the world, including the oil exporters.[38] After preparing an unconstrained emissions scenario in which the share of the industrialized nations in global CO_2 emissions drops from more than 70% to less than 50% (see Figure 6.4 above), Manne and Richels explored the impacts of a carbon emissions limit on each of the five regions. They considered scenarios that assumed a 20% reduction by the industrialized countries, a doubling or quadrupling by China, and a doubling by other Third World countries. This results in a 15–37% rise in global emissions between 1990 and 2030 but no further increase thereafter, so that by 2100 global emissions are 25–30% of what they would otherwise have been.

Using Global 2100, Manne and Richels analysed the impacts of rising energy costs on each region and estimated the annual losses resulting from the carbon constraint. Figure 6.9 illustrates these losses as a percentage of GDP for the case where China and the 'rest of the world' group limit their emissions to twice their 1990 levels. It is striking that whilst all regions begin to experience significant losses after 2000, the non-USA OECD countries suffer least over the full period, with losses in the range of 1–2% of GDP, while China's annual GDP losses would be more than 10% by the second half of the 21st century. For China, the principal alternatives to coal in a carbon-constrained energy future would be high-cost supply substitutes and price-induced conservation.

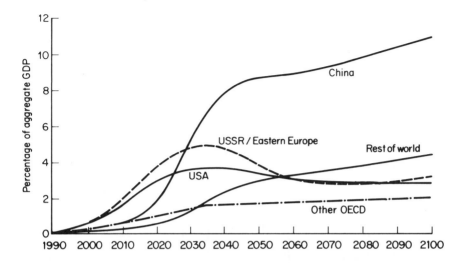

Figure 6.9 Annual losses due to carbon limit (Manne and Richels, 1991, Fig. 6, p. 100).

Suppose it were decided to adopt a criterion of equal percentage GDP losses across all regions. Manne and Richels' results suggest that a quadrupling of emissions would be required for China.[39] Interestingly, China would not necessarily do better under a criterion based on population. For example, a 20% global emissions reduction (Figure 6.10) would imply huge reductions by the industrialized countries, especially the USA, while the 'rest of the world' group could double their emissions but China would not even double—let alone quadruple—hers.[40]

Manne and Richels also investigated the size of the carbon tax that would be required to achieve the scenario depicted in Figure 6.9. The long-term equilibrium tax is the same in all regions, at $250 per tonne of carbon.[41] However, there are significant regional differences in the time paths to this long-term level. This suggests the opportunity for international trade in emissions rights, since the regions that are having the most difficulty in adjusting (and so experiencing higher tax rates) should be willing to buy emissions rights from regions that are experiencing less difficulty. For example, before 2020 all the industrialized regions would be net buyers of emissions rights.

A different set of estimates was produced by Whalley and Wigle (1991), using a computable general equilibrium model with trade effects, three regions ('developed world', 'developing world' and 'oil exporters'), and an assumed 50% reduction in CO_2 emissions. They estimated the impacts on regional welfare, tax revenues and trade of four different carbon tax regimes

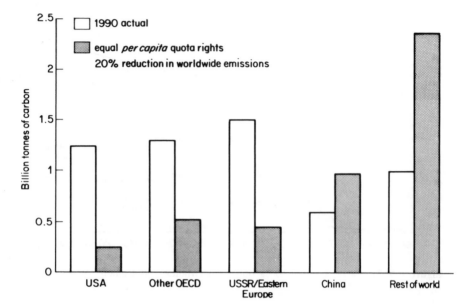

Figure 6.10 Actual carbon emissions in 1990 and with imposition of equal *per capita* quota rights.

designed to achieve this target. Amongst other conclusions, they suggested (Whalley and Wigle, 1991, p. 123) that while the use of:

> . . . *per capita* emissions ceilings may have an appeal from an equity point of view, such a policy could cause a severe distortion of trade patterns, with the production of energy-intensive products shifting from the developed to the developing countries . . . In terms of the sum of the region welfare changes criteria, the most equitable of the '*per capita* ceilings' approaches (. . .) fares the worst in terms of efficiency, perhaps partly due to the implied distortion.

Whalley and Wigle also observed that the oil exporters lose significantly (more than 20% of GNP) under all of the tax alternatives except for production taxes, which generate substantial revenue for them. As an article in the *Economist* suggested, in commenting on another paper by Whalley and Wigle,[42] this implies that the support of the oil exporters (including the Soviet Union and Saudi Arabia) for a carbon tax may need to be bought—and this adds further complexity to international negotiations towards GHG limitations.

There is no reason to assume that bold, speculative estimates such as those of Manne and Richels and of Whalley and Wigle, are an accurate representation of the future. Nonetheless, they do emphasize two points: that there is a very real concern that meeting stringent limitations on GHG emissions could be very costly for large Third World emitters; and that it will be difficult to find equitable strategies limiting GHG emissions that are also efficient.

XII THIRD WORLD PARTICIPATION IN GHG EMISSION LIMITATION STRATEGIES

It has been seen that there are good reasons why the industrialized countries that are concerned about the dangers of global warming should wish to secure the participation of Third World countries, particularly the big emitters, in GHG limitation strategies. There are also reasons why the big emitters are likely to be very disturbed about the potential impact of a 'carbon constraint' on their economic welfare. On the other hand, there are also numerous, often small, Third World countries that have little to offer in the way of GHG limitations but are vulnerable to the impacts of climate change and so might wish to see a successful limitations convention agreed. Elsewhere (Pearson, 1991b), I have looked in more detail at some of the reasons why many Third World countries might wish to set less stringent GHG emission limitation targets than industrialized countries.

Any agreement seems likely to involve some kind of compensation or assistance directed towards Third World countries. Such assistance could come in a number of forms. One is simply funding to enable Third World countries to pursue energy efficiency and fuel switching paths, including the purchase of imported technology. The other is facilitating technology transfer and local production of the latest energy- and pollution-efficient technology. Partly because of the problems that Third World countries already face in financing energy efficiency, it has been suggested that funding connected with reducing emissions should concentrate on assisting those energy projects which these countries would in any case find attractive, if it were not for barriers to implementation that tend to inhibit them (Festa and Cochrane, 1991). A problem here for the development of international agreements might be the reluctance of companies in the industrialized world to transfer their most up-to-date technology to the Third World.

What can be said here about the power of international funding to influence the pattern of Third World energy use and GHG emissions? Clearly it could influence project selection (e.g. towards energy investments that restrict CO_2 emissions) in a number of ways: international funding has done so in the past when, for example, the World Bank favoured particular types of energy project, such as big dam hydroelectricity. Suppose, for example, that a Third World government assesses a greenhouse-friendly project, using standard international *ex ante* discount rates, but rules it out on the grounds of capital scarcity. The decision might then be reversed if the capital constraint could be relieved through foreign borrowing and/or aid at preferential terms, offered by an international organization. But would this changed pattern endure? It has been argued that in times of economic difficulty, staff and funding for fledgling environmental agencies in Third World countries are the first to be cut back: for example, the Brundtland Commission suggested that conservation always takes a back seat in time of stress. Part of the reason for this may be that often only a part of the funding (or the early stages of the funding) is supported from overseas. Thus when the project is underway and if funds become short, Third World countries cut back on investments that would have been low on their list of priorities in the absence of external funding—now that the internal element dominates, they revert to the original priorities. Thus if international funding is agreed to promote energy efficiency and fuel switching, it is important that it be sustained over the long term.

XIII   CONCLUSIONS

There are a number of other important issues which would merit at least a chapter in themselves. Here I want simply to raise them and to acknowledge their importance:

(1)   What ought Third World countries, in the interests of their own sustainable development, to aim for in terms of GHG limitation strategies?

(2)   What should and will they negotiate for at UNCED in 1992 and in later negotiations? How far will action on GHGs be tied in with both wider environmental issues and with issues of poverty, trade and development, as many Third World countries would like and as a number of industrialized countries are seeking to avoid?

(3)   What are the Third World countries likely to be offered at UNCED? Will it, for example, be limited technology transfer but no cash? There is perhaps the possibility of a mutually satisfying compromise here: for example, Third World countries get the technology they want at prices they can afford, and possibly enhanced access to modern markets, while industrialized countries get acceptable limitations on Third World emissions growth. However, current impressions suggest that

the bargaining will be tough and may be polarized, thus reducing the likelihood of mutually satisfying outcomes.

(4) Finally, in what sense is global warming different from the problems of natural resource degradation that are exacerbated by external pressures of trade and debt? At first sight it looks to be a very different problem, but it is worth asking whether and how trade relations and debt burdens might be forcing Third World countries more rapidly down a particular GHG emissions path than they would otherwise choose.

Everything we know about the nature and scale of global warming suggests that it will be an unprecedentedly difficult problem to tackle. It remains to be seen whether appropriate and workable mechanisms to regulate the global atmospheric commons can be developed. The suitability of existing institutions for this task has been rightly disputed.

NOTES

1 See for example, Pearson (1991a).

2 This is sometimes known as the 'natural debt' argument.

3 For example, as the earth's surface gets hotter evaporation produces water vapour (a GHG—hence positive feedback), but also more cloud which could either (a) reflect incoming solar radiation (negative feedback) or (b) trap outgoing infra-red radiation (positive feedback) (Everest, 1989, p. 177).

4 Annex F of OECD/IEA (1991) contains a useful 'Summary of Key Commitments and Recommendations by Major International and National Entities on Climate Change as of April 1990', including brief descriptions of the major relevant international organizations and entities.

5 The discussions below of the findings of the IPCC Working Groups draw closely on the summaries in various issues of *The Environment Digest* (particularly numbers **35/36**, May–June 1990), and to a lesser extent on Touche Ross (1991).

6 Gribbin (1990a) provides an accessible outline of global climate models. For example, he describes the model set up by Schneider and others, which (Gribbin, 1990a, p. 127):

> . . . divides the surface of the Earth up into a grid of 1920 rectangles, a lattice in which each rectangle covers 4.5° of latitude and 7.5° of longitude (at a latitude of 40°—near Madrid, Beijing or Indianapolis—this corresponds to a rectangle of 500 by 640 kilometres). Then the atmosphere above each rectangle is divided into nine layers, giving a total of 17 280 boxes filling the atmosphere to an altitude of thirty kilometres. The climate parameters (temperature and so on) are specified at the corners of each box. Starting from an appropriate set of numbers spread through this grid to describe the instantaneous pattern of weather around the globe, a Cray XMP supercomputer can calculate a year's 'weather' in simulated thirty-minute steps in about ten hours of real time.

Global climate models obviously demand considerable computing resources and, partly in consequence, they have as yet very low spatial resolution (often 250–500 km-square grids) and simplified physical processes (e.g. several countries could be contained entirely in one box in the lattice, and cloud cover has to be represented as an average over each box). Consequently, such models cannot offer detailed, high-resolution simulations of weather patterns. Nevertheless, according to Gribbin, they (a) provide a reasonable guide to average conditions over the earth and can reproduce real world patterns of wind, rainfall and temperature, and (b) can reproduce patterns of past climates that can be confirmed from geological and other evidence (Gribbin, 1990a, p. 128). For a critical review of a number of the models that have been used to create global warming scenarios, see the *SCOPE 29* report (Bolin *et al.*, 1986).

7 See for example, George C. Marshall Institute (1989); see also Gribbin (1990b) for an outline and critical review of the Institute's approach.

8 OECD/IEA (1991, Fig. 2, p. 16) suggest, on the basis of one set of calculations, that in relative terms if the CO_2 emission per MJ from coal is 1, then oil = 0.82 and gas = 0.57. Estimates of emission factors vary, depending on the particular type of fuel (e.g. there are wide variations in the chemical composition of coals) and on assumptions made about combustion efficiencies (e.g. in the case of biomass fuels). For more detailed discussion and estimates, see OECD/IEA (1991, Annex B) and Grubb (1990, pp. 25–6).

9 See for example, Rosillo-Calle and Hall (1991), who also examine the significant role played by grassland burning in CO_2 emissions.

10 See also Touche Ross (1991, pp. 91–92), who cite estimates of 9% (USAID, 1990) and 18–19% (Houghton *et al.*, 1990) for the contribution of deforestation to global warming. Two of the reasons for the variations between estimates are differences in: (a) estimates of the rates and contributory causes of deforestation; and (b) estimates of biomass in forest stands. Examples given by Touche Ross concerning rates of deforestation include: that the range of estimates of deforestation in Brazil's Amazon (the most important forest area) vary between 1.7 and 8 million ha/year; and that estimates of deforestation rates in India differ by a factor of 23.

11 The potential impacts include increased risk of flooding, coastal erosion, salt-water intrusion and the loss of agricultural land, coastal fisheries and wetlands.

12 See OECD/IEA (1991, pp. 94–95) for a brief discussion of this approach. Although such methods appear currently to be very expensive, OECD/IEA quote a set of cost estimates for the removal of CO_2 from concentrated syngas in integrated coal-gasification combined-cycle power stations which suggest that power costs would rise by about 20% above the existing costs of coal-fired generation.

13 As yet, these options have not been attempted on any scale. As OECD/IEA (1991, p. 95) point out, the former might merely delay the transient build-up of atmospheric CO_2, while the latter is limited by the capacity of available natural reservoirs.

14 Static efficiency relates particularly to the minimization of the costs of limiting GHG emissions, and dynamic efficiency to the strength of incentives to continue to search for ways of limiting future emissions: see for example, Helm and

Pearce (1990); Oates and Portney (1991); Opschoor and Vos (1989); Pearce (1991); and Pearce *et al.* (1991).
15 *Environment Digest* **35/36** (May–June 1990), p. 8.
16 *Environment Digest* **35/36** (May–June 1990), p. 9.
17 *Environment Digest* **35/36** (May–June 1990), p. 9.
18 *Environment Digest* **44** (February 1991), p. 9.
19 The World Energy Conference figure for the Third World's share in global *total* (commercial plus biomass) energy consumption in 1985 was 30% (although the biomass figures for Third World countries are thought to be underestimates) (see OTA, 1991, Table 1.3, p. 9).
20 The potential influence of population growth is illustrated by this comment from the OTA review (1991, p. 11):

> The increase in population alone in developing countries would account for a 75% increase in their commercial energy consumption by 2025 even if *per capita* consumption remained at the same levels.

21 Cited in OTA (1991, p. 9, note 14). The source is the *Emissions Scenarios* document prepared by the Response Strategies Working Group of the IPCC, Appendix Report of the Expert Group on Emissions Scenarios (RSWG Steering Committee, Task A), April 1990. The OTA citation does not say whether the base is global commercial or commercial plus biomass energy consumption—the 23% 1985 figure suggests that it is probably the former.
22 See for example, Boyle (1990).
23 On a more dramatic note, the OTA report (1991, p. 13) comments that:

> The World Bank has estimated that investments of $125 billion annually (twice the current level) will be needed in developing countries to provide adequate supplies of electricity. *This figure represents virtually the entire annual increase in the combined GNP of the developing countries.*

24 Ledic (1991, pp. 382–6) developed scenarios for China up to the year 2030:

> By the year 2030 total power generated is expected to be around eight-and-a-half times the 1988 level, when thermal power from fossil fuel was 80% of the total. . . Thermal power from fossil fuel in 2030 accounts for between 60% and 80% of the total, depending on the assumptions made . . . There is likely to be much development in the production of gas, nuclear energy, hydroelectricity, and other renewables, but the considerable increase in energy demand expected will need large supplies of coal, of which ample reserves are available . . . It is difficult to envisage, even in the long term, under any scenario, any significant reduction in the importance of coal in the Chinese economy.

See also Sathaye and Ketoff (1991).
25 See the 1988–2030 scenarios in Mathur (1991). In his view:

> The most probable scenario is that Indian energy consumption will continue with rapid growth based on commercial fossil fuels dominated by oil for transport and coal for power production, in which case carbon emissions can be expected to increase six-fold over the next forty years (p. 398).
> Total energy consumption in the Indian economy under the business-as-usual

scenario is expected to increase by 60% (over the 1987–88 level) by the year 2000, and then more than treble between 2000 and 2030; CO_2 emissions would increase at a faster rate owing to the growing dominance of coal in the energy mix (p. 430).

See also Sathaye and Ketoff (1991).

26 WRI (1991, Tables 24.1 and 24.2, pp. 346–9).

27 WRI (1990, Table 24.1, note b, p. 347).

28 According to Hammond et al. (1991, p. 12), who developed the index:

> The method that gives rise to the index is straightforward and readily applied by policy-makers. Thus the greenhouse index is ideal for diplomatic (as opposed to scientific) purposes and could serve as the basis for international agreements.

(quoted by McCully, 1991).

29 According to McCully (1991, p. 158):

> A long time-horizon favours countries whose greenhouse gas emissions consist disproportionately of short-lived gases such as methane; a short time-horizon fails to take into account the future importance of long-lived gases such as CFCs. . . This time factor, while difficult to take account of, is of crucial importance in determining responsibility.

30 McCully (1991) provides further references, both to other criticisms of the WRI approach and to WRI responses to them.

31 As Touche Rosse (1991, p. 83) note:

> . . . similar listings for future emission levels under IPCC (or other) forecasts are not (to the best of our knowledge) available. Rather, a limited number of country case studies have been prepared as part of the EIS (Energy and Industry Sub-Group) reference scenario. Other studies have focused on energy projections.

It is, of course, possible to prepare highly aggregated scenarios, without relying on individual country data, on the basis of a few crucial assumptions: for example, split the world into the industrialized countries and the Third World, multiply each group's projected population by assumed future *per capita* energy use to get total energy for the chosen year, split it between different fuels, then apply carbon coefficients to get an estimate of CO_2 emissions.

32 For a variety of reasons, these data are not directly comparable with the WRI 1987 data shown in Table 6.7 above. This is a good illustration of the difficulties of working with GHG emissions data.

33 To quote (Nordhaus, 1991a, p. 930):

> In the damage estimates that follow, we will make the simplifying assumption that the damage applies to world GNP in 2050, and that the composition of 2050 world GNP is the same as United States GNP in 1981.

34 See also Nordhaus (1991a).

35 Nordhaus (1991b, p. 42) clarified the nature of the costs:

> Note the 'costs' in these estimates in principle represent the *gross* resource cost or dead-weight loss to the economy of imposing CO_2 constraints. They are gross in the sense that they do not include any correction, plus or minus, for improvements in economic

welfare due to slower climate change, nor do they include adjustments for any other externality, such as that due to CFC accumulation and ozone depletion. In addition the costs are distinct from the budget impact of any carbon or energy taxes that might be levied.

36 Nordhaus (1991b) showed the marginal and total cost curves in two separate diagrams.

37 Nordhaus (1991b, p. 63) noted, moreover, that:

This estimate is understated to the extent that the implementing policies are inefficient or that they are undertaken in a crash program.

He also emphasized the 'tentative nature' of the estimates but asserted that notwithstanding various weaknesses, his figures do provide a 'rough estimate' of the costs that must be met to slow the pace of global warming through conventional emission reductions.

38 In each region, the analysis is based on ETA-MACRO, a model which merges a process model for energy technology assessment with a macroeconomic growth model allowing for substitution between capital, labour and energy.

39 As Manne and Richels (1991) noted, the case of China highlights the difficulty of achieving even a 20% cut in global CO_2 emissions. Their calculations suggest that if China and the 'rest of the world' group were allowed to double their emissions, then to get a 20% global cut would require the industrialized countries to reduce their emissions by more than 70%. Moreover, if China were to quadruple its emissions, the industrialized countries would need to cut theirs to zero.

40 For further discussion of different types of emissions reduction criteria, see also Toman and Burtraw (1991).

41 This is much higher than would be indicated by the Nordhaus marginal cost curve in Figure 6.8 above.

42 *The Economist* (26 January 1991, p. 71).

REFERENCES

Agarwal, A. and S. Narain (1991) *Global Warming in an Unequal World: A Case of Environmental Colonialism*, Centre for Science and Environment, New Delhi.

Allen, M.R. and J.M. Christensen (1990) 'Climate Change and the Need for a New Energy Agenda', *Energy Policy* **18**, 19–24.

Bolin, B., Döös, Jäger, J. and Warrick, R.A. (1986) *The Greenhouse Effect, Climate Change and Ecosystems—SCOPE 29*, Wiley, Chichester.

Boyle, S. (1990) 'Energy and Development', *Oxford Energy Forum* **1**, 3–5.

CEC (Commission of the European Communities) [Directorate-General for Energy] (1990) 'Energy for a New Century: the European Perspective', *Energy in Europe – Special Issue*, July.

Darmstadter, J. (1991) 'Estimating the Cost of Carbon Dioxide Abatement', *Resources* (Spring 1991), 6–9.

Everest, D.A. (1989) 'The Greenhouse Effect: Issues for Policymakers', *Energy Policy* **17**, 177–81.

Festa, D. and J. Cochrane (1991) 'The Role of Aid and Off-Set Mitigation in Limiting CO_2 Emissions in Developing Countries' in P.J.G. Pearson (ed.), *Aid and Energy in the Third World*, Surrey Energy Economics Discussion Papers (SEEDS 56), University of Surrey, Guildford.

George C. Marshall Institute (1989) *Scientific Perspectives on the Greenhouse Problem*, George C. Marshall Institute, Washington, DC.

Gribbin, J. (1990a) *Hothouse Earth: The Greenhouse Effect and Gaia*, Black Swan, London.

Gribbin, J. (1990b) 'An Assault on the Climate Consensus', *New Scientist* 15, 26–31.

Grubb, M. (1989) *The Greenhouse Effect: Negotiating Targets*, Energy and Environmental Programme, Royal Institute of International Affairs, London.

Grubb, M. (1990) *Energy Policies and the Greenhouse Effect. Vol. 1. Policy Appraisal*, Royal Institute of International Affairs, Aldershot.

Hammond, A.L., E. Rodenburg and W.R. Moomaw (1991) 'Calculating National Accountability for Climate Change', *Environment* 33, 1.

Helm, D. and D. Pearce (1990) 'Assessment: Economic Policy Towards the Environment', *Oxford Review of Economic Policy* 6, 1–16.

Houghton, J.T., G.J. Jenkins and J.J. Ephraims (eds) (1990) *Scientific Assessment of Climate Change*, IPCC/Cambridge University Press, Cambridge.

Ledic, M. (1991) 'China: The Continuing Dominance of Coal' in M. Grubb, P. Brackley, M. Ledic, A. Mathur, S. Rayner, J. Russell and A. Tawbe (eds), *Energy Policies and the Greenhouse Effect. Vol. 2. Country Studies and Technical Options*, Royal Institute of International Affairs, Aldershot.

McCully, X. (1991) 'Discord in the Greenhouse: How WRI is Attempting to Shift the Blame for Global Warming', *Ecologist* 21, 157–65.

Manne, A.S. and R.G. Richels (1990) 'CO_2 Emissions Limits: An Economic Cost Analysis for the USA', *Energy Journal* 11, 51–74.

Manne, A.S. and L. Schrattenholzer (1989) *International Energy Workshop: Overview of Poll Responses*, Stanford University International Energy Project, Palo Alto, CA.

Marland, G. (1989) 'Fossil Fuel CO_2 Emissions: Three Countries Account for 50% in 1986', *CDIAC Communications*, Carbon Dioxide Information Analysis Center, Oak Ridge National Laboratory, TN.

Mathur, A. (1991) 'The Greenhouse Effect in India: Vast Opportunities and Constraints' in M. Grubb, P. Brackley, M. Ledic, A. Mathur, S. Rayner, J. Russell and A. Tanabe (eds), *Energy Policies and the Greenhouse Effect. Vol. 2. Country Studies and Technical Options*, Royal Institute of International Affairs, Aldershot.

Munasinghe, M. (1992) 'Efficient Management of the Power Sector in Developing Countries', *Energy Policy* 20, 94–103.

Nordhaus, W.D. (1991a) 'To Slow or Not to Slow: The Economics of the Greenhouse Effect', *Economic Journal* 101, 920–37.

Nordhaus, W.D. (1991b) 'The Cost of Slowing Climate Change: A Survey', *Energy Journal* 12, 37–65.

Oates, W.E. and P.R. Portney (1991) 'Economic Incentives for Controlling Greenhouse Gases', *Resources* (Spring 1991), 13–16.

OECD/IEA (1991) *Greenhouse Gas Emissions: The Energy Dimension*, OECD, Paris.

Ogawa, Y. (1991) 'Economic Activity and the Greenhouse Effect', *Energy Journal* 12, 23–36.

Opschoor, J.B. and H.B. Vos (1989) *The Application of Economic Instruments for Environmental Protection in OECD Member Countries*, OECD, Paris.

OTA (1991) *Energy in Developing Countries, Office of Technology Assessment*, OTA-E-486, US Government Printing Office, Washington, DC.

Pearce, D. (1991) 'The Role of Carbon Taxes in Adjusting to Global Warming', *Economic Journal* 101, 938–48.

Pearce, D.W., E. Barbier, A. Markandya, S. Barrett, R.K. Turner and T. Swansen (1991) *Blueprint 2: Greening the World Economy*, Earthscan, London.

Pearce, D.W., A. Markandya and E.B. Barbier (1989) *Blueprint for a Green Economy*, Earthscan, London.

Pearson, P.J.G. (1991a) 'Common Property, Privatisation and Environmental Policy: The Case of Natural Resource Degradation in the Third World' in W. Weigel (ed.), *Economic Analysis of Law—A Collection of Applications*, Oesterreichischer Wirtschaftsverlag, Vienna.

Pearson, P.J.G. (1991b) 'Externalities, Energy and Environmental Control in the Third World', European Association for Research in Law and Economics: Eighth Annual Conference, Copenhagen, August (mimeo).

Rosillo-Calle, F. and D.O. Hall (1991) 'Biomass Energy, Forests and Global Warming', *Energy Policy* **20**, 124–36.

Sathaye, J. and A. Ketoff (1991) 'CO_2 Emissions from Major Developing Countries: Better Understanding of the Role of Energy in the Long-Term', *Energy Journal* **12**, 161–96.

Skea, J. (1991) 'Editor's Introduction' to 'Climate Change: Policy Implications', *Energy Policy* **19**, 90–93.

Toman, M.A. and D. Burtraw (1991) 'Resolving Equity Issues in Greenhouse Gas Negotiations', *Resources* (Spring 1991), 10–13.

Touche Ross (1991) *Global Climate Change: The Role of Technology Transfer*, report for the United Nations Conference on Environment and Development, HMSO.

USAID (1990) *Greenhouse Gas Emissions and the Developing Countries: Strategic Options and the USAID Response – A Report to Congress*, US Agency for International Development, Washington, D.C.

Whalley, J. and R. Wigle (1991) 'Cutting CO_2 Emissions: the Effects of Alternative Policy Approaches', *Energy Journal* **12**, 109–123.

WRI (World Resources Institute) (1991) *World Resources 1990–91: A Guide to the Global Environment*, Oxford University Press, Oxford.

7 | Aid Effectiveness and Policy*

PAUL MOSLEY,
JOHN HUDSON
and
SARA HORRELL

I INTRODUCTION

Having oscillated between extremes of optimism and pessimism over the last 30 years, the debate over the effectiveness of overseas aid has now settled onto a more pragmatic footing, in which it is accepted that aid effectiveness may vary between countries, reflecting differences both in the economic policy preferences of governments and in the constraints to which aid spending is subject. Intercountry variations in aid effectiveness, it appears from the more recent literature, may be the consequence of variations in (1) the rate of return on projects financed by aid, (2) the allocation of aid by sector, (3) the allocation of aid between capital and recurrent budgets, (4) the influence of aid on relative prices—and thence on private investment—and (5) the rate of return on private capital (Mosley *et al.*, 1987; Cashel-Cordo and Craig, 1990). Any of the factors (2) to (5) may swamp (1), and hence the so-called 'micro–macro paradox': i.e. that most micro results on aid effectiveness are good whereas most macro results are bad, is no real paradox, even if one accepts for the purposes of argument that both micro and macro results are based on sound data. However, some serious gaps remain both in our knowledge of aid effectiveness and in the translation of that knowledge into policy. At the former level, although much effort has been invested by donors in an attempt to persuade

* Paper presented at ESRC Conference on The Economic Analysis of Aid Policy, University of Leicester, 3–4 April 1991.

recipients to liberalize and reform their economic policy, on the presumption that this will have a favourable impact on factors (2) to (5) above and thus on aid effectiveness, there is little information on whether this has in fact happened. Despite the bleak macro evidence on the performance of aid so far, all prescriptions for Sub-Saharan Africa, at least, concur in recommending that its problems can be eased only if there is an *increase* in aid flows. It is urgent to ascertain whether this represents a potentially meaningful strategy, or simply the triumph of hope over experience.

Within this broad field of enquiry, the contribution which this chapter seeks to make is quite deliberately modest. In the first place it uses, for the first time we believe, data for the entire decade of the 1980s, a period during which major changes in development policy were effected which potentially bear on aid effectiveness. Second, it sets out explicitly to ascertain the impact of policy regime on aid effectiveness. Third and last, it seeks to initiate a new approach to the long-term study of aid effectiveness by examining changes in aid effectiveness status between decades, and looking for a pattern in these changes. This last enquiry should be seen as a step towards a procedure in which the structure of lags in the effect of aid—a key empirical issue in the debate—is determined within the model rather than being imposed from outside as at present.

II THE INFLUENCE OF AID AND POLICY REFORM: PRELIMINARY RESULTS

The results of regression analysis of aid and other possible determinants on the growth rate of GDP for the period 1980–8, subdivided by geographical region and income group, are set out in Table 7.1. Note first that the partial regression coefficient of aid on growth is, for the first time according to our measurements,[1] positive and (just) significant. The coefficient is small (for example, if it were to be treated as stable, it would take an increase of 10% in the ratio of aid to GDP for recipient countries to add 1% to their growth rates); also, the fact that the coefficient collapses into insignificance when the sample is subdivided into its geographical component parts is a warning not to expect that a sudden structural change has taken place. There is, however, a hypothesis which is worth pursuing. One of the major threats to the effectiveness of aid is switching into unproductive uses (hypothesis (3) in the Introduction), but switching of aid expenditure into unproductive uses becomes progressively more difficult as the share of aid in the recipient country's development budget increases: finally, a point is reached when the entire development budget is being financed by aid, and switching of aid expenditure out of the use intended by the donor becomes impossible. In Africa, which accounts for nearly one-half of the present sample, this point was reached during the 1980s (Table 7.2); fungibility in most of the continent, therefore, has effectively vanished.

We now consider the role of policy orientation in determining aid effectiveness. It has long been the contention of the World Bank (e.g. World Bank, 1981, 1984, 1987) that an outward-oriented development policy, which opens the economy to international trade and investment, is the key to an effective use of public expenditure, including that part of it which is financed by aid flows. The logic of this position is that only in an open economy can domestic resources be allocated to the uses in which they are relatively most productive, and in pursuit of this logic the Bank and other donors have in recent years made a large proportion of their aid money conditional on the adoption of 'outward-looking' policies (Mosley *et al.*, 1991). However, not all developing countries have been willing to accept conditional aid of this type, and those that have been willing have by no means always implemented the conditions even in a literal sense.[2] A large gap therefore persists between the outward-looking and the inward-looking developing countries, and it is natural to ask whether the level of measured aid effectiveness correlates in any way with the level of outward orientation.

The results of Table 7.1, which incorporate a dummy variable into the regressions which takes the value 0 to 3 according to whether the country in question was classified as 'outward-looking' or 'inward-looking' by the World Bank in its *World Development Report 1987*, appear to contradict the hypothesis that policy orientation has a significant independent influence on aid effectiveness. The regression coefficient of this dummy variable on growth is positive but insignificant for the sample as a whole and for all regional groups; it is *negative* for low-income countries and positive and almost significant for middle-income countries (a point discussed below). However, these results are vitiated by the fact that (as a look at the correlation matrix for the independent variables confirms[3]) there is substantial multicollinearity between the dummy variable and several of the other independent variables. Policy orientation, in other words, although it may appear to have little direct influence on growth, may exercise an indirect influence through its impact on exports, non-concessional financial flows and (as described earlier) aid.

It is not possible to attack a multicollinearity problem directly; however, it is possible to throw some light onto the matter by splitting the scatter of aid and growth observations into four quadrants and then classifying the inhabitants of each quadrant according to their aid effectiveness status, as is done in Figure 7.1. The results are as follows. All of the 'strongly outward-

Table 7.1 Least-squares regression analysis of possible determinants of GDP growth rate 1980–8 for different groups of developing countries.

Sample	Number of observations	Regression coefficients on independent variables:							
		Constant	Aid (as % of recipient GDP)	Other financial flows (as % of recipient GDP)	Savings (as % of recipient GDP)	Growth rate of exports	Growth rate of literacy	Policy openness dummy[a]	r^2
All developing countries in sample	71	−0.10 (0.14)[b]	0.10† (2.19)	0.06 (0.81)	0.08†† (2.70)	0.23†† (6.41)	0.002 (0.05)		0.50
		−0.26 (0.34)	0.096† (2.07)	0.057 (0.77)	0.07† (2.26)	0.21†† (5.23)	0.001 (0.03)	0.28 (0.80)	0.51
Africa only	32	1.52† (1.97)	0.02 (0.46)	0.22† (1.89)	0.01 (0.37)	0.28†† (4.71)	−0.001 (0.19)		0.52
		1.44 (1.62)	0.02 (0.47)	0.22 (1.76)	0.12 (0.36)	0.28†† (4.39)	−0.001 (0.02)	0.08 (0.20)	0.52

Asia only	18	1.75† (0.71)	0.02 (0.10)	−0.21 (0.82)	0.07 (1.00)	0.31† (2.59)	−0.01 (1.16)		0.58
		1.88 (0.73)	−0.002 (0.11)	−0.30 (0.86)	0.06 (0.70)	0.28† (1.95)	−0.01 (0.98)	0.38 (0.40)	0.59
Latin America and Caribbean	21	−2.56 (1.23)	0.25 (1.18)	0.094 (1.18)	0.10 (1.22)	0.21† (2.46)	0.01 (0.47)		0.59
		−3.04 (1.36)	0.29 (1.28)	0.097 (1.20)	0.10 (1.18)	0.19† (2.06)	0.01 (0.37)	0.41 (0.69)	0.49
Low-income countries	33	0.67 (0.83)	0.08 (1.14)	0.12 (0.83)	0.10† (2.46)	0.33†† (5.79)	−0.02 (0.32)		0.69
		0.71 (0.85)	0.09 (1.16)	0.13 (0.87)	0.10† (2.43)	0.34†† (5.35)	−0.02 (0.33)	−0.15 (0.31)	0.69
Middle-income countries	38	−1.25 (1.00)	0.04 (0.61)	0.12 (1.42)	0.10 (2.17)	0.21†† (3.70)	0.01 (0.23)		0.56
		−1.92 (1.49)	0.05 (0.73)	0.08 (1.00)	0.09 (1.83)	0.15† (2.18)	0.003 (0.59)	0.85 (1.58)	0.59

Sources: growth: World Bank, *World Development Report 1990*, Table 2; aid, other financial flows: OECD, *Geographical Distribution of Financial Flows to Developing Countries 1981–88* (Paris, 1990); savings: World Bank, *World Development Report 1990*, Table 9; exports: World Bank, *World Development Report 1990*, Table 14; literacy: UNICEF, *The State of the World's Children 1990*, Table 4. All data are annual averages over the period 1980–8. The dependent variable in the regression was the growth of real GDP (% per annum).

[a] Policy openness dummy is the indicator given in the *World Development Report 1987*, p. 83 and characterized as: 0 for 'strongly inward-looking' economies, 1 for 'moderately inward-looking', 2 for 'moderately outward-looking', 3 for 'strongly outward-looking'.

[b] Figures in parentheses are Student's *t*-statistics.

Table 7.2 Overseas aid flows in relation to public expenditure, 1980–7.

	Average per capita income (US$) 1987	Overseas aid inflows as % of:					
		GDP		Public expenditure		Public capital expenditure	
		1980	1987	1980	1987	1980	1987
Sub-Saharan Africa	330	3.5	8.2	19.1	32.0	77.8	138.0
Côte d'Ivoire	740	2.3	3.3	7.4	10.3	22.9	58.9
Ethiopia	130	5.7	13.2	20.3	33.6	145.2	154.8
Kenya	330	6.5	8.1	21.5	25.1	92.9	136.8
Malawi	160	12.7	25.2	33.8	76.0	70.6	368.4
Nigeria	370	0.3	0.3	0.4	1.0	0.8	3.2
Tanzania	180	14.8	28.6	46.0	67.7	113.9	186.5
South Asia	290	2.8	1.9	13.3	8.2	24.3	17.2
All low-income economies	290	3.1	3.0	12.4	11.1	25.8	21.4

Sources: World Bank (1989), Tables 3, 18, 25; *IMF Government Finance Statistics Yearbook 1989.*

looking' economies and a high proportion (55%) of the 'moderately outward-looking' countries are in the low-aid, high-growth quadrant IV; meanwhile, a significant proportion (35%) of the 'strongly inward-looking' countries are in the low-aid, low-growth quadrant I. The differences in apparent policy orientation between the high-aid, low-growth quadrant II and the high-aid, high-growth quadrant III are, however, minimal: the percentage frequency distribution for the two quadrants is shown in Table 7.3. Already, however, Figure 7.1 suggests that it may be appropriate to think of aid effectiveness status as well as policy orientation in terms of a progression determined by stage of development, an idea which provides the key to the approach taken in the Section which follows.

III THE STAGES OF AID EFFECTIVENESS

One problem which remains unresolved in the aid effectiveness literature is the question of the lag structure which should be used. The early literature (e.g. Griffin, 1970; Papanek, 1973) assumed no lags at all; our own procedure (Mosley *et al.*, 1987, and also Table 7.1) has been to assume that all aid (and indeed all other financial flows) operate with the same lag structure as that of World Bank projects, as estimated by the Bank's Operations Evaluation Department in 1984, with the effects being

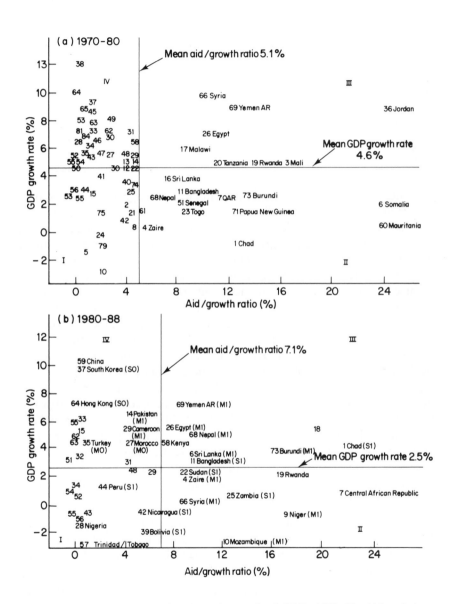

Figure 7.1 Scatter diagrams for aid and growth of GDP, 1970–88. Abbreviations: SO = strongly outward-oriented; MO = moderately outward-oriented; MI = moderately inward-oriented; SI = strongly inward-oriented.

Table 7.3 Percentage frequency distribution for high-aid, high-growth versus high-aid, low-growth countries according to degree of outward orientation (refer to Figure 7.1).

	Strongly outward-oriented	Moderately outward-oriented	Moderately inward-oriented	Strongly inward-oriented	No data
Quadrant III (high-aid, high-growth)	0	14	56	14	14
Quadrant II (high-aid, low-growth)	0	10	50	30	10

distributed over a 7-year period. This is in fact only slightly less heroic than the assumption of no lags at all, since some aid takes effect instantaneously (e.g. food aid, some varieties of import support) and some operates with a very long lag indeed (e.g. agricultural research, aid for family planning, some forms of policy advice). Our particular concern is that the lag structure we are currently using may be biased on the low side, since, to rehearse an old argument, the major function of aid is to build up a framework of infrastructure and knowledge which will allow the market mechanism to operate properly; and this may take many years. To take two positive examples, the success of industrial development in South Korea in the 1970s, and of the Green Revolution in India in the same period, is widely ascribed to aid flows into infrastructure and agricultural research, respectively, that took place two decades previously (Cassen *et al.*, 1986, Chap. 1). To take a negative example, aid flows into Sub-Saharan Africa in the 1980s increased by comparison with the 1970s, while growth rates have fallen; arguably that should be expected, since aid is at present going into the rehabilitation of the export and infrastructure sectors, and until that process is accomplished, a net return on aid should not be expected. Indeed, it is possible to postulate four stages of aid effectiveness, corresponding to the four quadrants of Figure 7.1:

Stage I: here a near-subsistence economy is cut off in large measure from international aid flows through war, political instability and/or mismanagement (e.g. Cambodia and Somalia at present, Uganda and Ghana in the 1970s); hence low aid, low growth.

Stage II: there are increased aid flows, but these take time to filter through into influence on growth rates because of gestation lags, inadequate infrastructure, lags in leverage on policy and so on; hence the measured effect is high aid, low growth (e.g. Tanzania and Mozambique at present).

Stage III: continuing high aid flows become more effective as lags unwind (e.g. Sri Lanka and Papua New Guinea).

Stage IV: some countries graduate out of the need for aid, and hence aid diminishes as growth continues at a high rate (e.g. Botswana, Mauritius, Thailand, and classically South Korea).

Obviously this is an idealized picture, since a number of countries have remained in particular stages for a long time rather than progressing (others indeed, as will be seen, have slipped back); it is also an oversimplified picture, as it omits even those non-aid influences on growth for which it was possible to control in the regression analysis of Table 7.1. Nonetheless, if there is any substance at all to this kind of cycle, then the kind of scatter observed in Figure 7.1, and indeed the partial regression coefficient close to zero which has been observed for 30 years now, are what is to be expected: since at a given time there will be countries in all four quadrants of the cycle, if the number of countries in each quadrant remains more or less equal the aggregate result will be aid neutrality. We now therefore focus on the transitions in aid effectiveness status between decades and put to the test the hypothesis that anticlockwise movement around the quadrants will dominate clockwise movement. The cases of transition in both directions are listed in Table 7.4. It is apparent that:

(1) In both decades, the anticlockwise transitions dominate the clockwise transitions (by 11:4 in the first period and by 13:2 in the second), as the hypothesis predicts.

(2) Broadly speaking, the transitions in aid effectiveness which appear to occur are those which would be expected from background knowledge of the countries concerned; for example, it will surprise few people to know that between the 1960s and 1970s Malawi and Egypt made the transition from quadrant II to quadrant III; and Pakistan, South Korea and Taiwan from quadrant III to quadrant IV. The transitions which occurred between the 1970s and 1980s (Burkina, Bangladesh, Senegal and Papua New Guinea from quadrant II to quadrant III; Egypt and North Yemen from quadrant III to quadrant IV) are more debatable, but are not obviously at odds with available case-study evidence on those countries.

IV INTERPRETATION AND POSSIBLE WAYS FORWARD

The data presented in Table 7.4 are of course purely illustrative, and should be seen as a stimulus to a proper econometric reconsideration of how long a

Table 7.4 Aid effectiveness status transitions from the 1960s to the 1980s (refer to Figure 7.1).

Anticlockwise transitions	Clockwise (perverse) transitions
(a) 1960–70 to 1970–80	
Quadrant I → Quadrant II (increasing aid, continuing low growth)	Quadrant IV → Quadrant III
Nepal	Syria
Quadrant II → Quadrant III (continuing high aid, increased growth in relation to mean level)	Quadrant III → Quadrant II
Mali	Togo
Malawi	Liberia
Tanzania	
Egypt	
Rwanda	
Quadrant III → Quadrant IV (continuing high growth, aid diminishing in relation to mean level)	Quadrant II → Quadrant I
Pakistan	Madagascar
Morocco	
South Korea	
(b) 1970–80 to 1980–90	
Quadrant I → Quadrant II (increasing aid, continuing low growth)	Quadrant IV → Quadrant III
Mozambique	none
Zambia	
Quadrant II → Quadrant III (continuing high aid, increased growth in relation to mean level)	Quadrant III → Quadrant II
Chad	Tanzania
Bangladesh	Syria
Burkina Faso	
Senegal	
Nepal	
Papua New Guinea	
Burundi	
Quadrant III → Quadrant IV (continuing high growth, aid diminishing in relation to mean level)	Quadrant II → Quadrant I
Egypt	none
Yemen	
Kenya?	

lag in effect is to be expected from different types of aid, and to an estimation process in which these lags are generated from within the model rather than imposed from outside. Nonetheless, even at this stage it is possible that the schema presented can contribute in two ways to the aid effectiveness debate. In the first place, it focuses attention on the real problem, which is the countries that do *not* make the transition from quadrant II to quadrant III (or who slip back) even though the other exogenous influences on growth listed in Table 7.1 remain favourable. Examples of countries which fit into this category from the 1960s through the 1980s are Zaire, Togo, Central African Republic, Niger, Tanzania, Haiti and Mauritania. In some of these cases a reason for persisting ineffectiveness has been found in the shape of one or more of the factors (1) to (5) listed in the Introduction (see for example, Mosley *et al.*, 1987, Table 2); where that explanation will not work, there will be a temptation to ascribe the residual to 'policy'.

This is the line of approach adopted in introducing a 'policy openness dummy' into Table 7.1, and the initial results, as has been seen, were not promising, although better in middle-income countries where the policies of liberalization and privatization favoured by aid donors have more relevance than in low-income countries. In any case, there are many more dimensions to development policy than simply the closed/open dichotomy, some of them very mundane—such as the extent to which government is able to maintain basic economic services, and the level of corruption in the civil service. The second way in which we hope to be able to point a way forward is in demonstrating the need for an analysis of the interaction between aid and development policy in this broader sense. The old nostrums which used to pass for knowledge in this area (e.g. 'aid does not augment resources, it merely centralizes power') have now been swept away, without having been replaced by anything else. Analysts in this field are therefore in the uncomfortable position of having to say that aid may sometimes serve as a stimulus to difficult and necessary economic policy decisions, and sometimes as a means of postponing those decisions, but that there is no way of forecasting which way the cat will jump. An understanding of this branch of political economy may therefore be the next bridge which aid donors need to cross if the yield on the money they spend is to be increased.

NOTES

1 In estimates of the same equation against databases for previous decades we obtained the following partial regression coefficients (*t*-statistics in parentheses):

1960–70: $-0.04^{\star}$ (2.12)
1970–80: -0.02 (0.32)

2 The World Bank's estimate (1988, 1990) of the proportion of conditions on their policy-based loans that have been fully carried out is 60%; our own belief is that this is not only an underestimate, but ignores the large number of demands to liberalize policy which have been complied with in a formal sense but evaded by means of countervailing actions (Mosley et al., 1991, Vol. I, Chap. 5).

3 Coefficients for major country groups are:

	1970–80	1980–88
Africa	-0.09	0.22
Asia	0.46	-0.21
Latin America and Caribbean	1.01	0.09

(source: Mosley et al., 1987, Table 3; Table 7.1 above).

REFERENCES

Cashel-Cordo, P. and S. Craig (1990) 'The Public Sector Impact of International Resource Transfers', *Journal of Development Economics* **34**, 17–42.

Cassen, R. and associates (1986) *Does Aid Work?*, Oxford University Press, Oxford.

Griffin, K. (1970) 'Foreign Capital, Domestic Savings and Economic Development', *Oxford Bulletin of Economics and Statistics* **32**, 99–112.

Mosley, P., J. Hudson and S. Horrell (1987) 'Aid, the Public Sector and the Market in Developing Countries', *Economic Journal* **97**, 616–42.

Mosley, P., J. Harrigan and J. Toye (1991) *Aid and Power*, Routledge, London.

Papanek, G. (1973) 'Aid, Private Foreign Investment, Savings and Growth in Less Developed Countries', *Journal of Political Economy* **81**, 120–30.

World Bank (1981) *Accelerating Growth in Sub-Saharan Africa*, World Bank, Washington, DC.

World Bank (1984) *World Development Report 1984*, World Bank, Washington, DC.

World Bank (1987) *World Development Report 1987*, World Bank, Washington, DC.

8 | Is There Still a Latin American Debt Crisis?*

STEPHANY GRIFFITH-JONES

and

RICARDO GOTTSCHALK

I INTRODUCTION

During the decade of the 1980s the external debt of Latin America became a major obstacle to the growth and development of the majority of the countries in the region. In late 1991, 9 years after the external debt crisis started and 2½ years after the Brady initiative was launched, finally significant progress has begun to be made in overcoming this obstacle in a number of these countries, though clearly not yet in all of them. There is now some preliminary evidence that in 1990, there was actually a reversal of the negative net transfer of resources from Latin America and the Caribbean to the creditor countries: a recent OECD study (OECD, 1991) estimated that during 1990, net resource transfers were positive, at $10 billion, for the first time since 1983. The main reason for this reversal was the significant increase in private flows to the region, estimated to have grown by over $8 billion between 1989 and 1990, to reach $24 billion in the latter year. These large increases are reported to have benefited only a small number of countries (essentially Mexico, Chile, Colombia and Venezuela). Should this trend continue, and be spread far more widely throughout the countries of the region, a central element of the region's debt crisis (the

* Paper presented to the Conference on International Aspects of Economic Development, University of Surrey, 18 September 1991.

crippling burden of negative net transfers and their negative effect on the region's development) would be overcome.

Amongst the main reasons for the newly increased private flows to some countries in the region, is the fact that these countries are perceived to have solved their 'old debt' problem; however, this does not seem to be the only reason or precondition, because other domestic conditions (e.g. stable macroeconomic policies, renewed growth prospects, creditworthy private borrowers), as well as international changes (as in the case of Mexico, where there is increased trade integration with the US), also seem to play an important role (CEPAL, 1991). It is furthermore interesting that Brazil, which had not yet reached a Brady or other deal in the first half of 1991, is reported[1] to have attracted far higher private flows than in previous years.

The causal link between satisfactory 'debt deals' and increased private new inflows, though it is clearly very important, is perhaps not unequivocal, as some of the academic literature has argued (see for example, Dooley, 1989; Van Wijnbergen, 1991). In any case, there is now evidence, particularly from Mexico, that at least for some countries there can be a strong *complementarity* between some debt service reduction (for example, via a Brady deal or more traditional debt restructuring) and increased capital inflows, leading to an increase in net external savings for the country. As Massad (1991) pointed out, one of the key preconditions for restoring GDP growth in Latin America in the 1990s to levels around 5% annually, is to increase total savings by around 7% of GDP; to achieve this, both domestic and external savings would have to increase significantly in the region. A significant increase in external savings can best be achieved if *both* significant debt service reduction and increased new capital inflows can be achieved, as now seems increasingly feasible, at least in some countries. There may be a particularly strong case for greater debt reduction in those countries (e.g. possibly smaller ones, which do not have so many large, creditworthy and internationally known corporations) that are more likely to have greater difficulty in attracting greater capital inflows.

It is in this wider, generally more optimistic context that recent progress on debt management needs to be assessed. The next Section examines in some detail and attempts to evaluate the experience of some of the countries in the region. The heterogeneity of current debt management strategies is stressed, differentiating especially between those countries that have entered Brady deals, those which—like Chile—have rescheduled debt outside the Brady context, and those countries which at the time of writing continue with arrears to the commercial banks. Despite the heterogeneity of the situation, some more general conclusions about recent progress can be extracted. Section III attempts to identify outstanding problems and to make policy suggestions, relating mainly to commercial debt but referring also to other categories of debt.

II EVALUATION OF DEBT MANAGEMENT SINCE 1989

As pointed out above, there is greater heterogeneity than in the past in the way in which different countries in Latin America have approached debt management and the extent to which they have, or are perceived to have, overcome the debt problem.

II.1 The Brady deals, with special reference to Mexico

The first category of countries are those that have already signed Brady deals: in Latin America, these include Mexico, Venezuela, Costa Rica and Uruguay. As it would be difficult to evaluate each of these deals in some depth, the present discussion centres on Mexico (which was the first to sign a deal, and for which there is therefore a longer period in which to assess the results and the influence on other deals), with some reference also to Costa Rica, due to its special characteristics.

In December 1988, the Mexican government initiated talks with its various external creditors. Amongst its important objectives (Aspe, 1990) were to reduce the flow of net external resource transfers and to obtain a multiannual agreement in order to reduce the uncertainty caused by recurrent negotiations. The need to reduce negative net transfers was linked to the need to provide more external savings to fund investment and growth. Increasingly emphasized in some of the academic literature, and particularly in *ex post* evaluations, have been the positive indirect effects of what is widely accepted as a satisfactory deal, on both the domestic and the foreign private sector. A multiannual deal which not only reduced debt service but also shifted amortizations for a significant number of years, was seen to reduce uncertainty and provide confidence, for example on the perceived sustainability of the exchange rate, which strongly influences debt service; it was thus hoped that a satisfactory debt deal would significantly lower high domestic interest rates, and also that it would attract additional private flows from abroad (not linked to the deal) and encourage private capital to return. As will be seen, it is this second category, of indirect benefits on domestic interest rates and on capital flows (by foreign and domestic private actions), which have been especially positive in the case of the Mexican deal.

The details of the Mexican deal have been described elsewhere[2] and are summarized in Section IV. The estimates of resulting cash flow savings, based on figures produced by the Mexican Minister of Finance, can be seen in Table 8.1. Total average cash flow savings for 1990–4 are estimated to reach around $4 billion: of these, over one-half are due to restructuring of amortization, and new money, which could have been achieved through the previous conventional restructuring process. However, the savings on interest payments, at around $1.6 billion, are reported to have provided sufficient financing to accommodate a growth target of an average of 4% over 1990–4 (Van Wijnbergen, 1991); naturally, the validity of such a link is based not only on the realism of the econometric macro-model used, but also on developments in the world environment relevant to Mexico, such as the price of oil and international interest rates.

So although the Brady deal obtained by Mexico implied a fairly limited external debt and debt service reduction, and a significantly smaller reduction than Mexico had initially requested,[3] it did seem to provide enough additional foreign exchange liquidity to sustain meaningful growth, given certain assumptions. It should be stressed that the debt service reduction was relatively limited: it represented only around 6% of the country's exports and only around 20% of average interest payments on medium- and long-term debt in the period 1983–8.[4]

The indirect positive effects linked to the removal of uncertainty and restoration of confidence generated by a deal which implies no repayment of amortizations until the one-shot payment in 2019, have been even more important, at least in the short term. Firstly, soon after the announcement of the Mexican Brady package, domestic interest rates fell by almost 20%, presumably because of a reduction in pressure on the exchange rate; they have remained at this level since. Given that the Mexican governments' domestic debt reached $54 billion, domestic interest payments were reduced

Table 8.1 Cash flow savings from the 1989 debt and debt service reduction agreement in Mexico.

Saving	Average 1990–4 ($ billion)
Interest savings	1.6
New money cash flows	0.3
Savings from restructuring of amortizations[a]	2.1
Total cash flow savings	4.1

Source: Aspe (1990).
[a] This includes the deferment of amortizations, originally falling due in this period, to 2019.

by over $9 billion (around 4.5% of GDP) as a result of the decline in interest rates. This both allows higher public investment and encourages higher domestic private investment. Van Wijnbergen (1991) estimated the *additional* positive effect on GDP growth of the decline in domestic interest rates at around 1% initially, increasing to more than 2% by 1994. A note of caution needs to be sounded here; as Reisen (1991) correctly points out, there is room for debate about the extent to which it was just the debt deal which pushed interest rates down in Mexico; furthermore, as the factors determining interest rate declines are not fully established, it is not completely certain that lower interest rates will be maintained throughout the whole period.

A second, but important indirect positive effect, is that on increased foreign private flows, especially foreign direct investment, and return of capital flight. There has been substantial return of capital to Mexico, estimated at $2.5 billion in 1989 and around $5 billion in 1990; additionally, private capital flows (through different non-commercial bank lending modalities) have also increased significantly. The debt deal was thus a very important factor helping to catalyze new flows and return previously fled capital (thus confirming the forecasts of the Mexican government and of writers such as Dooley (1989), Reisen (1991), Sachs and Kneer (1990) and others); however, as pointed out in the Introduction, other factors (such as prospects of FTA with the US and Canada) also seem to have played an important part.

Thus, although they are clearly very welcome, the indirect beneficial effects will not necessarily continue, especially at the same high levels of inflows, particularly should external or internal shocks hit the Mexican economy. The terms of some of these inflows (e.g. cost, maturity) may also not be so appropriate. Further monitoring and research seems to be · required, to determine what factors influence different categories of private inflows, to analyze their suitability to fund development needs, and so on. Finally, as regards other (especially smaller) countries that may sign similar debt deals, doubts must remain whether the indirect positive effects would be as important as have occurred in Mexico.

The Brady deals reached by Venezuela and Uruguay (for details, see Section IV) seem to follow roughly the pattern set by Mexico. The Venezuelan deal had some interesting innovations, such as a new instrument designed to provide debt service relief in the medium term by *temporarily* reducing interest to below-market fixed rates in the first 5 years after the deal. As regards cash flow relief, the Venezuelan Brady deal seems even less favourable than the Mexican deal, with relief estimated by the World Bank to reach only $460 million for the period 1990–4: this amounts to only 2.5% of the country's exports. Although it is too early to judge the indirect effects, there is evidence that at least as regards new private capital inflows, the debt deal in 1990 has had a positive effect.

The Costa Rican debt deal, even though in the context of the Brady Plan, was significantly different from the Mexican, Venezuelan and other packages. The two main features were that the deal has only the options of debt and debt service reduction (and *not* a new money option), and that the level of debt and debt service reduction, in relation to contractual obligations, is very large (it is estimated at around two-thirds of contractual obligations). As regards cash flow savings on interest payments, it should be stressed that they are very close to zero (the World Bank estimates an average yearly net reduction of $70 million for 1990–4) because the country had not been servicing the debt in full for several years. However, the major reduction of debt and debt service achieved may improve private sector expectations (both domestic and foreign) and has also eliminated the highly demanding and time-consuming activity of external debt negotiation, which is particularly costly for small countries, from senior policy-makers' agendas.[5]

The interesting deal achieved by Costa Rica, the bargaining tactics used by the Costa Rican authorities to achieve its debt management objective (including large arrears accompanied by a permanently conciliatory approach to bargaining with creditors), and simultaneous sustained efforts at carrying out prudent macroeconomic policies, seem to offer other small country debtors in the region interesting lessons. Indeed, as Devlin and Guerguil (1991) correctly pointed out, unilateral action to reduce or stop debt servicing is likely to yield better results if it is seen as a step towards reaching a consensual and definitive deal with the creditors, if it is accompanied by a coherent macroeconomic programme, and if a conciliatory attitude is adopted with different categories of creditors, including the commercial banks. Costa Rica skilfully met these preconditions and this seems to have helped it achieve a successful definitive deal. It should perhaps be mentioned that Costa Rica had at the time of the deal specific geopolitical features which made the US government wish to maintain friendly relations.

In the context of the preceding analysis, it is important to examine whether the potential beneficial indirect effects of the other Brady deals analysed—on return of capital flight and increased new inflows of private capital—will be in some way impaired by the fact that Costa Rica was in arrears to the commercial banks for a long time and obtained such a large discount in its debt and debt service reduction. It is still too early to give a definitive judgement but it seems that this will not be a major factor, provided that Costa Rica pursues appropriate economic policies in the future. Possibly a more problematic aspect, in terms of attracting future private flows in some categories (e.g. bonds), may be the limited size of the economy and the limited size of large companies in the country that can attract such funding.

II.2   Other deals

Outside the context of the Brady initiative, more traditional reschedulings of commercial debt slowed down. An important exception was Chile's rescheduling in September 1990. The unique approach by the Chilean authorities can be explained largely by certain particularly favourable features of Chile's recent economic evolution. Chile has for several years had prudent macroeconomic policies and its export growth has been extremely dynamic since 1985. The latter was one important factor responsible for the fall in debt service ratio. The other factor was that before the Brady Plan was announced, Chile drastically reduced its commercial debt, mainly through an active programme of debt–equity swaps and debt buy-backs; indeed, using 1989 data, Chile's debt indicators had improved enough for the World Bank to take Chile out of the severely indebted country category!

Chile's deal was special, not only because it did not include debt and/or debt service relief (but merely the postponement of amortization payments), but also because of the different mechanism through which 'new money' was raised. Instead of obtaining new money via so-called 'involuntary new money', distributed more or less proportionally among existing back creditors, Chile placed bonds (for $320 million) amongst a small number of large creditor banks which have a long-term commitment to funding the country. This mechanism represented an important step in Chile's return to the international capital market; it had the disadvantage of slightly worse conditions (short amortization and somewhat higher interest rate) than more conventional 'new money'.

It is interesting that Chile's debt deal (like that of Mexico) contributed to triggering very important private capital inflows into the economy, which—together with other factors—led by mid-1991 to a sharp increase in foreign exchange reserves. Indeed, in the case of portfolio investment in its various modalities, Chile and Mexico are reported to be the two countries in the region that have attracted most flows. Furthermore, Chile is the first country in the region since 1982 to have attracted a completely voluntary credit (that is, a credit without guarantees, and granted independently of a restructuring of existing debt) from a bank. Though very small, this credit signals the practical return of Chile to creditworthiness; another indicator of this return to creditworthiness is of course the secondary price of Chile's debt, which is at 90% of face value. Indeed, Sachs and Kneer (1990) defined full re-establishment of creditworthiness of a debtor country as occurring when its debt is once again trading at 100%. Chile seems very close to that aim! The overcoming of the debt crisis in Chile is naturally measured not only by balance of payments indicators; more important has been the ability of the Chilean economy to grow at a fairly rapid pace in recent years.

The recent experiences of Chile, Mexico, Venezuela and Costa Rica show that there is perhaps no single optimum path for debtors to return to creditworthiness and growth, but that different paths are better suited to different countries according to their specific circumstances. However, common features of countries apparently returning to creditworthiness and growth after the debt crisis, are fairly prudent macroeconomic policies and relative clarity and consistency about the way in which they wish to handle their external debt problems.

There are other countries in the region where neither of these conditions has been fully met, although significant efforts are being made in both directions. This is particularly well illustrated by the case of Brazil, where at the time of writing there were still serious fiscal and other macroeconomic imbalances *and* an agreement on debt had not been reached with the creditor banks, even though negotiations with the latter were reported to be progressing towards a Brady-type agreement[6] (a preliminary agreement to clear Brazil's arrears with the commercial banks has already been reached). However, even if Brazil were to reach an agreement with its creditor banks for debt and/or debt service reduction of the type and order of magnitude of the Mexican or Venezuelan deal, it is not yet clear—given the magnitude of existing imbalances—whether this would by itself be sufficient to restore creditworthiness and growth. Parallel efforts would be required on the domestic front to reduce macroeconomic imbalances. Should these take place, and should the deal grant enough debt service reduction to make growth likely, then the indirect beneficial efforts described above in some detail for Mexico may also hopefully occur for Brazil. It is encouraging in this sense that there has already been a general increase in private flows to Brazil in 1991, despite the difficult macroeconomic conditions and the unresolved debt situation.[7] Particularly interesting is the fact that a Petrobas Eurobond issue was oversubscribed in August 1991: this was reportedly the first time that a country technically in arrears and with no agreement with its creditors has been able to return to the world capital markets.[8]

Once a deal with Brazil is signed (as now seems likely), the focus of attention of the international banks is likely to turn towards reaching agreement with Argentina. Should such a deal also be concluded by mid-1992, deals for all the major debtors in Latin America would have been reached. Two issues remain unresolved. Will the deals reached in the last 2 years (and particularly those for Brazil and Argentina) imply enough debt reduction, and will they be accompanied by sufficient domestic efforts for stabilization, to allow a sustained return of those countries to growth and creditworthiness? Though there are many grounds for optimism, uncertainties remain whether the positive trends emerging for countries such as Mexico, Chile and Venezuela will be sustained, and will be generalized to the other debtors. Perhaps a cause of even greater concern is the case of the relatively smaller Latin American debtors (except for Costa Rica and Bolivia, which have solved their debt overhang problem). Because smaller countries matter less to the banks,[9] there is a risk that Brady or other deals will not be reached, and these countries will continue to 'muddle through' with partial arrears, little access to new private flows, and so on. Even if these countries reach agrement with their commercial creditors, there is a major risk that they will not be able to attract new private flows from other sources.

It therefore seems important for international financial institutions (IFIs) to make a special effort to support attempts by small debtor governments to resolve their commercial debt overhang. Because of the small likelihood that they will attract new flows, a stronger case can be made by the IFIs and the debtor governments for a larger debt and/or debt service reduction than was achieved by countries such as Mexico and Venezuela; the cost to the banks would be far smaller, and they have in many cases already provisioned heavily against exposure in those countries.

A number of small Latin American countries also have very heavy exposures to official sources, both bilateral and multilateral. This is an issue which is beginning to lead to action, especially on the bilateral side; these actions need to be broadened. As regards official bilateral debt, more generous terms have been granted in the Paris Club since September 1990 for severely indebted middle-income countries such as El Salvador and Honduras. ODA debt is rescheduled with a 20-year maturity and 10 years of grace; and consolidated export credits with 14–15 years maturity and 7–9 years of grace. In addition, these agreements, like all Paris Club agreements for lower middle-income countries, have a clause for debt reduction through debt–equity swaps and/or debt for nature or development swaps, to be organized with each creditor country on a voluntary basis, up to a ceiling of 10% of total export credit claims or $10 million.

Along a similar line, the US government has undertaken bilateral action in the context of the 'Enterprise for the Americas'. This allows substantial reduction and restructuring of US concessional loans (e.g. PL-480) to Latin American countries, and the sale of a portion of outstanding bilateral commercial credits under Eximbank and Commodity Credit Corporation programmes in order to facilitate foreign investment and to fund environmental programmes. Part of this initiative has already been approved by the US Congress and has started to operate. No parallel initiative for Latin American countries has been taken by non-US creditors, except that in the context of the broadened Paris Club deals.

It is important to stress here (because of the potential precedent effect) that two middle-income countries have received far more significant bilateral official debt reduction than Latin American countries: these are Poland and Egypt. These agreements—reached in early 1991—will achieve, when fully implemented, the equivalent of a *50% reduction* in the present value of scheduled debt service payments for bilateral official debt. There are several features of the Polish and Egyptian agreements that are new, and which may be of interest as precedents to Latin American debt negotiators, especially in lower middle-income and even in some cases low-income countries: for the first time since 1974, the Paris Club has agreed to consolidate the *entire* stock of eligible debt; interest repayments will be uniformly reduced during the first 3 years of the agreement; non-ODA debt is rescheduled on highly concessional terms (this again is a first for middle-income countries); the basis of debt relief is the present value of scheduled debt service payments; principal repayments start at a very low level and increase steadily; and debt relief is phased over 3 years, so as to reinforce IMF conditionality.

Poland and Egypt, like other seriously indebted lower middle-income countries, may enter into agreements with creditor countries to swap eligible debt for local currency obligations. It is interesting that in this context Poland has taken a far-reaching initiative: in June 1991, it announced its wish to create a large environmental fund for around $3 billion to combat pollution, which would be financed out of bilateral official debt reduction, going beyond the 50% debt reduction already granted.[10] Although creditor country officials have stated, at a formal level, that Poland and Egypt are special cases and should not be taken as a precedent, many recognize informally that new ground has been broken by these two deals, and that for cases where debt reduction is needed urgently to restore growth in lower middle-income countries, more generous terms than currently granted are called for.

III CONCLUSIONS

As outlined in the previous Sections, in the last 2 years significant progress has finally been made in external debt management in several countries of

Latin America. Preliminary evidence also indicates that where debt deals have been reached which are seen as leading probably to sustained growth, positive indirect effects have actually begun to materialize, especially for the larger countries in the region. Although voluntary bank lending to the region has not returned (except for a small loan to Chile), other private flows seem to have grown significantly since 1990. Thus, for several of the larger countries (Mexico, Chile and Venezuela), prospects for growth have improved significantly; though more uncertain, prospects for Brazil and Argentina are also relatively encouraging, especially at the level of reaching debt deals and attracting new private flows. For heavily indebted small countries (except for Costa Rica and Bolivia), progress on the debt front is far slower, and special efforts are required to accelerate progress.

Although debt management has finally made quite significant progress, actions are still required to help the region's countries return to creditworthiness and growth. The following suggestions are based on actions (mainly by industrial governments) that would improve the current debt management strategy rather than change it, under the assumption that it is working in a relatively satisfactory manner; naturally, such an attitude would need to be reviewed should, for example, major external shocks hit the region, which at present seems unlikely.

III.1   Commercial debt and private flows

One line of action which seems to be desirable, but is unlikely to be implemented, is for industrial governments to increase the sums available, mainly from the IMF and World Bank, for debt reduction operations. Large claims being made by Eastern Europe—and the Soviet Union—make this even less likely than in the past, as does relatively satisfactory progress with the debt strategy as currently structured.

Perhaps more important is the continued and increased backing and technical assistance which the IFIs can give to debtor countries in their negotiations with creditor banks, to help ensure that deals are speedily finalized and that there is sufficient debt reduction to allow the country to return to adequate growth and creditworthiness; as pointed out above, this support is particularly crucial for small debtors. ECLAC (1990) contained an interesting proposal that the IMF pronouncement on a debtor country's payments capacity should be the basis for determining the required debt and debt service reduction by private creditors; the IMF could even go further in special cases by tolerating arrears to commercial banks, while granting new loans itself, or even possibly sanctioning arrears as an exchange restriction under its *Articles of Agreement*. Pressure by the IFIs on banks seems perhaps a better way of achieving sufficient debt reduction quickly than using additional public flows for this purpose: additional public flows to the region could be better used to finance essential investment in new projects or to rehabilitate existing capacity, than to provide additional guarantees to the commercial banks.

If additional guarantees by the IFIs are used, they would be most useful if they were employed to encourage new private capital flows (Snowden, 1991).[11] A specific example could be a broadening of the World Bank's Expanded Cofinancing Operations Programme, set up to support and improve access by middle-income countries to industrial countries' credit and capital markets. Currently, this programme excludes countries that have rescheduled debts in the last 5 years (such as Mexico and Chile); it would clearly seem desirable for the World Bank to make its eligibility criteria more flexible, to include countries that have recently had successful debt reduction operations. This, and similar measures, would offer a desirable incentive to countries which pursue sensible economic policies and relevant agreement with creditor banks, and would encourage others to follow a similar path. More generally, further action is required by the countries of the region to further co-financing and other facilities of the IFIs as a mechanism to attract new private flows, as well as to make suggestions for the development and broadening of such mechanisms where necessary.

More generally, support not just by IFIs but by industrial governments and others is required to encourage improved access by the region to different types of private flows. An example relevant to the encouragement of commercial bank funding, would be that where countries are seen to have overcome their debt problems, industrial country bank regulations remove those debtors from the 'debt rescheduling list' so that new money no longer has to be effectively penalized (for banks) by automatic incremental loan-loss provisions. An encouraging step in this direction is the removal of Chile in early 1991 from the US banks' list of debt rescheduling countries. Similarly, for those countries emerging from the debt problem, it would be desirable to reduce the capital requirement (within the context of BIS capital guidelines) linked to new loans, which currently require 100% capital back-up for all loans to developing countries and thus provide quite a large disincentive for new lending. Similar changes may well be required to encourage other private capital flows to the region and/or eliminate existing regulatory biases against such flows to developing countries.

As pointed out above, the new nature of these private flows requires not just their encouragement by industrial and recipient governments, but also monitoring and evaluation of their nature and their appropriateness for funding of different types of projects in the region, together with possible regulatory action to attempt to channel them to desirable activities and to avoid (where relevant) excessive flows. Such regulatory actions should be carried out both by industrial and Latin American governments.

Returning to the regulatory issues on bank flows and debt, it seems desirable for changes to be introduced in Western Europe and Canada (where relevant) to encourage tax changes that would only allow banks to keep tax relief on their provisions against potential losses on developing country loans, *if within a certain period* (e.g. 3 years) they grant at least as large debt reduction as they have provided and been given tax relief for (see Griffith-Jones and Van der Hoeven, 1991; Bouchet, 1991). The United Kingdom has made a partial though positive move in this direction but other countries have not yet followed. Such a measure should be attractive to industrial governments because it has no fiscal cost for them and may imply additional fiscal revenue. Latin American governments could therefore effectively lobby for such a change.

We have referred mainly to actions to be taken by industrial country actors. However, as discussed in Sections I and II, a crucial role needs to be played by debtor governments in overcoming their debt problems. Particularly important are actions by small debtors, many of them currently in a situation of arrears to commercial banks. It is important that they search energetically for consensual 'deals' that will reduce debt sufficiently to allow for renewed growth; the second-best solution, of maintaining arrears, though clearly legitimate, may in the new circumstances deprive them from some access to new inflows. Backing by international financial and other organizations (as well as advisers from other debtor countries) should provide much-needed expertise. Certainly, Costa Rica and Bolivia provide valuable lessons on bargaining tactics and of desirable solutions to the debt overhang.

Amongst the elements which may attract commercial banks to reach agreements with their debtors is the possibility of debt conversion programmes. To the extent that these programmes are consistent with national objectives (e.g. provide additional incentives to start attracting foreign direct investment and/or to fund privatization), the debtor government may wish to offer the possibility of creating or developing a debt conversion programme as an incentive for banks to reach a more comprehensive agreement on debt reduction.

III.2 Official debt reduction

For severely indebted countries, where bilateral official debt is significant, it is important that further progress is made towards debt reduction. In this sense, it would be desirable if the US 'Enterprise for the Americas' could be complemented by a parallel initiative by the European, Canadian, Japanese and otehr creditor governments. Alternatively, severely indebted countries (and especially lower middle-income and low-income ones) could bargain for a significant improvement in their Paris Club reschedulings, legitimately arguing that they should get at least as good terms as Poland and Egypt. International financing institutions should back them in such a position. However, those countries that are already returning to creditworthiness and growth (e.g. the larger debtors) may not necessarily wish to apply for the Paris Club rescheduling, if they estimate that this would make access to new officially guaranteed credits more difficult in the future.

For lower middle-income countries with large bilateral official debts, an imaginative and rapid response is desirable to take advantage of the clause in Paris Club deals that allows up to 10% of bilateral official debt to be reduced if used for debt–equity, debt for nature and debt for development swaps. As in the case of commercial debt, it is important that the operations thus designated fundamentally suit national development objectives and not just creditor preferences. Such operations may not only provide some foreign exchange cash relief and domestic support for important objectives, but may also be a bridge to encourage further international financing (or new flows) for the same objectives, for example via foreign direct investment.

IV ANNEX: DEBT DEALS WITHIN THE BRADY PLAN: MEXICO, COSTA RICA AND VENEZUELA

The information that follows is extracted from the *World Bank World Debt Tables Statistics and Supplement*, except when otherwise indicated.

IV.1   Mexico (February 1990)

Mexico's debt deal was the first comprehensive deal within the Brady initiative. Three options were offered to banks involved in the negotiations. First, old loans could be exchanged for new bonds at a discount of 35% of their face value, keeping interest rates at market levels. Second, as an alternative, old debt could be exchanged for new bonds at face value, bearing fixed interest rates of 6.25%. Both alternatives encompassed 30-year bonds, whose principal was guaranteed with loans provided by the IMF, World Bank, Japan and Mexican reserves and deposited with the US Treasury as zero-coupon bonds. Interest payments had a guarantee for 18 months. Finally, new money could be provided. This would have to be equivalent to 25% of the banks' medium- and long-term loans (Askari, 1991).

The agreement included a clause of value recovery, making a link between debt service payments and oil prices, the country's main source of foreign exchange. From July 1996 onwards, if the oil price surpasses the barrier of $14 per barrel (at

1989 prices), up to 30% of the additional revenues will accrue to creditors. This additional payment, however, will not exceed 3% of the nominal value of the debt converted into new bonds.

At the time the deal was signed, the country's total debt stock was $95.6 billion (*World Debt Tables 1990–91*), only the share of the long-term debt with the commercial banks being subject to restructuring. The debt value involved in the agreement was about $49 billion, that is, roughly one-half of the total debt. Most banks (approximately 60%) opted for interest rate reduction ($22.8 billion, or 46.7% of the total); the others chose to reduce the principal ($19.7 billion) and a few offered new loans ($6.4 billion, or 13.1% of the total).

IV.2   Costa Rica (May 1990)

Costa Rica's debt deal was far more successful than Mexico's in that it reduced the country's debt with commercial banks by 61.5%, according to the *World Debt Tables 1990–91*. The buy-back mechanism was employed at a discount of 84%. From a total of $1.61 billion (this excludes unregistered debt converted into local currency), $1.2 billion was negotiated within this option: this value includes past due interest, and is equivalent to 75.3% of the total value. Banks which had over 60% of their claims negotiated could exchange the remainder for bonds at par value, of 20 years, with interest rates of 6.25%. Arrears on interest could be exchanged for bonds of 15 years with interest at market levels (LIBOR plus 13/16%). In both cases interest payments were collateralized; in the first case over 12–18 months, and in the second case over 36 months. This option (principal plus past due interest converted) involved $290 million, corresponding to 18% of the total debt. Banks where less than 60% of their claims were sold, received bonds with no collateralization. The converted principal would bear a fixed 6.25% interest rate and arrears of LIBOR plus 13/16%. This option involved resources amounting to $289 million, corresponding to 17.9% of the total.

Finally, a recovery clause was included. Payments of interest on bonds with interest arrears would be accelerated and other bonds would receive higher interest rates once the country's GDP increased by more than 20% of its 1989 level, in real terms.

IV.3   Venezuela (August 1990)

The Venezuelan agreement (see Alvarez, 1990) was similar to that of Mexico but included a wider menu of options. The first option consisted of debt buy-backs. Short-term bills (91 days) were offered in exchange, at 55% discount, fully collateralized. Only $1.4 billion was finally involved in this option, or 7.2% of the debt eligible for restructuring. As in Mexico's deal, the second and third options consisted of discount bonds and par bonds, respectively, fully collateralized. The second option had a discount of 30%, bearing interest rates of LIBOR plus 13/16%. A guarantee for interest of 14 months was provided. $1.79 billion was chosen within this option, that is, 9.2% of debt subject to negotiation. A par bond was offered in the third option with interest rates of 6.75%, interest payments also having a guarantee of 14 months. $7.4 billion (37.9% of the total) was involved in this option, the most preferred of all. The fourth option was the offer of 'step-down, step-up' bonds, that is, bonds with temporarily lower interest rates. They would bear an interest rate of 5% in the first 2 years, 6% in the following 2 years and 7% in the fifth year. From the sixth year onwards the bonds would bear LIBOR plus 7/8%. Unlike the other options, the principal was not collateralized but would have an interest guarantee for 12 months during the periods with fixed interest rates. The debt retired under this option amounted to $2.9 billion, or 14.9% of the total involved. The fifth option encompassed new money, which would have to be provided by creditors at the amount of 20% of the value of restructured debt. Conversion rights for debt–equity swaps were also included. This option attracted 30.7% of the total debt retired.

Finally, as the cases cited above, a recovery clause associated with oil price fluctuation was included. Part of the interest payment can be recovered by creditors if oil prices exceed $26 per barrel, from 1996 onwards.

NOTES

1 *Latin American Economy and Business* (September 1991).
2 See for example, Aspe (1990); several CEPAL publications; World Bank, *World Debt Tables 1990–91*; Van Wijnbergen (1991).
3 The Mexican government initially requested 55% debt relief; the final agreement included a debt relief option with 35% debt relief.
4 The former figure is based on World Bank (*World Debt Tables 1990–91*) calculations; the latter on own calculations.
5 For a description of how time-consuming, distracting and costly the Costa Rican debt negotiations were, see Rodriquez (1988).
6 Interview material and 'Brazil: Debt Talks Get Off to an Untraditionally Harmonious Start', *Latin American Economy and Business* (September 1991).
7 See 'Latin American Borrowers Set to Re-enter the Market', *Financial Times* (27 August 1991).
8 'Brazil Seeks to Come in From the Cold', *Financial Times* (4 September 1991).
9 Interview material.
10 Interview material.
11 Snowden argues rather persuasively for the importance that 'new debt' has senior guarantees to restructured 'old debt'; see also Devlin and Guerguil (1991) for a similar point.

REFERENCES

Alvarez, A.M. (1990) 'Venezuela En Los Años Noventa: Acuerdo De Reduccion De Deuda y Politica de Ajuste' in *Seminario sobre Reconversion Productiva con Equidad*, prepared by el Foro sobre Deuda y Desarrollo (FONDAD) jointly with CEPAL and PREALC, Santiago.

Askari, H. (1991) *Third World Debt and Financial Innovation, the Experiences of Chile and Mexico*, OECD, Paris.

Aspe, P. (1990) 'The Renegotiation of Mexico's External Debt' in M. Faber and S. Griffith-Jones (eds), *Approaches to Third World Debt Reduction*.

Bouchet, M. (1991) 'Developing Countries' External Indebtedness to International Banks', Mimeo, Paris.

CEPAL (1991) 'El Regreso de Paises Latino Americanos al Mercado Internacional de Capitales Privados: Una Nota Preliminar', CEPAL, Santiago.

Devlin, R. and M. Guerguil (1991) 'America Latina y las Noevas Corrientes Financieras y Comerciales', *Revista de la CEPAL* **43**.

Dooley, M. (1989) 'Market Valuation of External Debt' in J. Frenkel, M. Dooley and P. Wickhan (eds), *Analytical Issues in Debt*, IMF, Washington, DC.

ECLAC (1990) *Latin America and the Caribbean: Options to Reduce the Debt*, ECLAC, Santiago.

Griffith-Jones, S. and R. Van der Hoeven (1991) 'La Deuda—Le Herencia no Descada de los Niños de Hoy', *CIEPLAN, Nota Tecnica 139*.

Massad, C. (1991) 'Hechos Externos, Politicas Internas y Ajuste Estructural', *Revista de la CEPAL* **43**.

OECD (1991) *Financing and External Debt of Developing Countries*, OECD, Paris.

Reisen, H. (1991) 'The Brady Plan and Adjustment Incentives', *Intereconomics* (March/April).

Rodriquez, E. (1988) 'Costa Rica: A Quest for Survival' in S. Griffith-Jones (ed.), *Managing World Debt*, Wheatsheaf, London.

Sachs, J. and J. Kneer (1990) 'Debt Reduction: The Basis and Shape of a New Strategy', *Intereconomics* (January/February).

Snowden, P. (1991) 'Reviving Capital Inflows are Debt Reduction', mimeo, University of Lancaster.

Van Wijnbergen, S. (1991) 'Mexico and the Brady Plan', *Economic Policy* (April).

9 | Reviving Capital Inflows after Debt Reduction: Seniority and Incentives under the Brady Strategy

P.N. SNOWDEN

I INTRODUCTION

Following official endorsement by US Treasury Secretary Brady in March 1989, debt reduction has become the accepted strategy in attempts to revive the international creditworthiness of debtor countries. Recent agreements have involved the issue of bonds which either have a lower face value or carry a lower interest rate than the debt instruments for which they are exchanged. Enhancement of the attraction of these bonds by externally supplied collateral has helped to achieve almost complete participation by commercial bank creditors. A further inducement has been the status of the new bonds as senior claims, which implies exclusion from future debt rescheduling exercises: they are 'exit' bonds.

Whereas a significant literature has developed on the positive incentive effects of debt reduction, mainly from the viewpoint of the government of the country concerned, Dooley (1989a) emphasized the depressing effects of a debt overhang on new investment by domestic and foreign residents. This chapter investigates the extent to which debt reduction agreements have addressed the problem which Dooley raised. Investment incentives following Mexico's 1989 agreement certainly appear to have improved. The country was able to raise $4 billion on international financial markets in 1990, and around $5 billion in flight capital is estimated to have returned (Van Wijnbergen, 1991). While acknowledging these gains, it is argued here that certain forms of financial inflow may still be obstructed by the seniority structure of old and new claims implied in typical debt reduction agreements.

The basis of the argument is a familiar diagrammatic analysis extended to provide a clarification of the theoretical case for combining debt reduction with new lending. Although the inclusion of new money options in recent agreements with, for example, Mexico and Venezuela was not motivated by this reasoning, its relevance in the present context is to highlight the relationship between the seniority structure of *existing* claims and the incentives for *new* provision. The analysis has more general interest as a response to the objection which has been raised in principle to the combination of debt reduction with new lending under the Brady strategy: 'the linking of these two policies shows confusion in the underlying thinking behind the proposal' (Lomax, 1989, p. 111). While this objection is based on the need to distinguish clearly between illiquidity and insolvency, the latter typically requires a financial restructuring after which new lending becomes appropriate. The basic question addressed by this paper is whether the restructuring in recent debt reduction agreements has been optimal with respect to a resumption of external private financing.

After a brief review of the original incentives case for debt reduction, Section II explains the theoretical argument for combining debt reduction with new lending. While in this presentation the new loans are supplied by creditors who are simultaneously offering debt reduction, it is argued that the same incentives could be brought to bear by a restructuring of old claims which encouraged new creditors to participate. This observation leads to Section III where the incentives provided to new external investors by debt reduction are discussed.

II THEORETICAL ARGUMENTS FOR DEBT REDUCTION/RELIEF

Recent Brady-type agreements, as typified by those with Mexico and Venezuela, have persuaded creditors jointly to offer debt reduction defined as a reduction in the present value of contractual payments due (Sachs, 1989, p. 1). The discount rate implied in this definition is the opportunity cost of funds to the *creditor*: a detail which distinguishes debt reduction from debt relief in the sense used by Corden (1988). This would be a change in the contractual stream of payments agreed to by the creditors which is favourable to the debtor (Sachs, 1989, p. 2). On this definition, the *debtor's* discount rate is implied and could allow loan rescheduling, which simply delays repayment, to qualify as relief. Provided that the rescheduling is at the *creditor's* discount rate, it is favourable to the debtor in view of the latter's higher (crisis-induced) rate.

Arguments for debt reduction as opposed to, say, rescheduling must recognize that the discounted market price of the debt will include a probability-weighted allowance for the possibility of full (or relatively full) repayment. Creditors will be disinclined to relinquish this 'option' value of the current level of contractual claims. Debt reduction effectively imposes a ceiling on the maximum possible future receipts (Corden, 1988, p. 5). However, incentives arguments, which rely on creditor gains arising from improved performance by the debtor, have been advanced to suggest that creditors may offer debt reduction despite the ceiling effect (e.g. Krugman, 1988, p. 259).

The most well-known incentives mechanism has also given rise to the notion of a 'debt relief Laffer curve' (Krugman, 1989, p. 265). A large debt overhang, involving legal claims which the country is unlikely to be able to honour in full, acts as a 100% marginal rate of tax on any adjustment effort aimed at raising export earnings. While adjustment policies may be politically painful, they are less likely to be followed if creditors are in a position to demand the full dividend of improved net export earnings. A joint decision to cut the outstanding claims could, by offering the country a share in its potentially improved position, provide the necessary incentive to undertake painful reforms. Since these policies may improve the probability of creditor repayments they amount to an opportunity for Pareto improvements.

The 100% marginal tax rate reflects an extreme assumption whereby foreign creditors are able to coerce all of the resources which an economic adjustment programme may be capable of generating. If only a share can be extracted, the tax rate is merely a high one, suggesting a low national return on adjustment policies. This less extreme version may also be applied to the situation that confronts potential new investors. The overhang-induced discount on the country's outstanding debt can be interpreted as a threat to the future returns on existing and *new* financial claims held against residents both by foreigners and by other residents (Dooley, 1989a, p. 76). Without any seniority structure for claims, new investors do not know whether their returns will be pre-empted in an attempt to satisfy existing creditors. Their own claims may therefore share the same discount and, given the world price of investment goods, a very high real interest rate for new projects is implied. Dooley's argument therefore emphasizes that a resolution of the debt problem will require the substantial elimination of the discount on outstanding claims.

While the above arguments explain why the discount rate applied by agents in the debtor country will be higher than that prevailing in world capital markets, it is this difference in discount rate which creates the possible motivation for existing lenders to offer debt (liquidity) relief. In the situation described, other outside lenders are unlikely to make new loans available, and the existing creditors would be in a position to internalize any benefits which may accrue to their *overall* claims as a result of new lending. If the country could be obliged (or persuaded) to invest the proceeds of a new loan at its own high rate of discount, the surplus over the opportunity cost of funds would accrue to the creditors through an increased ultimate payment on their total outstanding claims. However, since resources are to be handed over immediately, there is the potential principal-agent problem for the creditors in ensuring that the country invests rather than consumes the funds. At this point, the liquidity argument for debt relief cannot be separated from the incentives argument for debt reduction. This is the basis of the case for combining debt reduction with new lending to be developed in the next Section.

III   INCENTIVES FOR COMBINING NEW LENDING WITH DEBT REDUCTION

The case for combining debt reduction with new lending can most simply be portrayed in the context of the popular two-period optimization framework (e.g. Corden, 1989; Dooley, 1989b). The country is assumed to have a large inherited debt at the beginning of Period 1. A central planner determines how much of the resources available are to be consumed in Period 1 and how much are to be invested. The invested resources will make output available in Period 2, during which the debt becomes repayable with accumulated interest. Creditors are assumed to be able to extract all Period 2 output above a subsistence minimum up to their full contractual claims. The transformation functions between present and future production and consumption are as displayed in Figures 9.1 and 9.2.

The horizontal distance between A_1A_2 and P_1P_2 in each case is set equal to $(1+i)D$, which is the debt plus interest to be paid in Period 2: assuming full repayment, the planner must choose a consumption combination on the boundary of the inner curve. On the further assumption that an interest payment (iD) on the inherited debt has been set aside, and is about to be paid by the country at the beginning of Period 1, Figure 9.1 displays the effect of an offer by creditors to (effectively) capitalize this payment. A new money loan permits the amount to be deferred until Period 2.

The production transformation boundary facing the planner is now allowed to shift by the vertical amount iD (from P_1P_2 to R_1R_2) to absorb the newly released resources. The new boundary B_1B_2, showing the

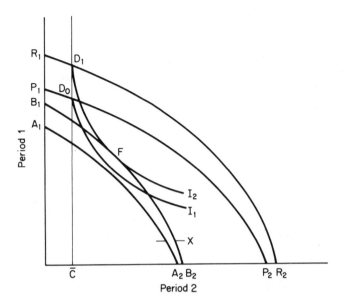

Figure 9.1 Interest capitalization in the two-period optimization model.

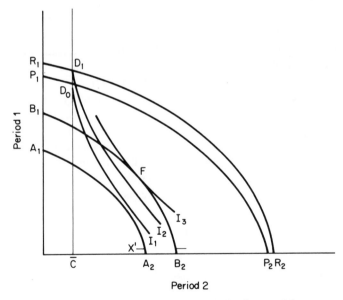

Figure 9.2 Debt reduction in the two-period optimization model.

resources available for the country on the assumption of full repayment, is derived by subtracting the amount $(1+i)^2D$ horizontally from R_1R_2 and suggests that potential domestic resource availabilities have been augmented. The gain arises from the assumption that the debtor's discount rate (r) is higher than that applied by the lenders (i). The former is equated with the marginal return to investment *at the point chosen by the planner*, and suggests that the extra resources available to the country in Period 2 (if all the new funds were invested) would be:

$$(1+r)iD - (1+i)iD = (r-i)iD \qquad (1)$$

This amount, shown as X in Figure 9.1, is made up of the difference between the gross return on the invested funds and the repayment (with interest) of the new loan. Thus, liquidity relief is favourable to the debtor even when full repayment is expected.[1] The diagram further suggests that a gain of this magnitude could produce the incentive to renounce default at D_0 in favour of full repayment at F. However, the analysis also confirms the intuition that a new money loan has the potential of generating *perverse* incentive effects. Especially if the assumption that creditors are able to coerce all new resources is retained, the enhanced liquidity of iD represents the maximum impact on Period 1 consumption arising from Period 2 default, represented by point D_1.

Immediate liquidity provision is clearly much smaller in the case of a debt reduction offer by lenders (dD), portrayed in Figure 9.2. The gain in immediate resources (equal to an amount $i|dD|$, or the vertical distance P_1R_1) represents the reduced Period 1 interest payment which the debt reduction offer permits. It has a Period 1 liquidity value compared with the new money loan of $i|dD|/iD = |dD|/D$ (the proportionate debt reduction), reflecting the argument that (for a 10% reduction) 'a dollar of debt reduction would lead to only about ten cents of liquidity relief' (Claessens and Diwan, 1989, p. 220). There is less incentive to default in this case. However, to gauge the effect on resource availabilities to the country *on the assumption of full repayment*, B_1B_2 is horizontally separated from R_1R_2 by the distance $(1+i)(D-|dD|)$. Again, representing the marginal rate of return on investment which the country undertakes as $r > i$, the maximum increase in Period 2 consumption on the assumption of full repayment would be:

$$(1+r)i|dD| + (1+i)|dD| \qquad (2)$$

This amount, shown as X' in Figure 9.2, is made up of the return on the reduced Period 1 interest payment and the Period 2 amount (with interest) which will no longer be paid. Despite the smaller gain in immediate liquidity, debt reduction of dD would normally be of greater value to the country (given full repayment of the remaining debt), than a new loan (iD) of the same amount. Comparing equations (1) and (2) above, and neglecting the first part of the latter, $(1+i) > (r-i)$. The implication is that the incentive effects of debt reduction will be more powerful than the equivalent value of new loans.

Given the differing magnitudes of the incentive and liquidity effects involved in new money loans and debt reduction, the question arises as to whether lenders can gain from combining the two policies. Figure 9.3 indicates the conditions under which this would be possible. Recognizing the relative attraction of the default option at point D_1, an offer of debt reduction which would allow the planner to reach point F would be in the creditors' clear interests by promoting full repayment of the remaining loan. If, however, creditors were to offer debt reduction combined with a new loan, the required debt write-off could be reduced. The effect of one such new loan offer is displayed in the diagram. As before, the outer schedule is displaced vertically by the amount of the loan, L. Similarly, a new loan shifts the consumption transformation curve by the horizontal distance $(r-i)L$. Provided that this distance is greater than that between the two

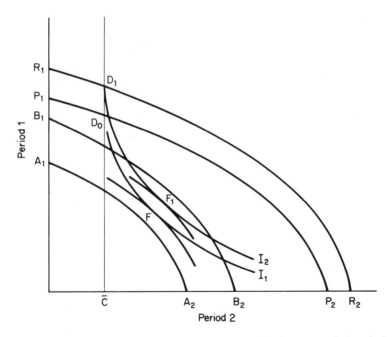

Figure 9.3 Debt reduction combined with new loans in the two-period optimization model.

indifference curves shown, the loan can be combined with less old debt reduction than is required at F while leaving the country with a sufficient improvement in Period 2 welfare to avoid default. Diagrammatically, the transformation curves shown can be shifted backwards to produce a tangency at F_1.

More formally, successive loan offers could be combined with reduced old debt forgiveness as follows:

$$D_2(1+i) = D_1(1+i) + (r-i)L - U(L) \tag{3}$$

The term on the left is the old debt (with interest) which can be paid with a new loan L. It is made up of the initial (reduced) debt at a point like F plus the extra amount the country would just be willing to repay. The surplus is measured with r and $U(L)$ (the required Period 2 welfare gain), evaluated at the tangency point reached on acceptance of the offer. Differentiating this expression with respect to L shows that new loans maximize the repayments on the old debt when:

$$(r-i) = U'(L) \tag{4}$$

or when a further loan generates just enough surplus over service cost in Period 2 to compensate the country for not exercizing the Period 1 default option.[2]

IV   INCENTIVE EFFECTS FOR NEW INVESTORS OF RECENT DEBT REDUCTION AGREEMENTS

Although the analysis above has abstracted from uncertainty, it clarifies the interest of original creditors in the supply of new finance. Whereas debtors must keep a share of the improved economic performance which the new loans make possible, the analysis shows that creditors have implicitly opted to take a share in this improved outcome as well. While the new loan receives normal interest, the real motivation for the lender is the improved ultimate payment on the remaining old debt. Compared with the situation in which debt is simply forgiven, the new loan attracts an overall return which reflects the future performance of the debtor. The analysis thus highlights a possible externality of new lending which may be appropriated by existing creditors.

In view of the current reluctance of commercial banks to make new loans to sovereign debtors, it is important to note an alternative route which could help to appropriate this externality. Original lenders could opt to swap their existing claims for new instruments which permitted some sharing of improved economic performance with the debtor. Given this restructured claim, it would be in their interests to facilitate new money inflows by agreeing to allow seniority to be granted to new loans and investments from whatever source. Such an agreement would roughly parallel some domestic bankruptcy settlements where creditors take over the ownership of an insolvent enterprise. When this option is chosen, the ability of the financially reconstructed firm to raise new loans allows the firm to resume normal activities in the joint interests of the new owners.

In the light of this parallel with familiar bankruptcy settlements, the structure of claims following the implementation of debt reduction agreements is of interest. A recent study of the Mexican agreement by Van Wijnbergen (1991) noted that the earlier discounted bank debt represented a *de facto* junior claim on the country's foreign exchange resources. The fact that such debt had been rescheduled in the past suggested that its priority was below that of Mexico's loans from the official sector (including the IMF and the World Bank). Moreover, since outstanding bonds are not easily subject to rescheduling (due in part to the 'bearer' status of eurobonds), commercial bank debts were also effectively junior to these claims. More curiously in view of normal financial patterns, this debt was also subordinate to foreign direct (i.e. equity) investment. Since these investors typically have prior access to their foreign exchange earnings from Mexican operations, they could not easily be pre-empted by other creditors. It is worth noting that this effective insulation of direct equity and bond investments from the defaulted claims of commercial banks weakens somewhat Dooley's 'contamination' argument as a case for debt reduction.

How was this effective structure of claims influenced by the agreement reached with Mexico? Almost one-half (49.8%) of the $45.8 billion of foreign commercial bank debt covered by the agreement was exchanged for par bonds carrying the same face value as the debt exchanged, but with a reduced fixed interest rate of 6.25% (for those of dollar denomination). An alternative bond with face value discounted by 35% but carrying a market-based interest rate was exchanged for 40.7% of the amount involved. The unconverted remainder, representing 9.4%, committed the holders to the provision of new money amounting to 25% of their claim over 3 years (Van Wijnbergen, 1991).

With respect to the seniority issue, the agreement made clear that the new bonds were not subject to rescheduling; they were 'exit' bonds. Moreover, the unexchanged debt was declared to be junior to the new claims. While the relatively insulated position of foreign direct investors is unchanged by the agreement, it seems clear that the exchanged bank debt has become less clearly junior to other existing and potential Mexican bond holders. This impression is reinforced by the collateral supporting the new bonds. Using largely borrowed funds, Mexico has financed the purchase of

US Treasury obligations which will cover their principal on maturity at the end of 2019. In addition, Mexico has financed a second escrow account to cover 18 months of rolling interest guarantees. Both would be at risk in the event of further default. While these provisions seem to strengthen the claims of holders of the new bonds against those of other types, it has been noted that these are registered rather than bearer bonds. Since current ownership will therefore be known, the securitized bonds may yet be vulnerable to further rescheduling (Fidler, 1990).

The uncertainty of the relative status of Mexico's bond obligations following the agreement suggests that the contamination issue raised by Dooley may still be of relevance for the revival of bond financing. The terms on which Mexico will be able to issue bonds in future may be influenced by the yields currently obtained on the restructured debt. Table 9.1 reports relevant data for the new instruments. The reported prices are based on a face value of 100, while the 'stripped' yield estimates reflect the bonds' yields to maturity after removal of the collateralized component of the returns: they are an estimate of the yield on Mexican risk. While the market valuation of these claims increased significantly over their first year of trading, the yield data suggest that they are still regarded as risky assets. As dollar-denominated claims, for instance, the figures may be compared with the 7.4% yield on US Government 10 year bonds in September 1991 (Goldman). To what extent do these yields reflect the cost of new bond finance for Mexico after the debt reduction agreement? While new claims of equivalent status would presumably be valued by the market in a similar manner, the cost of the most recent Mexican bond issues does appear to have been lower than indicated in the table.

An issue by Pemex in early July 1991 carried an interest coupon of

Table 9.1 Price and yield data for Mexican collateralized bonds.

	6 October 1990[1]	11 September 1991[2]
Discount bonds		
Price (bid)	63.25	76.00
Current yield	14.64%	9.68%
'Stripped' yield	17.21%	10.60%
Par bonds		
Price	42.75	60.00
Current yield	14.53%	10.80%
'Stripped' yield	19.05%	12.58%

Source: (1) Salomon Brothers, reported in *International Financing Review* (Issue 847, p. 29; Oct. 1990). (2) Supplied by Continental Bank, London to the author.

11.5%. Although this is higher than for recent issues by large commercial borrowers based in the developed countries (e.g. 9.25%), the Pemex bonds seem currently to be regarded as a better risk than the debt reduction issues. While some rescheduling risk is probably attached to the latter, a distinguishing feature of the Pemex issue is the oil company's ability to generate foreign exchange directly for debt service. The recent recovery of bond issues by Latin American borrowers appears to be based on this requirement (London, 1991). Tentative evidence, therefore, suggests that large private sector entities which have ready access to foreign exchange may be able to raise international bond finance on terms which are less stringent than those attached to the sovereign obligations of their governments. Unfortunately, the number of potential borrowers in this class is limited—perhaps only a dozen in Mexico (London, 1991).

The figures in Table 9.1 suggest that a recovery of the traditional form of international financing—bond issues by government borrowers—may be more difficult. Such claims are less easy to insulate from those attached to the existing issues arising from debt reduction, and may be expected to receive a similar valuation. To this extent, new sovereign bond issues may still be affected by the contamination problem to which Dooley drew attention in the context of debt overhang.

V CONCLUSIONS

While debt reduction agreements of the type recently negotiated with Mexico and Venezuela[3] have made a significant contribution to resolving the debt-related problems of the countries concerned, a large external debt remains. Mexico's debt service ratio is projected at 30% over 1989–94 and debt service may amount to 5% of GDP at the end of that period. Moreover, the reduced debt has a more senior claim on Mexican resources than that which it has replaced. Current market valuations confirm the bonds' status as high-yield assets and suggest that future bond issues by the Mexican government may be viewed similarly.

On the basis of the earlier analysis, however, the interests of both new and old creditors may be better served if the status of the debt reduction bonds could be more satisfactorily clarified with respect to new issues. If the latter could be defined as having a senior claim over the stock of debt reduction instruments, access to the bond market could probably be improved, with positive implications for holders of existing bonds. One suggestion would be for creditors in further debt reduction agreements to be induced to accept junior status with respect to *future* bond issues by augmenting their claims in the event of improved economic performance in the country concerned. By permitting better access to international capital markets, the potential gains identified in the previous analysis could then be realized. Although a minor recapture clause based on movements in future oil prices has been included in the Mexican agreement, a more substantial provision based on future export earnings would be required for this purpose.

NOTES

1 This expression also suggests that as r declines X becomes smaller, justifying the increased steepness of the consumption transformation curve displayed in the diagram.
2 A more formal mathematical derivation of this result is contained in the appendix of Claessens and Diwan (1989, p. 223). For comparison, $f'[I\star(L^c)] = (1+r)$ in the present paper, and world interest rates (i, here) are assumed to equal zero.
3 A similar type of agreement, with similarly arranged collateral, was reached with Venezuela covering the bulk of her public sector debt ($21 billion out of $27 billion) in March 1990.

REFERENCES

Claessens, S. and I. Diwan (1989) 'Liquidity, Debt Relief and Conditionality' in I. Husain and I. Diwan (eds), *Dealing with the Debt Crisis: A World Bank Symposium*, World Bank, Washington, DC.

Corden, W.M. (1988) 'Is Debt Relief in the Interests of Creditors?', *IMF Working Paper WP/88/72*.

Corden, W.M. (1989) 'Debt Relief and Adjustment Incentives' in J.A. Frenkel, M.P. Dooley and P. Wickham (eds), *Analytical Issues in Debt*, IMF, Washington, DC.

Dooley, M. (1989a) 'Market Valuation of External Debt' in J.A. Frenkel, M.P. Dooley and P. Wickham (eds), *Analytical Issues in Debt*, IMF, Washington, DC.

Dooley, M. (1989b) 'Debt Relief and Leveraged Buy-Outs', *International Economic Review* **30**, 71–5.

Fidler, S. (1990) 'Bond Market Renaissance in Latin America', *Financial Times* (11 May 1990).

Goldman (1991) *International Economic Indicators*, October 1991, Goldman Sachs.

Krugman, P. (1988) 'Financing vs. Forgiving a Debt Overhang', *Journal of Development Economics* **29**, 253–68.

Krugman, P. (1989) 'Market Based Debt Reduction Schemes' in J.A. Frenkel, M.P. Dooley and P. Wickham (eds), *Analytical Issues in Debt*, IMF, Washington, DC.

Lomax, D. (1989) *Memorandum to Treasury & Civil Service Committee (Appendix 4, 25/7/89)*, HMSO, London.

London, S. (1991) 'International Capital Markets Survey', *Financial Times* (22 July 1991).

Sachs, J. (1989) *New Approaches to the Latin American Debt Crisis (Essays in International Finance No. 174)*, International Finance Section, Princeton University, Princeton, NJ.

Van Wijnbergen, S. (1991) 'Mexico and the Brady Plan', *Economic Policy* (April), **6**, 14–56.

10 | The Bretton Woods Institutions and Developing Countries: Analysing the Past and Anticipating the Future

GRAHAM BIRD

I INTRODUCTION

Such is the diversity amongst developing countries that it is almost certainly of little use to talk about them as one single, and therefore by implication, homogeneous group. The causes of balance of payments and developmental difficulties and the appropriateness of specific policies vary across developing countries and a more disaggregated approach is required. While diversity will mean that it is unwise to generalize about the details of policy, it may still be legitimate to generalize about the institutional framework within which policy is designed and implemented. This paper examines the existing structure of international financial institutions (IFIs)—concentrating on the sister Bretton Woods institutions, the International Monetary Fund (IMF) and the International Bank for Reconstruction and Development (IBRD) or World Bank—and investigates their input into the process of economic development.

The changing size and nature of balance of payments problems in many developing countries has created a significant challenge to the IFIs. However, much of the available evidence suggests that the institutional response has been inadequate, with the result that the IMF and World Bank are not making their full potential contribution. At the same time as there are shortcomings with the IFIs, however, there are also significant weaknesses associated with both the private sector, whether in the form of commercial bank lending or foreign direct investment, and bilateral aid.[1] It would therefore be misguided to conclude that the Bretton Woods institutions have outlived their usefulness. A more positive response is to explore how the basic institutional structure might be reformed in order to realize more fully any potential beneficial impact on economic development. An important element in this exploration is to examine the extent to which the traditional division of labour between the IMF and the World Bank has broken down in the context of their dealings with developing countries. If the old specializations no longer exist, wherein lie the new comparative advantages of the two institutions? And is the existing institutional structure likely to exploit these advantages efficiently? Since both institutions are heavily involved with developing countries in a lending as well as in an adjustment role, a further question to ask is whether there is scope for institutional rationalization. If there is, then it is also relevant to ask whether this may be best achieved by merging the IMF and the World Bank, or by some alternative means.

II   RESOURCE FLOWS, FINANCING GAPS AND ADJUSTMENT NEEDS

Many developing countries encounter severe financing and adjustment difficulties. Various criteria may be used to assess such difficulties and to give an indication of the size and nature of the balance of payments problems that developing countries face. These criteria include movements in the terms of trade, export concentration and export instability, reserve holdings and adequacy, access to international financing, debt, and the scope for and costs of payments adjustment. Examination of the empirical evidence suggests unsurprisingly that not all less developed countries have encountered equivalent difficulties; the problems are often most acute for the low-income countries.[2]

Other indicators of economic performance suggest that developing countries, in general, encountered severe difficulties during the 1980s, and the 1990s. Table 10.1, for example, provides evidence on the growth of real output and real output *per capita* during 1973–91. With the exception of the Asian developing countries—dominated by Hong Kong, Korea, Taiwan and Singapore—growth performance was significantly less good during the 1980s than it was in the 1970s; and even for Asia, growth rates declined significantly during 1989–91. For many developing countries poor growth performance translated into a marked decline in living standards. For African less developed countries, living standards fell in six of the years between 1983 and 1991. For less developed countries in the Western hemisphere, a moderate growth in living standards between 1984 and 1987 was reversed between 1988 and 1991; and for those in the Middle East, the decline was most dramatic, reaching almost 27% over 1983–91.

Combined with such a poor output record, developing countries experienced a significant increase in inflation rates. While inflation in industrial countries fell by about a half during the 1980s in comparison with the 1970s, inflation in less developed countries rose from an annual average rate of about 25% during 1973–82 to almost 118% in 1990. For less developed countries in the Western hemisphere the increase was even more pronounced, rising from 50% to 768% (see Table 10.2). Such macro-economic trends create immense problems.

Rapid inflation will clearly have ramifications for the balance of payments. A failure to allow the nominal exchange rate to depreciate adequately will result in currency overvaluation and will therefore create disincentives for the tradeables sector. Further, depreciation at the speed and to the extent required to prevent this will itself lead to cost-based inflationary pressures, causing an inflation–devaluation–inflation spiral from which it is very difficult to break out. Escape from the spiral is almost certain to mean that domestic demand has to be deflated severely, but this will exacerbate poor performance on the supply side of the economy and will create domestic political problems as living standards continue to fall. Measures to raise output and encourage economic growth, if successful, may alleviate inflation and balance of payments problems in the long term by raising aggregate supply but may raise aggregate demand in the short term and will therefore make such problems worse. For highly indebted developing countries the situation is even more problematic, since an increasing share of declining domestic output has, in effect, to be directed towards debt servicing.

The problem is shown succinctly by the familiar income–expenditure equation for an open economy:

$$X - M = Y - [C + I + G]$$

In order to service outstanding debt, countries need to generate a payments surplus with exports (X) greater than imports (M). This will inflict least pain if domestic output (Y) is rising more rapidly than aggregate demand in the form of consumption (C), investment (I) and government expenditure (G). If, however, domestic output is stagnant, domestic aggregate demand

Table 10.1 Real GDP and real *per capita* GDP in developing countries, 1973–92.[a]

	1973–82[b]	1983	1984	1985	1986	1987	1988	1989	1990	1991	1992
Developing countries											
Real GDP	4.5	2.1	4.3	4.2	4.1	3.8	4.4	3.1	1.3	2.2	4.8
Real *per capita* GDP	1.7	−0.3	1.9	2.0	1.5	1.8	2.2	1.0	−0.6	0.1	2.7
By region											
Africa											
Real GDP	2.9	−1.1	0.7	4.0	1.7	1.3	2.9	3.3	1.9	2.0	4.8
Real *per capita* GDP	–	−3.8	−1.9	1.2	−1.2	−1.5	–	0.4	−0.9	−1.0	1.7
Asia											
Real GDP	5.7	8.1	8.4	6.8	6.9	8.1	9.0	5.5	5.3	5.0	5.2
Real *per capita* GDP	3.2	6.1	6.6	5.0	5.1	6.3	7.3	3.5	3.5	3.4	3.6
Europe											
Real GDP	4.0	2.4	4.9	2.7	4.4	2.6	1.6	−0.7	−4.7	1.5	3.0
Real *per capita* GDP	2.8	1.4	4.0	1.7	2.9	1.7	0.8	−1.4	−5.5	0.7	2.2
Middle East											
Real GDP	4.9	1.1	–	1.7	−0.7	0.1	4.7	3.2	−1.5	−3.3	8.5
Real *per capita* GDP	0.5	−3.0	−3.8	−1.8	−4.3	−4.2	1.6	0.5	−4.7	−6.9	4.6
Western hemisphere											
Real GDP	4.3	−2.8	3.6	3.4	4.7	2.4	0.2	1.5	−1.0	1.0	3.3
Real *per capita* GDP	1.6	−4.8	1.2	1.3	1.6	1.2	−1.9	−0.6	−2.5	−1.0	1.3

Source: World Economic Outlook (IMF, May 1991).

[a] Data are compound annual rates of change and exclude China.

[b] Arithmetic averages of country growth rates weighted by the average US dollar value of GDPs over the preceding 3 years.

Table 10.2 Inflation rates (%) in developing countries, 1973–92.[a]

	1973–82[b]	1983	1984	1985	1986	1987	1988	1989	1990	1991	1992
Developing countries	24.8	32.9	38.3	38.8	30.2	41.0	70.2	105.0	117.7	40.9	18.0
By region											
Africa	16.0	18.0	20.5	13.3	14.2	14.8	19.3	20.0	15.6	21.9	9.9
Asia	11.7	6.6	6.1	6.0	8.7	9.5	14.3	11.7	7.9	9.1	9.2
Europe	18.7	23.0	26.2	27.3	26.8	35.9	63.5	169.7	166.4	60.8	22.8
Middle East	15.2	12.3	14.8	12.2	13.3	17.1	16.1	14.4	13.3	13.7	13.9
Western Hemisphere	49.6	108.7	133.5	145.1	87.8	130.9	286.4	533.1	768.0	122.9	35.9

Source: World Economic Outlook (IMF, May 1991).
[a] Data are compound annual rates of change and exclude China.
[b] Percentage changes of geometric averages of indices of consumer prices for individual countries weighted by the average US dollar value of their respective GPDs over the preceding 3 years.

will have to be depressed, and this depression will need to be even more pronounced where output is declining.

This bleak macroeconomic picture has direct consequences as far as the future international financing needs of developing countries are concerned. Conventionally these needs can be conceptualized and estimated using dual gap analysis. International borrowing (and aid) helps to close domestic savings and foreign exchange gaps. There has always been a degree of unease about the notion of a financing gap, since it presupposes a specific 'target' rate of economic growth. A gap can always be opened by simply raising this target sufficiently. By the same token, a domestic savings gap can, in principle, equally well be closed by a reduction in domestic investment; and a foreign exchange gap can be closed by reducing imports. The calculation of a financing gap therefore becomes an essentially normative exercise. During the 1980s developing countries indeed lowered their claims on international financing by reducing domestic investment and compressing imports. A median estimate of gross capital formation shows that as a percentage of GDP this fell from 21.5% in 1983 to 20% in 1989. Similarly, import volume, which had grown on average by 7.3% per annum during 1973–82, shrank by almost 4% during 1983–86. This way of closing *ex ante* gaps has been made more costly by the fact that domestic savings have frequently been declining and export performance has often been poor, calling for even sharper reductions in investment and imports.

While the normative aspect of dual gap analysis has to be accepted, it also has to be seen against the statistical picture drawn so far in this Section. In principle, developing countries could eliminate their demand for international finance by reducing economic growth. Although never appealing, this option becomes even less acceptable where growth has been negative for a number of years and where living standards have been falling. Nor does one have to accept the humanitarian dimension of financing gaps in order to be moved to close them. Arguments that are both strictly economic and more in the sphere of international political economy may also be persuasive.

The economic argument is that the rate of return to capital in developing countries is higher than that in developed countries, even where international financial markets may require (excessively) high risk premia. Moreover, at a relatively early stage of development, and with high social discount rates, it is rational for less developed countries to import capital. The political economy argument is that closing a financing gap by reducing the demand for foreign exchange will create greater political instability than would closing it by increasing the supply of foreign exchange through borrowing. It may then be in the interests of creditors that developing countries do not carry domestic sacrifices too far.

A summary of financial flows to developing countries is provided in Table 10.3. Again, care needs to be taken in interpreting any such a summary table but a number of trends are relevant to the discussion here. It emerges that during 1981–9 there was a very significant reduction in total net resource flows. At 1988 prices and exchange rates these stood at $202 billion in 1981, but had fallen to only just over $100 billion by 1987. Within this overall picture there were significant changes in the composition of resource flows. Official Development Finance (ODF), both of a bilateral and multilateral type, remained approximately constant over the period as a whole, although aid from the DAC (Development Assistance Committee) countries increased. Since total resource flows were declining, the share of aid in total flows almost doubled. In current prices, export credits fell from $17.6 billion in 1981 to −$2.6 billion in 1987. Similarly, bank lending declined dramatically. Participation by developing countries in international bond markets remained only very modest throughout 1981–9, although direct investment showed some increase. Net credits from the IMF were positive during 1981–5 but were negative for the remainder of the period. Matching this decline in net resource flows, developing countries also experienced a significant fall in the size of their current account deficits: these fell by more than 50% between 1983 and 1990, although they increased very sharply again in 1991.

In terms of the future financing needs of developing countries, it is the interpretation of these resource and balance of payments figures which is important. Superficially, one interpretation could be of strengthening economic performance permitting the simultaneous achievement of economic growth and export expansion. Within this context it is the increased generation of domestic resources which allows the reliance on foreign resources to be reduced. Here negative net transfers become a sign of strength rather than of weakness. However, the information presented earlier suggests that this interpretation of developments is far from the truth. The more accurate interpretation is one where the declining availability of external finance has forced developing economies to pursue adjustment policies which reduce their demand for foreign exchange mainly by the compression of imports. Here it is the availability of finance which has been an effective constraint on economic development. What measure of concern is placed upon this depends on how importantly one views the reactivation of economic development. Although there are economic elements in such an assessment including, for example, the 'mutuality of interest' argument which featured centrally in the Brandt Report (1980), the principal elements are likely to remain political, and even moral.

Clearly, it would be possible to derive a constellation of specific assumptions which would provide a range of estimations of the financing

Table 10.3 Total net resource flows to developing countries, 1981–9 (current $ billion).[a]

Source	1981	1982	1983	1984	1985	1986	1987	1988	1989
Official Development Finance (ODF)	45.5	44.2	42.4	47.7	48.9	56.3	61.6	66.0	69.0
Official Development Assistance (ODA)	36.8	33.9	33.9	35.0	37.3	44.5	48.3	51.6	53.1
Of which: Bilateral disbursements	28.9	26.3	26.3	27.2	28.8	34.9	38.2	40.3	40.5
Multilateral disbursements	7.9	7.6	7.6	7.8	8.5	9.6	10.1	11.3	12.6
Other ODF	8.7	10.3	8.5	12.7	11.6	11.8	13.3	14.4	15.9
Of which: Bilateral disbursements	3.0	3.7	1.3	4.5	3.7	4.0	6.6	7.9	9.0
Multilateral disbursements	5.7	6.6	7.2	8.2	7.9	7.8	6.7	6.5	6.9
Total export credits	17.6	13.7	4.6	6.2	4.0	-0.7	-2.6	-0.5	1.2
DAC countries	16.2	12.7	3.9	5.2	3.4	-0.9	-2.9	-0.9	1.0
Of which: Short-term	2.9	3.0	-3.5	0.3	3.2	3.0	4.1	2.0	1.0
Other countries	1.4	1.0	0.7	1.0	0.6	0.2	0.3	0.4	0.2
Private flows	74.3	58.2	47.9	31.7	31.4	28.2	34.5	40.4	40.2
Direct investment	17.2	12.8	9.3	11.3	6.6	11.3	21.0	25.1	22.0
Of which: Offshore centres	4.1	4.1	3.7	3.8	3.7	6.8	13.5	9.9	–
International bank lending	52.3	37.9	35.0	17.2	15.2	7.0	7.0	5.8	8.0
Of which: Short-term	22.0	15.0	-25.0	-0.6	12.0	-0.4	5.0	2.0	4.0
Total bond lending	1.3	4.8	1.0	0.3	5.4	2.7	0.5	0.4	1.0
Other private	1.5	0.4	0.3	0.3	1.3	3.9	2.5	4.9	5.0
Grants by non-governmental organizations	2.0	2.3	2.3	2.6	2.9	3.3	3.5	4.2	4.2
Total net resource flows	137.4	116.1	94.9	85.6	84.3	83.8	93.5	105.9	110.4

Source: Development Cooperation Report (OECD, Paris, 1990).
[a] Includes flows from all sources, i.e. DAC, Eastern European countries, Arab and other less developed country donors. Figures exclude Taiwan.

constraint that developing countries will encounter during the 1990s. For our purposes we do not need to make such forecasts. All we need to do is to make a number of observations and broad assumptions. These are first, that the record of economic development during the 1980s has been unsatisfactory: we should aim to avoid falling output and declining living standards in developing countries. Second, that the future export performance of developing countries in general is unlikely to be sufficiently strong to generate adequate amounts of foreign exchange to support development, and that flows of finance from abroad will therefore be required. And third, that commercial banks will continue to look to reduce their exposures to developing countries or, at least, will not wish to increase them significantly; and that international bond lending, foreign direct investment and aid will not increase sufficiently to fill the lending vacuum left by the banks. These assumptions lead us to focus attention on the role of the IFIs and in particular the IMF and the World Bank.

Indeed, concentration on the Bretton Woods institutions may be justified in a more direct way than simply by eliminating the alternatives. There is little doubt that the data provided above show developing countries to be in need of a combination of macroeconomic stabilization, economic adjustment and international financing. History suggests that the Bretton Woods institutions are uniquely placed to provide an input into the development process which involves such a combination. Concentration on the IMF and the World Bank does not, however, imply that it would be wise to ignore other ways in which the adjustment and financing needs of developing countries might be met. There is significant scope for reform in other areas.

III THE BRETTON WOODS INSTITUTIONS AND THE EROSION OF THEIR TRADITIONAL SPECIALIZATIONS

The division of labour between the IMF and the World Bank used to be fairly clear-cut. The IMF was a balance of payments institution. Its focus was short term, with an orientation towards the demand side of the economy, the monetary sector and programme lending. The World Bank, in contrast, was a development institution. Its focus was long term, with an orientation towards the supply side of the economy, the real sector and project lending. Although it has never been possible to draw a sharp distinction between the balance of payments and economic development, for as long as the distinction had some legitimacy it was equally legitimate to draw a distinction between the roles of the IMF and the World Bank.

Developments during the 1980s clouded this distinction. Essentially, the recognition that many countries needed to undertake structural adjustment made the distinction between the balance of payments and economic development more opaque. To the extent that structural adjustment sought to improve export performance and strengthen the tradeables sector of economies, it was clearly a balance of payments policy. At the same time, since structural adjustment was a long-term process which aimed to raise domestic aggregate supply, it also formed a central component of economic development. It was therefore in the context of structural adjustment that the roles of the IMF and the World Bank began to overlap.

The overlap is illustrated by institutional changes within the two organizations. The World Bank, under the umbrella of Structural Adjustment Loans (SALs), began policy-based lending at the beginning of the 1980s. Although certainly different from IMF conditionality in some respects, the World Bank now began to make some loans conditional upon the pursuit of a programme of policies. In its attempt to 'get prices right' the Bank, not uncommonly, became concerned with the exchange rate, an issue that had traditionally been the concern of the IMF. Meanwhile, through the Extended Fund Facility (EFF) introduced in 1974, the IMF had begun to place greater emphasis on longer-term balance of payments difficulties which were in large measure associated with supply-side weaknesses. The overlap with the World Bank was completed terminologically during the second half of the 1980s when the IMF introduced first the Structural Adjustment Facility (SAF) and then the Enhanced Structural Adjustment Facility (ESAF). Each sister institution now had its own structural-adjustment lending programme.

The shifting areas of activity and the increasing overlap are illustrated in Figure 10.1. Figure 10.1(a) shows the operational spheres of the IMF and the World Bank during the 1960s. The IMF still had a systemic, regulatory role in the context of the Bretton Woods system, as well as its involvement

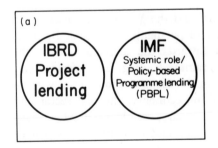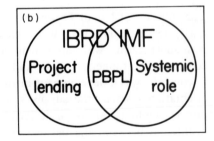

Figure 10.1 Division of institutional responsibilities: the past and present.

in policy-based lending. The World Bank was almost exclusively a project lending agency. During the 1970s and the 1980s the IMF largely lost its systemic role. Exchange rates were now flexible and balance of payments deficits were financed (certainly up until the early 1980s) through the private sector via the commercial banks. A relatively larger part of its activities therefore became related to policy-based lending. Meanwhile, the World Bank also began policy-based lending. The sphere of operations of the two institutions now overlapped, as shown in Figure 10.1(b). The overlap was, however, significantly more pronounced than that shown in Figure 10.1. It was not simply that the two institutions were both involved in policy-based lending but that they were both involved in policy-based lending in the same countries. Throughout the 1980s the IMF lent exclusively to developing countries. At the beginning of the 1980s its involvement was with the low-income countries that had been deemed uncreditworthy by the private international financial markets. After the debt crisis in 1982, the IMF also became involved with the highly indebted middle-income countries that were now no longer seen as creditworthy. Both in terms of function and country involvement the sisters came into closer proximity. Some observers even suggested that to all intents and purposes the IMF had itself become a development agency. Are these changes something about which we should be concerned? Have they created problems which have resulted in impaired efficiency? Is some sisterly reorganization called for?

IV ASSESSING THE CURRENT SITUATION

The success of the *de facto* institutional changes may be judged in a number of ways. Without undertaking a detailed review of the operations of each institution, some broad factors may be considered. Table 10.4 provides information on the amount of credit developing countries have been drawing from the IMF. According to this, less developed countries ceased to receive net credit from the IMF after 1984, in circumstances where as the data we have already examined show, their economic performance was poor and other sources of international finance were drying up. Nor can net repayments to the IMF be explained as a consequence of averaging, since it is a feature of almost all the subgroups' dealings with it: only the 'net debtor fuel exporters' category remained net recipients of IMF resources.

The disaggregation of net credit provided under various IMF accounts also serves to challenge any idea that the IMF has made a significant contribution to meeting the financing needs of the developing world.

Table 10.4 Net credit from IMF to developing countries, 1983–90 ($ billion).[a]

	1983	1984	1985	1986	1987	1988	1989	1990
Developing countries	11.0	4.7	—	-2.7	-5.9	-5.0	-2.4	-1.8
By region								
Africa	1.3	0.6	0.1	-1.0	-2.4	-0.3	0.1	-0.6
Asia	2.5	0.3	-1.0	-0.9	-2.4	-2.4	-1.1	-2.4
Europe	1.1	0.5	-0.6	-0.9	-1.6	-1.3	-1.1	—
Middle East	—	—	—	-0.1	0.1	-0.1	—	-0.1
Western hemisphere	6.1	3.4	1.5	0.1	-0.8	-0.9	-0.2	1.2
Net credit provided under:								
General Resources Account	11.1	4.9	0.3	-2.2	-5.7	-4.9	-3.1	-2.1
Trust Fund	—	-0.2	-0.3	-0.6	-0.7	-0.7	-0.5	-0.4
SAF	—	—	—	0.1	0.5	0.4	0.9	0.1
ESAF	—	—	—	—	—	0.1	0.3	0.6

Source: World Economic Outlook (IMF, May 1991).
[a] Includes net disbursements from programmes under the General Resources Account Trust Fund, Structural Adjustment Facility (SAF) and Enhanced Structural Adjustment Facility (ESAF). The data are on a transactions flow basis, with conversions to US dollar values at annual average exchange rates.

Between 1988 and 1990 the SAF and ESAF facilities, designed specifically to assist developing countries, in total provided them with net credit of only $2.4 billion. Under the EFF net purchases were negative during 1986–90, and under the Compensatory Financing Facility they were negative during 1984–88, and were only positive to the tune of SDR 131 million in 1989. During 1988–91 the payments balance on goods, services and private transfers for developing countries was −$176.7 billion.[3]

Not only has the IMF been a quantitatively insignificant source of finance for developing countries, it is also difficult to establish any clear pattern of lending. Attempts to estimate a demand function for IMF resources and to identify the characteristics of those developing countries that do and do not turn to the IMF have been largely unsuccessful. A regression analysis of drawings on the IMF covering the period 1980–85 for example yields the following results:

$$D^{IMF} = \underset{(4.93)}{54.0} \quad - \underset{(-0.51)}{0.23} \; DSR + \underset{(2.59)}{0.22} \quad INF - \underset{(-2.58)}{0.16} \; GNP$$

$$- \underset{(2.4)}{1.02} \; TRAD + \underset{(2.63)}{0.094} \, BOP + \underset{(3.23)}{0.0018} \, CRE + \underset{(1.11)}{0.028} \, RES$$

$$R^2 = 23.1 \qquad F = 9.73$$

where D represents drawings by developing countries on the IMF, DSR the debt service ratio, INF the rate of inflation, GNP gross national product *per capita*, TRAD total trade, BOP the balance of payments deficit, CRE borrowing from the private international finance markets and RES denotes reserve holdings. Imports are used here as a scaling variable. The coefficients on INF, GNP, BOP and CRE are all significant and have the anticipated sign, but the low R^2 value suggests that the model cannot be used as a basis for prediction.

This finding is confirmed by a logit analysis of those countries that negotiated programmes with the IMF during the early 1980s (Joyce, 1990). Here the model used is:

$$Z^t = B_0 + B_1 DCG_{t-1} + B_2 GDV_{t-1} - B_3 CUR_{t-1} + B_4 INF_{t-1} -$$
$$B_5 RES_{t-1} - B_6 INC_{t-1} - B_7 COM_{t-1} + B_P TDS_{t-1} + e_t$$

where Z^t takes the value of unity or zero depending on whether a country has an IMF-supported programme, DCG is the percentage growth in the central bank's holdings of domestic assets, GDV is the ratio of government expenditure to GDP, CUR is the ratio of the current account balance to exports, INF is the annual growth rate of consumer prices, RES is the ratio of reserves to imports, INC is *per capita* GDP, COM is the ratio of commitments for loans from private sources signed during the year in relation to imports, TDS is the ratio of total debt service to exports, and e_t is a disturbance term with a zero mean. Indicator variables are lagged to allow for information lags and to avoid simultaneity bias.

The results of the maximum-likelihood estimation of the above equation for 1980–84 which are presented in Table 10.5, are largely consistent with *a priori* theorizing. Countries that pursue relatively expansionary domestic policies, with more acute payments problems, and with more depleted reserves are more likely to turn to the IMF. Similarly, the poorer a country is, the more likely it is to draw from the IMF. However, estimation of the model gives a log-likelihood ratio which ranges between 0.14 and 0.18, which implies that the model has low predictive capacity. Other studies also conclude that drawings on the IMF cannot be explained purely in terms of economic variables. On the assumption that the use of the IMF is not simply random, it therefore appears that additional social, institutional and political factors need to be taken into account, although as yet attempts to do this have not been very successful either.[5]

While the IMF's financing role in developing countries is therefore in question, there has also been frequent criticism of its adjustment input: this has ranged from the theoretical basis upon which IMF-supported programmes are designed, through to the actual impact that they have upon the countries that negotiate them. Criticism of the theoretical basis of IMF conditionally encompasses a number of elements. For many years a view has been expressed by some observers that the theoretical underpinnings of the IMF are of monetarist extraction and that the policy recommendations that are derived from this will be inappropriate for developing countries where payments difficulties are caused primarily by structural deficiencies.[6] A more recent variant on this theme is that the IMF's model has failed to keep pace with advances in economic theory (Edwards, 1989). An illustration of the IMF's underlying model is provided by the following set of equations:

$$M = D + R \tag{1}$$
$$M^{\mathrm{d}} = P f(y) \tag{2}$$
$$D = D^{\mathrm{P}} + D^{\mathrm{g}} \tag{3}$$
$$Y = P\bar{y} \tag{4}$$
$$P = wP^{\mathrm{D}} + (1 - w)EP^\star \tag{5}$$
$$R = ER^\star \tag{6}$$
$$\Delta R = \bar{X}^\star - Z^\star + \Delta\bar{F}^\star \tag{7}$$
$$\Delta\bar{F}^\star = \Delta\bar{F}^\star P + \Delta\bar{F}^{\star\mathrm{g}} \tag{8}$$
$$Z^\star = P^\star V \tag{9}$$
$$V = g(y, EP^\star/P^{\mathrm{D}}) \tag{10}$$

Table 10.5 Maximum-likelihood estimation of data for countries that negotiated IMF programmes in the early 1980s (see text).[a]

Variable	(a)	(b)
Constant	-2.147★★★	-0.711
	(0.772)	(0.513)
DCG_{t-1}	0.011★	—
	(0.006)	—
GOV_{t-1}	8.199★★	—
	(3.393)	—
CUR_{t-1}	-1.278★	-1.286★
	(0.741)	(0.715)
INF_{t-1}	0.002	-0.004
	(0.009)	(0.008)
RES_{t-1}	-1.785★★	-2.139★★
	(0.885)	(0.847)
INC_{t-1}	-0.0003★	-0.0003★
	(0.0002)	(0.0002)
COM_{t-1}	-2.306	-2.024
	(2.391)	(2.276)
TDS_{t-1}	-0.691	0.021
	(1.975)	(1.888)
DUM80	1.232★★	1.203
	(0.546)	(0.533)
DUM81	0.876★	0.903★
	(0.519)	(0.509)
DUM82	-0.007	0.068
	(0.537)	(0.526)
DUM83	1.506★★★	1.596★★★
	(0.508)	(0.499)
Log-likelihood statistic	52.65★★★	42.21
Log-likelihood ratio	0.18	0.14

Source: Joyce (1990).
[a] Standard errors are reported in parentheses. Asterisks indicate the following significance levels: ★ 10% level; ★★ 5% level; ★★★ 1% level.

$$\Delta M = \Delta M^{P} \tag{11}$$

where M represents the nominal stock of money, R the stock of international reserves of the monetary system expressed in domestic currency, D is domestic credit (D^{P} to the private sector, D^{g} to the non-banking government sector), P is the domestic price level, Y is nominal income, y is real income, P^{D} are prices of domestic goods, E is the nominal exchange rate, $P^{\star}$ the world price of imports expressed in foreign currency, $R^{\star}$ the stock of international reserves in foreign currency, $\Delta R^\star$ the balance of payments in foreign currency, $\bar{X}^\star$ represents exports in foreign currency, $Z^\star$ imports in foreign currency, $\Delta F^\star$ the change in net foreign assets in foreign currency ($\Delta F^{\star P}$ the change for the private sector, $\Delta F^{\star g}$ the change for the public sector), and V is the volume of imports.

It is relatively easy to see how this model, and in particular the key assumption of monetary equilibrium contained in equation (11), has generated criticism of the IMF on anti-monetarist grounds. If the model is modified to incorporate a constant-velocity demand for money equation ($M^d = kPy$) and a linear import demand function, then, with given values for foreign prices, capital flows, real income and exports, the target values for the balance of payments (ΔR) and inflation (ΔP^D) generate appropriate values for the instrument variables ΔD (domestic credit) and E (the nominal exchange rate).[7] According to this interpretation, the model provides a ready explanation of why the IMF conventionally supports programmes of devaluation and demand deflation based on controlling domestic credit, as a means of improving the current account of the balance of payments and reducing the rate of inflation. Edwards (1989) has claimed that if prices and imports are assumed to be given, and the exchange rate is assumed not to change, then this recent IMF model actually collapses into the simplest version of the so-called Polak model devised more than 30 years ago where balance of payments deficits perfectly reflect excesses in domestic credit creation.[8]

While the IMF model presented above has been criticized for failing to incorporate advances in open economy macroeconomics[9] and for being too simplistic, a criticism which is of more direct concern to developing countries is the assumption that real income is exogenous and unaffected by changes in exchange rate and credit creation instruments. This assumption is at odds with the discussion undertaken earlier and, indeed, is also at odds with some assessments of IMF-supported programmes undertaken by the IMF itself. Certainly, the new structuralist critique of IMF conditionality has for some time maintained that devaluation will have a recessionary as well as a cost inflationary impact and that credit controls will be cost inflationary as well as being demand deflationary.[10] Since adjustment with growth clearly requires an increase in real income, it may be unwise to leave aggregate supply in a theoretical vacuum by assuming exogenity. In an analytical framework based on the absorption approach to the balance of payments, it may easily be demonstrated that assuming domestic real output to be given will ensure that policy has to be directed towards reducing domestic expenditure.

Another way of showing the potential unsuitability of the conventional

IMF-supported programme is by using the so-called Swan diagram[11] (Figure 10.2). Here the internal and external balance schedules (IB and EB) divide the diagram into a number of regions showing various combinations of inflation or unemployment and balance of payments deficit or surplus. The appropriate policy mix, however, depends on the economy's location *within* a region. Thus, although the same signals are given at both points M and N, the appropriate blend of policy differs. Let us now assume that an economy turns to the IMF when it is at point X. Moving horizontally to the EB schedule through demand deflation will create unemployment, while moving to it vertically through devaluation will cause inflation. The appropriate action seems to be to combine deflation with devaluation and move in a northwesterly direction along the IB schedule. At first sight the conventional IMF-supported programme appears to be vindicated. However, initial appearances may be deceptive.

First, although the typical IMF-backed policy is appropriate in the vertically shaded region, it is inappropriate in the horizontally shaded and cross-hatched regions: in the horizontally shaded region devaluation needs to be combined with demand expansion, whereas in the cross-hatched region demand contraction needs to be accompanied by revaluation. Second, the Swan framework itself rests on some rather restrictive

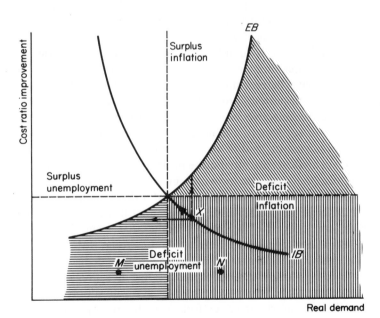

Figure 10.2 Swan diagram.

assumptions: for example, it ignores the effect of expansionary fiscal policy on the rate of interest and thereby on the capital account, and it uses a demand-based theory of inflation which implies that inflation and unemployment cannot coexist. Third, and even accepting these theoretical restrictions, it is possible that devaluation will cause a horizontal as well as a vertical movement, and that demand management will cause a vertical as well as a horizontal movement. In the extreme, devaluation may, in principle, fail to affect the real exchange rate because of the additional inflation it generates, but may, via its effects on the real money supply and aggregate domestic spending, reduce demand and create unemployment. Where devaluation fails to induce the conventionally assumed response, the reasons for failure need to be identified. Is it that foreign trade elasticities are low, in which case how can they be raised? Is it that there is real wage resistance, in which case how can this be overcome? In other words, the supply side is important.

Returning to basics, what emerges is again the conclusion that the superiority of a package of devaluation and deflation rests too uncritically on the assumption that, whatever the circumstances, a combination of expenditure-switching and expenditure-reducing policies is appropriate. The Swan diagram reinforces the point that different conditions in fact warrant different policy measures. If the policy package which the IMF supports is not modified in accordance with the economic conditions existing in individual countries, it will not be surprising to find that IMF-supported programmes meet with only mixed success.

This is exactly what is found. Although assessing the impact of IMF conditionality creates immense methodological problems, it is hard to ignore the fact that whatever method is used a similar conclusion is usually reached.[12] IMF-supported programmes have few if any statistically significant effects. Selective reference to empirical studies could provide some evidence in support of a beneficial effect on at least a component of the balance of payments, and of at least a short-term negative effect on real output, but such effects are often quite difficult to discern. At the aggregate level therefore the evidence provides only a very weak case for IMF conditionality, based largely on the claim that it does not appear to do much harm. But what is the point of IMF involvement if it is essentially neutral? Developing countries may reasonably argue that even if the empirical evidence for a negative output effect is not strong, IMF conditionality should not passively set out to reduce aggregate demand in order to compensate for assumed exogenous reductions in aggregate supply, but should be seeking more aggressively to raise aggregate supply. If the IMF is institutionally uncomfortable or ineffective in this role, perhaps it is a role that should be played by a different institution.

Disaggregation across IMF facilities does not soften this conclusion, since it is precisely those facilities that are apparently more specifically designed for use by developing countries that are either least used or least effective. The 1980s, for example, saw a sharp reduction in the number of EFF programmes. At the same time, using the extent to which credits are drawn down as an indicator of the extent of implementation, it is revealed that EFF programmes had a relatively high failure rate (Killick and Manuel, 1991).

Developing countries have been reluctant to use either the ESAF or the CCFF facilities largely because of what they perceive to be faults in their design, in particular relating to the conditionality that they involve. The World Bank's financing role is also called into question by data presented in its 1991 *Annual Report*, which reveals that while the World Bank was a net provider of finance to African and Asian developing countries over 1987–91 to the extent of $5.9 billion and $4.9 billion, respectively, it was a net recipient during the same period in the case of developing regions in Europe, Middle East and North Africa (−$6.4 billion) and in Latin America and the Caribbean (−$2.1 billion). The *Report* also shows how disbursements fell from $9.3 billion in 1990 to $6.3 billion in 1991.

It is more difficult to make a detailed assessment of World Bank lending to developing countries since there is less evidence upon which to draw. The project lending side of its operations seems, in large measure, to generate a satisfactory rate of return, but policy-based lending has been a more recent phenomenon. Moreover, while (as seen earlier) it is possible to criticize the IMF's underlying model, the World Bank does not appear to have a model that may be exposed to criticism, or at least it has not formally specified what it is. Of course, precision may not always be a good thing: it may be better to be vaguely right than precisely wrong. An indication of how right World Bank conditionality has been may be gleaned by examining the impact of its structural adjustment lending. First, it may be useful to look briefly at the pattern of World Bank lending.

An interesting, if somewhat cursory, analysis of this was made by Frey *et al.* (1985). In attempting to model World Bank behaviour they conceptualized the Bank as a unified actor possessing well-defined preferences. These they rather unambitiously claimed are to assist developing countries while avoiding default and thereby staying in business. This led them to test empirically two hypotheses. The first was that relatively poor countries will get relatively more loans *per capita* than relatively rich countries. The second was that a relatively high probability of default will result in relatively low loans *per capita*. Of course these hypotheses may conflict, and Frey *et al.* also attempted to estimate which of the two predominates in these circumstances.

They tested the first of the two hypotheses by estimating the following regression equation for 1981 and 1982:

$$LC_i^t = a_0 + a_1 \ GNPC_i^{t-1} + a_2 \ IICR_i^{t-1} + e_i$$

where LC is the amount of World Bank loans *per capita*, $GNPC^{t-1}$ is GNP *per capita* in the previous year, and IICR is the country's Institutional Investors Credit Rating, also in the previous year; e_i is a white-noise error term and the subscripts index each separate country in a 55-country sample. A summary of the results is presented in Table 10.6. The equation explains 37–40% of the variance of World Bank loans, which the authors claim to be quite satisfactory for a cross-sectional analysis where a time trend is absent. The beta coefficients in Table 10.6 suggest that the risk differences contribute more to explaining the pattern of World Bank lending than do differences in *per capita* income, a result that is confirmed by using covariance analysis. The model tested may be criticized for its assumptions of typifying the World Bank as a unified actor, for its failure to distinguish more systematically between demand and supply factors in explaining Bank lending, and for its failure to distinguish between project and programme lending, but the significant coefficient on GNP *per capita* does at least confirm the Bank's developmental orientation and tends to emphasize this role by comparison with the respective coefficient in the regression analysis of Fund drawings reported earlier.

A problem in assessing the impact of the World Bank's policy-based

Table 10.6 Cross-sectional analysis of World Bank loans to 55 developing countries: OLS estimates of loans *per capita* for 1980, 1981 and 1982.[a]

Year	Intercept	Income (GNP *per capita*)	Risk of default	$\bar{R}^2$	Standard error	F	d.f.
1981	2.032	−0.384**	0.425*	0.37	14.47	3.99	52
	(1.56)	(−2.99)	(2.61)				
		−0.301	0.415				
1982	1.984	−0.417**	0.497**	0.40	17.41	4.71	52
	(1.65)	(−3.12)	(2.99)				
		−0.323	0.455				

Source: Frey *et al.* (1985).
[a] The figures in parentheses below the estimated coefficients are the *t*-values; underneath the *t*-values are the beta coefficients. * Statistically significant at the 95% level of confidence, ** statistically significant at the 99% level of confidence (both one-tailed test); $\bar{R}^2$, coefficient of determination corrected for degrees of freedom; F, F-value for testing the significance of the independent variables on the dependent variable.

lending is its almost perfect positive correlation with IMF lending. It is therefore difficult to attribute effects. Statistical analyses of World Bank lending have, however, generally failed to discover strongly positive results.[13] Slippage in the implementation of agreed policies is not uncommon, although the evidence suggests that the less is the slippage, the more beneficial are the effects. In general, World Bank programmes seem to have a neutral or weakly positive effect on real GDP growth, a positive effect on export growth and on the balance of payments, but a negative impact on investment. The results of one major study are summarized in Table 10.7. They do not offer compelling support for the superiority of World Bank over IMF conditionality. However, in this respect the evidence is difficult to interpret. As noted above, the 1980s saw greater overlap between the two institutions. If this generated net negative externalities, programmes designed by either institution might be expected to be relatively ineffective. Moreover, if it could be argued that the negative impact on investment is associated largely with IMF conditionality, then the effects of Bank conditionality on the supply side become more unambiguously successful, if still only modest, and Bank conditionality may therefore remain a better base upon which to build.

Attempts to minimize negative externalities and indeed to maximize positive ones have taken the form of codifying the primary responsibilities of the IMF and the World Bank, and of closer cooperation. As part of the IMF's SAF and ESAF programmes it is envisaged that the World Bank makes a contribution to the design of the programme as presented in the Policy Framework Paper (PFP). However, some observers have suggested that this procedure has created a number of problems and has sometimes resulted in duplication, delay and confusion (Goreux, 1989). In

Table 10.7 Effects of World Bank policy-based lending.

Method	Real GDP growth	Real export growth	Investment GDP	Balance of payments	Private foreign finance
Tabular comparisons with control	neutral/ weak −ve	+ve	−ve	+ve	N/A
Multiple regressions	weak +ve	+ve	−ve	+ve	Neutral
Single-country simulation (Malawi)	N/A	Ambiguous	N/A	−ve	N/A

Source: Mosley et al. (1990).

any case, the SAF/ESAF has not proved a popular facility with developing countries and the framework it provides for cooperation has therefore not been heavily exploited. In practice, the effectiveness of cooperation may depend on the personal chemistry of those involved. While this factor will never be totally absent, it may be wise to reassess any institutional structure which relies on it too much. Certainly, some insiders report that relations between the IMF and the World Bank became acutely strained towards the end of the 1980s, even though agreements on cooperation were already in place. Whatever the institutional framework under which cooperation is envisaged, a nagging doubt is left that problems between the Bretton Woods sister institutions will always exist because of their historically different orientations. The World Bank, with its developmental, long-term, supply-side background, is always likely to favour the correction of payments deficits by means of expanding domestic output. The IMF, on the other hand, is always likely to take the view either that there is insufficient time to raise aggregate supply, or that to raise supply in the long term may imply raising aggregate demand in the short term. Demand expansion will then be viewed as exacerbating immediate balance of payments disequilibria.

In the same way the World Bank might be expected to favour the correction of payments deficits by means of expanding exports—the adjustment with growth path—the IMF may again regard this as both difficult to achieve in the short term and uncertain in the longer term. A more predictable short-term impact may be achieved by compressing imports. While the two institutions were involved in different countries, and while only one of them was providing advice on macroeconomic policy, this fundamental conflict was not exposed. However, with both institutions giving policy advice to developing countries, it was always probable that the conflict would become more transparent and that tensions and clashes between the institutions would result. Although it is possible that the outcome of such clashes will be programmes that are appropriately balanced overall—resolution of payments problems should ignore neither the demand nor the supply side—it is perhaps more probable that the programmes that emerge will lack cohesion and direction and that they will therefore be more likely to fail.

V VARIANTS OF INSTITUTIONAL REFORM

The range of alternative institutional methods of handling this potential conflict may be illustrated by referring again to the Venn diagram introduced earlier. In Figure 10.3, area A represents the traditional project

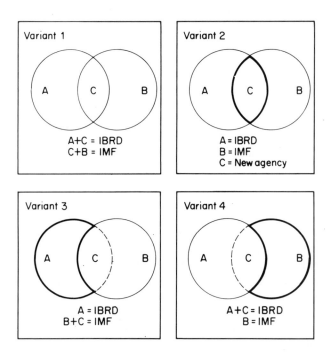

Figure 10.3 Division of institutional responsibilities: options for the future.

lending role of the World Bank, area B represents the systemic/regulatory role of the IMF, and area C represents the role of policy-based lending to developing countries shared between the Bank and the Fund. Variant 1 would be to retain the existing *status quo* and to endeavour to handle the overlap by closer consultation and coordination.[14] This coordination could be *ad hoc* and largely discretionary, possibly varying from case to case, or it could involve defining institutional spheres of competence. The exchange rate, the overall fiscal balance and monetary policy might, for example, be deemed to fall in the sphere of competence of the IMF, while measures to raise supply and demand elasticities in response to the relative price changes brought about by exchange rate depreciation, to alter the structure of taxation and government expenditure, and to introduce financial innovation might be defined to be within the sphere of competence of the World Bank. Variant 2 would be to return the World Bank to its project lending role, to return the IMF to its regulatory role, and to establish a new institution to carry out policy-based lending to developing countries. Variant 3 would again have the World Bank returning to exclusive project lending, but would call upon the IMF to take exclusive responsibility for policy-based lending to developing countries. Variant 4, in contrast, would remove policy-based lending from the IMF, allowing it to adopt a purely regulatory function. Policy-based lending to developing countries would become the preserve of the World Bank.

From amongst these alternatives Variant 1 suffers from the dangers discussed above. Besides, since this is, in essence, the existing situation, there is little evidence to suggest that it is working satisfactorily in terms of the effects of the policy advice that is being given. If this is the best that can be done, it does not seem to be very good. Variant 2 appears to be inefficient. The only advantage of building a new institution would be the opportunity to start from scratch. Although this is an initially appealing idea, deeper thought makes the appeal ephemeral. A new agency would face the same economic problems, would have a similar staff, and would encounter identical political constraints as the existing IFIs. Moreover, there is always the danger that institutional proliferation would dilute the effect of any one agency. To the extent that the chances of institutional disagreement also rose, the aggregate impact of the IFIs might even be reduced. Even so, Variant 2 remains more attractive than Variant 3. The record of the IMF in developing countries is not one of success, and the IMF appears to be uncomfortable with this role. Its attempts to incorporate supply-side measures into the programmes it supports have been half-hearted, and demand-side programmes often appear to be at odds with economic development. While developing countries must not ignore macroeconomic stabilization, neither must they ignore the level of economic activity which they are stabilizing. To extend the role of the IMF in developing countries would therefore imply either operational changes that will be extremely difficult to achieve, or the pursuit of policies that will be inappropriate and ineffective.

The superior choice therefore seems to be Variant 4. The World Bank has a tradition of dealing with developing countries and has more experience in designing policies to strengthen the supply side. Moreover, if it can be achieved, it is clearly more attractive to correct payments difficulties by raising aggregate supply rather than by depressing aggregate demand. Institutionally it is perhaps the World Bank that stands the best chance of achieving the elusive 'adjustment with growth' option. The Bank would clearly need to incorporate short-term stabilization into a longer-term balance of payments and development strategy, but it is probably easier and more appropriate to superimpose a short-term stabilization constraint upon a longer-term policy of economic development than to approach things the other way about. Many economists have argued that the balance of payments should not be regarded as a target variable at all but as a constraint. If it is accepted that the majority of balance of payments problems in developing countries in recent years require structural adjustment, then the World Bank is the more appropriate institution to bring this about.

The case for Variant 4 would have been stronger had the World Bank's record on policy-based lending itself been better. However, to some extent the limited impact of such lending may reflect the current institutional overlap and the imprecise institutional division of labour. The classification of institutional responsibilities incorporated in Variant 4, and a greater exclusivity of the World Bank in policy-based lending in developing countries, could be expected to result in better-designed programmes and an improvement in their performance. A potential difficulty with Variant 4 relates to policy-based lending to developed countries—should this also become the responsibility of the World Bank or be retained as the prerogative of the IMF? In practice, the problem seems unlikely to arise. Developed countries are disinclined to borrow from the IFIs, preferring to use the private international capital markets. While persistent payments deficits could of course ultimately undermine their creditworthiness and force them to turn to the IFIs, the input of the IFIs at this stage might more probably be in terms of adjustment advice and the restoration of commercial creditworthiness. Such a role could develop out of the regular *Article IV* consultations that would continue as part of the IMF's regulatory and systemic function.

VI CONCLUSIONS

When the Bretton Woods institutions were established there was a clear division of labour between them: the World Bank was charged with responsibility for economic development and the IMF with responsibility for international monetary issues. Time has eroded this division. Both institutions are now heavily involved with developing countries, an involvement that has frequently strained sisterly relations between them. There are, however, few indicators to suggest that this mutual involvement has resulted in success in terms of either economic development or the balance of payments.

Of course, it is no simple task to achieve simultaneously stability and development, and the structure of international financial institutions is unlikely to be the principal factor in determining success or failure. However, this is no reason for failing to seek the most conducive institutional framework. Although the specifics of policy will vary across countries depending on their particular circumstances, the institutional structure within which policy is designed will need to be more constant. It may be an appropriate time therefore to reassess the existing spheres of influence of the Bretton Woods institutions.

The analysis undertaken here casts some doubt on the ability of the IMF to play a central role in economic development. Although, in principle, there are many reforms that would enhance its contribution, there remains significant political resistance to seeing the IMF become more oriented towards developing countries. This resistance is much less apparent in the case of the World Bank. Since developing countries will continue to face financing and adjustment problems which will not be resolved adequately by private international capital markets, the involvement of an international agency such as the World Bank will be an important factor in influencing the future economic performance of many developing countries.

Up to now the institutional response to the problems that developing countries face has been an essentially *ad hoc* one. New facilities have been introduced to try to address particular difficulties: the result is that there are now an array of facilities on which countries may draw. However, in many cases these facilities are either little used or do not seem to be effective. This conclusion applies, for example, to the Buffer Stock Financing Facility, the Extended Fund Facility and the Compensatory and Contingency Financing Facility. It may be better therefore to go back to first principles and stop such ineffective proliferation.

The first step in an institutional reassessment would be to identify broad areas of institutional responsibility. The suggestion made in this chapter is that the IMF should concentrate more narrowly on a regulatory role and on macroeconomic management at the global level. This is a role that is likely to become more important as the global economy continues to move away from freely flexible exchange rates and towards closer coordination of macroeconomic policy. The World Bank, on the other hand, should take on more exclusive responsibility for policy-based lending to developing countries. This is not to say that the traditional input of the IMF into the design of policy should be lost. Indeed, although it is better to correct disequilibria by means of raising supply rather than by reducing demand, macroeconomic stability almost certainly remains a prerequisite for sustained economic development. The danger is that excessive reliance on the short-term management of demand will threaten long-term aggregate supply, and this is a danger that appears to have become more evident during the latter part of the 1980s and the beginning of the 1990s.[15]

An institutional reorganization along these lines would still mean that the IMF contributed to economic development, since the performance of developing countries in large measure depends upon the global economic environment in which they find themselves. However, it's contribution would be indirect, as compared with the World Bank's direct contribution.

The clear distinction between the direct role of the World Bank and the indirect role of the IMF would mean that more friendly relations between the Bretton Woods sister organizations could be established, as opposed to the squabbling that seems to have been a feature of much of the 1980s. The restoration of good relations would of itself be to the benefit of global economic development. The design of sustainable supply-side programmes would also offer the best chance of reactivating a catalytic effect on commercial lending and of restoring long-term creditworthiness to developing countries.

NOTES

1 For an analysis of commercial bank lending, see for example, Bird (1989) and Llewellyn (1990). Cassen et al. (1987) provide a review of the arguments for and against foreign aid.

2 A statistical examination of these criteria is given in Bird (1990a).

3 Of course, net flows from less developed countries to the IMF reflect previous lending, but from a developmental point of view the current flow of loans will be more important than the existing stock of loans except to the extent that this influences current flows.

4 Examples of such attempts include Bird and Orme (1981) and Cornelius (1987).

5 For an example of research into the use of the IMF from the perspective of international political economy, see Nelson et al. (1988).

6 For a brief assessment of the claim that the IMF is monetarist, see Bird (1990b). For a fuller assessment of the basis of IMF conditionality, see Bird (1984).

7 Edwards (1989) provides the necessary formal support.

8 Edwards cites Khan et al. (1986) as one source of a recent statement of the IMF's underlying theoretical model. There is some debate about the extent to which the formal model actually contributes to the design of policy.

9 Edwards (1989, pp. 19–20), for example, claims that: 'the Fund's basic model is fundamentally static, has a fairly rudimentary financial sector, ignores the existence of uncertainty, and has no fundamental role for expectations . . . (it) has failed to incorporate issues related to the inter-temporal nature of the current account, the role of risk and self insurance in portfolio choices, the role of time consistency and precommitments in economic policy, the economics of contracts and reputation, the economics of equilibrium exchange rates, the "Lucas critique" and the theory of speculative attacks and devaluation crises'.

10 The issue of whether devaluation is contractionary has spawned quite a large literature of its own: see Lizondo and Montiel (1989) for a careful analysis of the issue, and Kamin (1988) for a review of the evidence.

11 The conventional IMF-supported programme can also be analysed using the IS–LM–BP framework (Bird, 1990b).

12 Khan (1990) provides a detailed review of the literature, discussing the methodological problems and summarizing the results of the main studies.

13 Mosley *et al.* (1990) provide the most detailed published examination to date.

14 This is the conclusion reached by some of the other commentators on evolving IMF–World Bank relations: see for example, Feinberg (1988) and Gwin and Feinberg (1989). See also Goreux (1989). Gwin and Feinberg favour establishing the World Bank as the lead institution in the case of the poorest less developed countries.

15 The proposal is not to merge the two institutions completely but merely their policy-based lending operations. Such a change could contribute to restoring the financial reputation of the IMF that some observers argue has been lost in recent years (Finch, 1989), and could enhance its role as a monetary institution.

REFERENCES

Bird, G. (1984) 'Relationships, Resource Uses and the Conditionality Debate' in T. Killick *et al.* (eds), *The Quest for Economic Stabilisation: The IMF and the Third World*, ODI/Gower.

Bird, G. (1989) *Commercial Bank Lending and Third World Debt*, Macmillan, London.

Bird, G. (1990a) 'The International Financial Regime and the Developing World' in G. Bird (ed.), *The International Financial Regime*, Surrey University Press/Academic Press, London.

Bird, G. (1990b) 'Evaluating the Effects of IMF Supported Adjustment Programmes: An Analytical Commentary on Interpreting the Empirical Evidence' in K. Phylaktis and M. Pradham (eds), *International Finance and Less Developed Countries*, Macmillan, London.

Bird, G. and T. Orme (1981) 'An Analysis of Drawings of the IMF by Developing Countries', *World Development* (June).

Brandt, W. (1980) *North–South: A Programme for Survival*, Pan, London.

Cassen, R. *et al.* (1987) *Does Aid Work?*, Oxford University Press, Oxford.

Cornelius, P. (1987) 'The Demand for IMF Credits by Sub-Saharan African Countries', *Economics Letters* 23.

Edwards, S. (1989) 'The International Monetary Fund and the Developing Countries: A Critical Evaluation', *Carnegie Rochester Conference Series on Public Policy No. 31*.

Feinberg, R. (1988) 'The Changing Relationship Between the World Bank and the International Monetary Fund', *International Organisation* (Summer).

Finch, D.C. (1989) 'The IMF: The Record and Prospect', *Essays in International Finance* 175.

Frey, B.S., H. Horn, T. Persson and F. Schneider (1985) 'A Formulation and Test of a Simple Model of World Bank Behaviour', *Weltwirtschaftliches Archiv* 121.

Goreux, L.M. (1989) 'The Fund and Low-Income Countries' in C. Gwin and R.E. Feinberg (eds), *The International Monetary Fund in a Multipolar World*, US–Third World Policy Perspectives No. 13, Overseas Development Council, Washington, DC.

Gwin, C. and R.E. Feinberg (1989) *The International Monetary Fund in a Multipolar World: Pulling Together*, US–Third World Policy Perspectives No. 13, Overseas Development Council, Washington, DC.

Joyce, J.P. (1990) 'The Economic Characteristics of IMF Programme Countries', *Wellesey College Working Paper 118*.

Kamin, S.B. (1988) *Devaluation, External Balance and Macroeconomic Performance: A Look at the Numbers*, Princeton Studies in International Finance 62, Princeton University Press, Princeton, NJ.

Khan, M., P. Montiel and N.U.I. Haque (1986) *Adjustment with Growth: Relating the*

Analytical Approaches of the World Bank and the IMF, *World Bank Discussion Papers XX*, World Bank, Washington, DC.

Khan, M. (1990) 'The Macroeconomic Effects of Fund Supported Programmes', *IMF Staff Papers* (June).

Killick, T. and M. Manuel (1991) 'What Can We Know About the Effects of the IMF Programmes?', mimeo.

Lizondo, J.S. and P.J. Montiel (1989) 'Contractionary Devaluation in Developing Countries: An Analytical Overview', *IMF Staff Papers* (March).

Llewellyn, D.T. (1990) 'The International Capital Transfer Mechanism of the 1970s: A Critique' in G. Bird (ed.), *The International Financial Regime*, Surrey University Press/ Academic Press, London.

Mosley, P., J. Harrigan and J. Toye (1990) *Aid and Power: The World Bank and Policy Based Lending*, Routledge, London.

Nelson, J.M. *et al.* (1988) *The Politics of Economic Adjustment in Developing Nations*, Overseas Development Council, Washington, DC.

Index